The Nature of

COMPETITION
IN GASOLINE DISTRIBUTION

at the Retail Level

PUBLICATIONS OF THE

BUREAU OF BUSINESS AND ECONOMIC RESEARCH

UNIVERSITY OF CALIFORNIA

THE NATURE OF COMPETITION IN GASOLINE DISTRIBUTION AT THE RETAIL LEVEL

A STUDY OF THE LOS ANGELES MARKET AREA

RALPH CASSADY, Jr. and WYLIE L. JONES

1951

BERKELEY AND LOS ANGELES

UNIVERSITY OF CALIFORNIA PRESS

University of California Press, Berkeley and Los Angeles, California

Cambridge University Press, London, England

CONTENTS

vii

FIGURES

TABLES

The Nature of

COMPETITION
IN GASOLINE DISTRIBUTION

at the Retail Level

I

INTRODUCTION

A stage has now been reached in our economic thinking where intensive analysis of real competitive situations is essential to progress
toward a fuller understanding of competitive behavior. This approach—micro-economic analysis so called[1]—provides a more realistic picture of competitive behavior than that which results from
overview analysis only, hence can be expected to confirm, vitiate, or
refine some of our existing hypotheses, thus providing a sounder
body of theory of economic rivalry. The authors hope that this study
will prove to be a contribution along these lines. They hope, furthermore, that this will be only one of many such investigations.[2] There-

[1] Micro-economic analysis is not merely description in the usual sense (which often is
superficial); it is rather the detailed and penetrating breaking down of an economic
activity with the purpose of disclosing its innermost workings.

[2] Indeed this study might better be considered as an attempt by the authors to improve the technique of micro-economic analysis since this is not the first attempt in
this direction. The authors already have done a similar study of the Los Angeles wholesale grocery field although this was two-dimensional in nature—it was an historical
study of the changing competitive structure as well as an intensive analysis of the present competitive situation. See Ralph Cassady, Jr. and W. L. Jones, *The Changing Competitive Structure in the Wholesale Grocery Trade* (Berkeley and Los Angeles: University
of California Press, 1949). See also W. F. Brown and Ralph Cassady, Jr., "Guild Pricing
in the Service Trades," *The Quarterly Journal of Economics*, LXI (February, 1947),
pp. 311–328. In addition, the senior author used a technique similar to this in certain
respects in a study he made of the sugar industry for a large food firm several years ago.

3

fore this might be viewed as a methodological study as well as one designed to analyze the industry under consideration.

This investigation arose from a curiosity on the part of the authors as to the nature of competition in the retail gasoline field; it was independently conceived and executed, and at no point was there any other interest than to present an objective picture of competitive activity in this field. In this study, extensiveness of coverage was sacrificed in favor of a greater degree of intensiveness. Our analysis is circumscribed in at least three ways: (1) productwise—the study is confined to gasoline, (2) marketwise—it covers the Los Angeles area only, and (3) distribution-level-wise—it is confined largely to the retail level. We are thus placing a relatively small segment of the business structure under a high-powered microscope in order to observe minutely some of the more subtle aspects of competitive behavior.

The Los Angeles area was selected for analysis largely because of its proximity to the center of activity of the authors. Thus, the area should not be considered as necessarily typical of other areas. The fact is that in some ways it is atypical. This is not to say that the area is completely different from all others; basically it is much the same. But similar studies of other areas would have to be conducted before generalizations could be made concerning competitive behavior elsewhere.

Data for the study were obtained from bibliographical sources and from field investigation.[3] Thus, material was gathered from government publications (particularly U. S. Bureau of Mines output figures and California State Board of Equalization tax figures), industry sources (e.g., price quotations reported in trade papers), commercial agencies (e.g., metropolitan newspaper consumer-preference studies, testing laboratories' reports), as well as from hundreds of carefully planned interviews[4] with individuals representing all important com-

---

[3] The authors are happy to acknowledge the intelligent and invaluable aid given throughout the study by Miss Patricia Hay of the Bureau of Business and Economic Research, Southern Section. They wish to acknowledge also the equally intelligent but much less extensive help provided by Mr. Jack Northrup, a research assistant on certain aspects of the study.

[4] Interviews were conducted without formal questionnaires but with specific questions in mind. While the answers to some of the questions could be derived by direct questioning (e.g., the number of stations the company operates), many could be derived only by intensive probing (e.g., factors determining variations in dealer margins).

petitive factors in the industry,[5] and from an even greater number of market observations. Although factual data were obtained from every available source, the responsibility of classifying the material and drawing inferences from it was that of the authors except when otherwise indicated. In doing this, considerable use was made in this investigation of known generalizations (theory) about behavior patterns of consumers and vendors. Thus, the study is a blending of theoretical economic analysis and business policy.

Perhaps the major complication in this study was the difficulty encountered in attempting to observe accurately the increasingly dynamic conditions that developed in this market during the two-and-a-half-year period of the study. This made for measurement difficulties since time is required to gather material, and since conditions were changing before our eyes as we were making our observations. We were in somewhat the same position as the artist whose landscape of the countryside in late fall is interrupted by a snowstorm.

One main difficulty was the increasing number of aggressive price cutters appearing on the scene and the resulting change in the competitive behavior of certain types of vendors, particularly major-company dealers. As a composite picture would have been meaningless, it was necessary to consider what we think is "normal" behavior (where the conventional competitive tools are adequate in seeking or retaining custom) separately from "abnormal" behavior (where sharper weapons are required). It should be recognized, however, that these current dynamic developments have been a blessing in disguise since no analysis of the retail gasoline market would be complete without a consideration of the periodic price skirmishes which develop among rival sellers in markets of this type.

The main purpose of this study is to throw more light on the nature of competitive behavior. Therefore we are considering the economic position of various types of competitors, the psychological aspects of competitors' behavior, and the legal circumscriptions which condition competitive activities.[6] Before doing this, however,

---

[5] It might be stated, parenthetically, that the reports of interviews (recorded as soon as possible after taking leave of the interviewed person) are rich in background material and industry lore.

[6] Originally we planned to present a concentrated discussion of the legal aspects of competition as a part of the general discussion of the nature of competition. As the

account must be taken of the characteristics of the product under consideration, and the supply of and the demand for this product. The immediately following chapters will discuss these preliminary matters; subsequent chapters will describe supplier policies, the nature of the rivalry existing in retail gasoline distribution, and the price structure which develops from such a competitive struggle.

---

study developed, however, it was discovered that the legislative framework within which competition operates could best be understood in conjunction with the particular aspect of the study with which it is related. Consequently this latter plan has been followed.

II

CHARACTERISTICS OF THE PRODUCT
AND THE MARKET

Considerable light can be thrown on the nature of the competitive structure of an industry merely by studying the characteristics of the product under consideration. That is, the characteristics of the product have an important bearing on the amount of the product produced, the number and types of vendors found in the field, the appeals they may make for custom, the attitude of consumer-buyers toward various offerings, and other factors. The following brief exposition is the result of an attempt by the authors (1) to isolate all of the characteristics of the commodity which may have a conditioning effect on the nature of competition among retail vendors in the gasoline field and (2) to point out preliminarily for perspective purposes some of the distinctive market characteristics of this product.

Gasoline has been defined as: "a volatile, inflammable, liquid hydrocarbon mixture used as a fuel, especially for internal-combustion engines, as a solvent for oils, fats, etc., and as a carburetant; . . . It is made by the refining or the cracking of petroleum, by low-temperature distillation of coal, by recovery from natural gas, etc." [1] The product is jointly produced with other petroleum products in a limited number of refining areas of which Los Angeles is one.

---

[1] *Webster's New International Dictionary* (2d ed., unabridged).

Gasoline is a necessary transitory good for which no practicable close substitutes exist for most uses[2] (except, of course, in the broader sense of public transportation facilities which may be used in place of one's own automobile). The product is a repeat-purchase item which is physically consumed in use. Thus, unlike the demand for durable consumption commodities, demand for gasoline does not tend to be dissipated as a result of consumer purchases;[3] by the same token, there is no replacement market for this type of product, hence sellers are not faced with a turn-in problem. Wide quality variations may exist in the product, although in practice sellers offer their commodity at a few well-defined quality levels.[4] From the point of view of the present study, the commodity under consideration is a consumer good rather than an industrial item. Hence the buying side of the market is not well informed about the various offerings and their prices.

Gasoline is highly inflammable. Therefore its sale requires a considerable amount of regulation, both locational restrictions and safety facilities (although perhaps not as much as actually prevails). Gasoline is freely reproducible on a nonseasonal basis. It is a commodity of high enough value to justify long-distance transportation by mass means.

The product is purchased not by any one class of persons—according to sex, income group, age, and the like—but by practically

---

[2] This does not mean, of course, that no other fuels *could* be used in the operation of motorcars. Other fuels *are* used to a limited extent. For example, many heavy trucks are operated on Diesel fuel, and others use butane (or some other liquefied petroleum gas). Moreover, "souped-up" midget racers often use alcohol as a motor fuel. Despite these limited uses of other products as motor fuel, substitutes are by no means available in the same sense that lard can be used in place of vegetable shortening or vice versa. Actually the high cost of some such products (alcohol), the expense of adapting motorcars for others (Diesel oil), and the hazardous quality of still other fuels (butane) render free substitution impracticable.

[3] See Ralph Cassady, Jr., "The Time Element and Demand Analysis" in *Theory in Marketing*, edited by Reavis Cox and Wroe Alderson (Chicago: Richard D. Irwin, Inc., 1950), p. 199.

[4] However, the *quantity* of gasoline that a buyer obtains may vary considerably each time he makes a purchase. According to Dr. Waldo Kliever, director of research for the Minneapolis-Honeywell Regulator Company, the quantity of gasoline acquired varies according to the temperature at the time the purchase is made; hence he advocates purchase of the product by the pound. To illustrate from his findings: "One gas tank on a new plane holds 9060 pounds of fuel at 77 degrees Fahrenheit, but only 8700 at 120 degrees. At 25 below zero, it would hold 9603 pounds. . . . In every case, the tank would be full to the brim." (*Los Angeles Examiner*, July 24, 1949.)

all groups, except the very young. The demand for gasoline is derived (from the demand for transportation). The item is jointly demanded with other goods and services required in the operation of motor vehicles. Gasoline possesses no style or size element although it is usually sold at more than one quality level. All these factors have a bearing on the amount of stock which must be carried by a vendor.

Gasoline is largely a one-purpose commodity. Therefore, and because the use of gasoline as a motor fuel is so well established, no primary (as distinguished from selective) sales-promotional effort is required.[5] Actually, the generic product is not expansible to any great extent by sales-promotional efforts or even by price concessions.[6] Gasoline is a product which is usually sold under some brand name. Differentiation, however, as attempted by suppliers has met with only limited success,[7] although differentiation of the product-services of individual filling stations may be quite successful. This latter situation may result from the fact that the product-services of some sellers actually are superior to those of others in terms of the individual requirements of certain consumers.

At the refinery level, the product is sold by a relatively small number of producers in each area, among whom there is one or, at most, a few dominant sellers. Adequate distribution of the product demands a large number of scattered outlets to supply the needs of buyers wherever they may be at the time the product is required (despite the fact that it would be *physically* possible for a person to travel a fairly long distance to acquire supplies if he were so inclined).[8] Typically, close relations prevail between producer-vendors

---

[5] Primary sales effort is that used in expanding sales of the generic commodity; selective effort is that used in promoting sales of a brand of a commodity.

[6] The use of gasoline could possibly be expanded, however, by means of promotional effort designed to interest the motoring public in taking more and longer trips, thus increasing gasoline requirements. Such effort might best be effected through the use of coöperative advertising by gasoline refiners as a group. One individual firm, however —Continental Oil Company—has expended considerable promotional effort on attempting to interest motorists in (1) visiting the natural wonder spots of the country, (2) using the map service provided for them by the company, and (3) patronizing Conoco dealers during the tour.

[7] Although most buyers recognize the insignificance of any differences among the leading brands of gasoline, most are not well informed with respect to the quality of the non-major brands.

[8] The fact that he can do this and will do so if there is sufficient inducement makes possible the operation of large-volume stations.

and retailer-distributors in this industry.[9] Gasoline differs from most other nondurable commodities in that usually only one brand is offered in each outlet, although "split-pump" operations were the rule rather than the exception in early days.

The demand for gasoline is not postponable; at the same time, storage of any substantial amount of the commodity by consumers is impracticable and usually unlawful.[10] The need of specialized facilities for storing this commodity, and legislative restrictions limit the amount of the product that can be purchased by a consumer-buyer. Since stocks cannot be accumulated by consumers, gasoline is seldom offered by a dealer at special-sale prices.[11]

The retail purchase of gasoline, therefore, is on a hand-to-mouth basis, with practically all deliveries made at the point of sale. This means, of course, that sales are typically made in relatively small quantities at numerous convenient points. Since the product must be offered at many scattered locations, many fairly close-substitute supply sources are available to the average gasoline consumer. This suggests also that the possibilities of operating large-scale retail plants are limited.

Because of the hazardous nature of the commodity, retail distribution is confined to specialized outlets designed especially for this purpose; thus there cannot be any substantial amount of competition from other types of outlets distributing the same product (as in the case of groceries, drugs, hardware, etc.).[12] But as the retail gasoline field can easily be entered, competitors are plentiful in most submarkets. Like whisky and tobacco, gasoline is considered an excellent source of tax revenue; hence, taxes constitute a considerable part of the retail price of the product—approximately 25 per cent in California.

---

[9] This may be caused, in part at least, by the fact that retailers normally are only able to buy small quantities of the product at any one time; hence suppliers, unable to "stock up" their customers, use contractual means to effect a closer tie between buyer and seller.

[10] However, industrial users and farmers may store certain amounts of the product. Dealers, of course, must store gasoline in varying amounts; indeed, some retailer-buyers have an advantage over others because they have large storage facilities.

[11] Although sellers could offer gasoline books at a special price, which would have much the same effect as though the seller had been able to "stock up" the buyer on the commodity.

[12] Although it is not impossible for a retail grocer, for example, to operate a gasoline pump in connection with his grocery business, such operations are generally impracticable except in country general stores.

III

DEMAND FOR GASOLINE

"Demand" is a schedule of amounts of a product or service that would be taken at various prices in a market at a particular moment of time. Demand, then, is not merely the amount taken at a particular price; it is the whole series of amounts that would be taken at various prices. Thus, those appraising demand should consider not only the number of units that can be sold at existing prices but the number of units that would be taken at prices other than those presently existing. They should consider (1) the possible response from consumers ready to purchase the product at prices above those prevailing at the moment as well as (2) the vast market that may lie untapped below the current price.

The total demand for gasoline in the Los Angeles area includes all the product acquired for whatever purpose. That is, the total amount of gasoline taken in any market includes that purchased by farmers and mariners (which is not used on roads and therefore not taxable), that acquired by commercial companies directly from suppliers (and thus not sold through service stations), as well as that distributed through retail outlets. But this study is confined to the product falling into the last category which constitutes the bulk of gasoline sold in the Los Angeles market.

Demand for Gasoline Contrasted with That of Other Products

The demand for gasoline differs from the demand for certain other products in several specific ways:

1. Unlike some products (e.g., candy), gasoline as such is not a product for which the consumer has a *desire*. Gasoline is useful not in and of itself but because it makes possible the use of products which do directly satisfy wants.

2. Unlike the sale of certain types of products (e.g., automatic home laundries), the sale of gasoline does not have the effect of removing the buyer from the market, thus altering the demand curve. Rather, the product is a repeat-purchase type of commodity which must be acquired regularly and often.

3. Unlike some products (e.g., mouthwash), gasoline is a necessity of life in the American economy and one for which no close substitutes exist. Consequently, gasoline would probably be consumed in much the same quantity even if no sales-promotional effort were made.

4. Unlike certain types of commodities (e.g., copper), gasoline is largely a single-use product. The lower part of the generic-demand schedule includes few, if any, persons who would not buy at the higher price and, indeed, relatively few, who would buy less at the higher than at the lower price.

5. Unlike certain products (e.g., women's stockings), gasoline is used up in initial consumption. Because of this, and because consumer storage is not practicable, gasoline is a product for which postponement of purchase is normally impossible.

6. Unlike the buying habits affecting most products, perhaps, the habits of the consumer-buyer of gasoline may be radically different at one time than at another,[1] depending upon the nature of the

---

[1] According to a study made by Alfred Politz, Inc. for the Hearst Newspapers in 1947 (*Motorists Talk in 10 Hearst Newspaper Cities Coast to Coast*), the most important reasons for patronizing particular stations given by Los Angeles motorists were as follows:

When at Home	*When Touring*
1. Personality of attendant	1. Appearance of station
2. Convenient location	2. Brand of gasoline
3. Service given	3. Reputation for clean rest
4. Brand of gasoline	rooms

activity in which he is engaged at the time of the purchase. Thus, the buyer is likely to react differently to the offerings of gasoline dealers, depending upon whether he is on a trip or driving around town.

Consumption in the Los Angeles Area and in California

As in so many other fields few data are available on the demand for gasoline in its technical sense. One reason for this arises out of the concept of demand itself—it is impossible to determine precisely the amount of a product or service that would be taken at various prices as of a moment of time. Another is found in the fact that when one attempts to make actual price-quantity measurements over a period of time, presumably eliminating extraneous influences from the data, adequate basic data, particularly on the prices at which sales were made, are unavailable.[2] This does not mean, however, that we will summarily dismiss price-quantity relationships from our consideration; indeed, the immediately following section will deal with this subject; but the approach, of necessity, will be largely theoretical.

Although we have little definitive information on (1) the precise nature of the demand curve for gasoline as of a moment of time, or (2) the extent of any real changes in demand[3] over a period of time, considerable data for gasoline consumption are available (without reference to the prices at which the product was exchanged) through the gasoline tax records.[4] Even here there are some difficulties, however, because gasoline tax figures are not available for subdivisions within the state, and therefore figures for the Los Angeles market area (roughly coterminous with Los Angeles County) must be estimated on a basis of the proportion of automobile registrations in this area. Because of these data limitations, total California figures are more reliable than those for any subsection of the state and will be used for the major part of the consumption

---

[2] The posted retail price may or may not be a true reflection of the price at which sales are made. In some communities at certain times most sales will be made at the posted price; in other communities at other times most sales will be made at a discount.

[3] That is, more or less of the product taken at the same price, or the same amount of the product taken at a higher or a lower price.

[4] Annual reports made by the California State Board of Equalization on motor vehicle fuel tax assessments and taxable gallonage distributed.

analyses, especially for that phase which deals with changes in amounts taken over time. Before doing this, however, a word about the size of the Los Angeles gasoline market.

The Los Angeles gasoline market is the largest in the world. Los Angeles County has more cars registered than the four states of Arizona, Nevada, Oregon and Washington combined.[5] The number of motor vehicles (not including trailers) registered in the county in 1948 was 1,598,381.[6] In the same year an estimated 1,188,725,000 gallons of gasoline were consumed in this market for highway use, or about 41 per cent of the total consumption of the state.[7] The average amount of gasoline consumed per registered vehicle in this market in 1948 was 744 gallons.[8]

The need for gasoline is continuous, but consumption varies over time. Three types of temporal consumption behavior may be distinguished: (1) the trend of consumption, (2) cyclical behavior, and (3) seasonal fluctuations. As adequate consumption data for the Los Angeles market do not exist, analyses of these several types of changes are presented for the state of California as a whole, which we think may reflect fairly accurately consumption behavior in the Los Angeles market.

Trend of Consumption. Figure 1 shows the total and per-vehicle consumption of motor fuel in California for 1929–1948. The consumption of taxable gasoline in California[9] increased from 1,253,-337,000 gallons in 1929 to 3,190,346,000 gallons in 1948;[10] this was an increase of approximately 155 per cent in twenty years. In large

[5] Summary of Testimony on the Trial of Civil Action No. 6159-Y, *United States* v. *Standard Oil Co. of Calif., et al.,* (Wayne Goble Publications, May 4–27, 1948) Tenth Day, p. 2.

[6] Western Oil and Gas Association, Table K 45. 2, March, 1949.

[7] Estimated on a basis of the total motor vehicles (less trailers) registered in Los Angeles County as a percentage of the total registered in the state, times the taxable sales of gasoline for the state (i.e., taxable distributions of gasoline as reported by the State Board of Equalization minus 10 per cent—estimated amount of refunds for non-highway use).

[8] According to one student of gasoline consumption: "It is interesting to note that in California, however, the annual consumption per vehicle is sometimes less than the national average because of the high incidence here of two-car families. When a family gets a second car, they do not always double their mileage driven." (H. C. Grimsley, "The Application of Market Research to the Oil Business," p. 16 [an address before the American Marketing Association, October 19, 1949, Los Angeles, California].)

[9] Which excludes exports to other states.

[10] Report made by California State Board of Equalization.

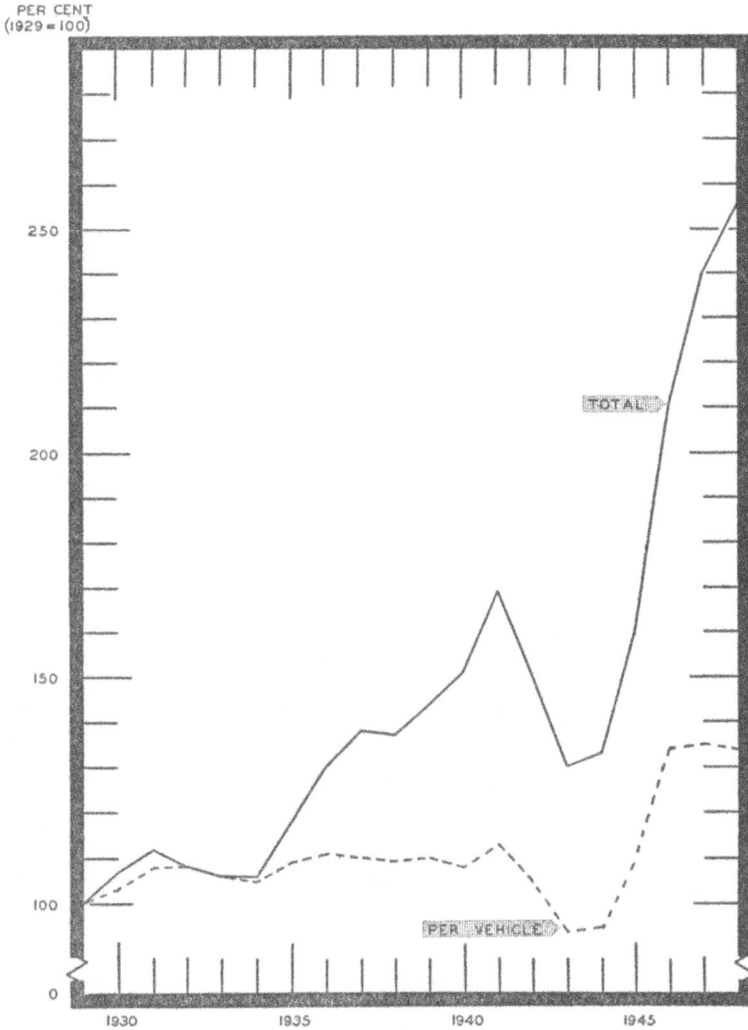

Fig. 1. Total and per-vehicle taxable distributions of gasoline in California, 1929–1948. Basic data from the California State Board of Equalization and the California State Department of Motor Vehicles.

part this increase was the result of population change rather than of increased use per automobile owner. Therefore, a more meaningful view of changing consumption from the standpoint of the individual consumer is the trend of consumption per vehicle; this

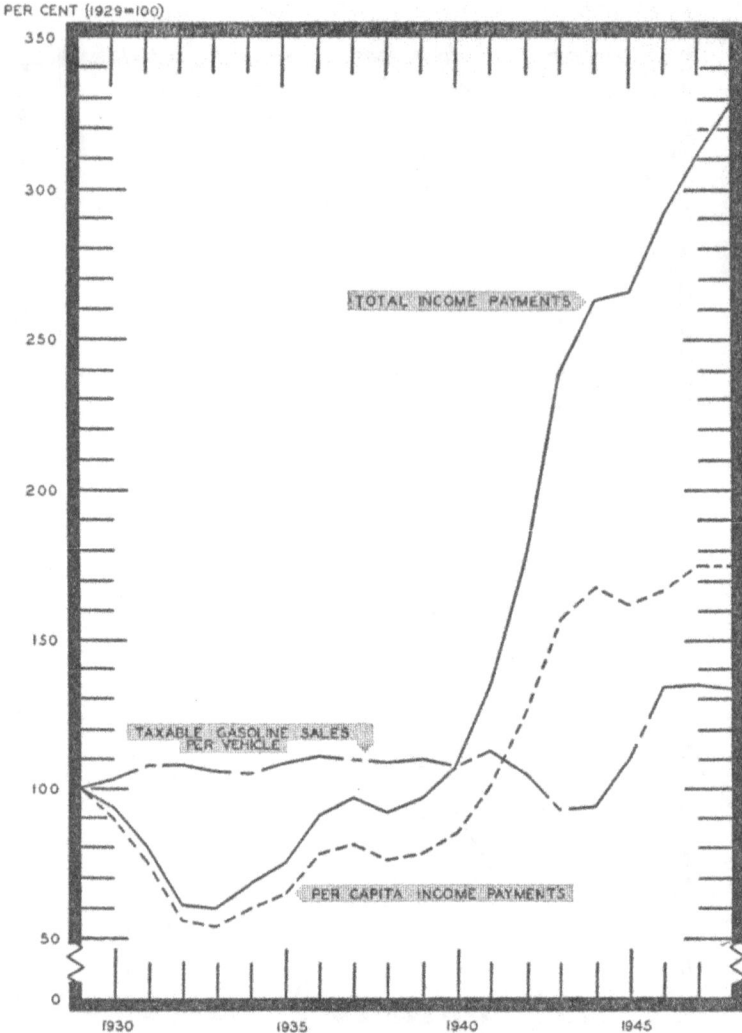

Fig. 2. Taxable gasoline sales (distributions of motor-vehicle fuel) per vehicle, and total and per-capita income payments in California, 1929–1948. Basic data from the California State Board of Equalization, California State Department of Motor Vehicles, and U. S. Department of Commerce (in *Survey of Current Business,* August, 1949, pp. 14–15).

indicates a modest but gradual increase in the average amount of gasoline used by California consumers over the same period. Actually, gasoline consumption per motor vehicle increased from approximately 620 gallons at the low point of 1929 to some 830 gallons at the high point of 1948 (unadjusted);[11] this was an increase of not quite 35 per cent for the twenty-year period or an average of a little less than 2 per cent per annum.

Cyclical Behavior. Figure 2 presents data on taxable gasoline sales per vehicle, and total and per capita income-payment figures. The latter are shown to provide a standard of comparison for the gasoline-consumption figures. From this presentation one may conclude that the consumption of gasoline in the state, as evidenced by the California taxable gasoline sales data, shows relatively little reaction to cyclical changes in business conditions. Total and per capita income payments to individuals in California dropped about 40 per cent from 1929 to 1933, but the consumption of gasoline per vehicle increased about 8 per cent from 1929 to 1931, and receded only 2 percentage points from 1931 by 1933; the average consumption dropped only an additional percentage point by 1934, and increased to a prewar peak in 1941. In 1943 and 1944 the per-vehicle average dropped below the 1929 level as a result of the wartime rationing program. The postwar peak of 35 per cent above the 1929 figure appears to be largely a continuation of the rate of growth which was interrupted by the war; but it may also be caused by the continued boom conditions combined with a reaction to the wartime restrictions. Figure 2 suggests that California residents must indeed consider gasoline a necessity.

Seasonal Fluctuations. Although gasoline consumption per vehicle shows little reaction to cyclical fluctuations in business (particularly to the downward swing), there is a considerable seasonal variation in California. This is due, possibly, to (1) heavy vacation- and other summer-travel by residents, and (2) the influx of out-of-state visitors, rather than to a contraction of consumption in winter time. This seasonal variation is shown in the moving-average analysis prepared for this study in figure 3.[12] The low point in average

---

[11] These data have not been adjusted for gasoline originally taxed as motor fuel and later used for other than highway purposes (such as tractors or stationary engines). The Board of Equalization estimates that in recent years the annual refunds of tax for motor fuel not being used on the highway have amounted to approximately 10 per cent of the total collected, but this figure was considerably lower in earlier years when the tax rate was much less. In any case, the figures do serve as an adequate basis for depicting the *trend* of consumption.

[12] The seasonal patterns of monthly sales of gasoline in California were plotted for the years 1933–1947. There were, of course, differences in some of the years but pre-

consumption in California is in February, the high point in August. The range between these two months is almost 20 percentage points. Consumption increases sharply from February to March (12 percentage points) and then rises gradually, with the exception of

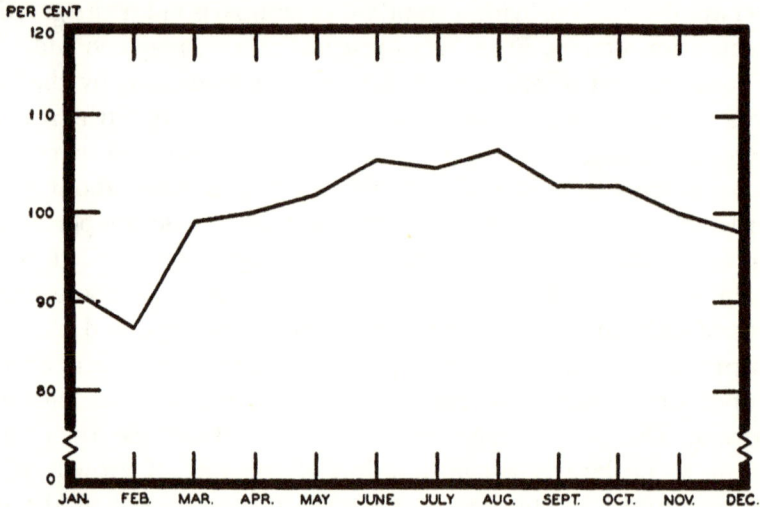

Fig. 3. Seasonal behavior of gasoline consumption in California. Based on monthly distributions of taxable motor-vehicle fuel as reported by the California State Board of Equalization, 1932–1948.

one month, to the August peak; then it declines gradually to December, and sharply to January. The behavior of consumption in the state is somewhat the same as that for the United States as a whole,[13] but considerably different from that for some other states.[14]

---

war years generally showed a low point in February and the peak in the summer months. The method used to determine the seasonal patterns was to express the original sales data as percentages of the centered twelve-month moving average. This has the effect of removing trend, cyclical, and irregular fluctuations and giving equal importance to each of the years. The data for figure 3 were obtained by computing the arithmetic average for each month separately, after eliminating the high and low values for each month.

[13] Taking the United States as a whole, the low point of consumption is in February (25 percentage points below "normal"), followed by a sharp rise for one month and a more gradual rise which crosses the average line in April, until a peak is reached in August (17 percentage points above "normal"). A gradual decline follows this peak which crosses the average line in November and is 20 percentage points below "normal" in January. (From *Survey of Current Business* data as published in T.N.E.C. Monograph No. 39, *Control of the Petroleum Industry by Major Oil Companies* [Washington:

One may summarize at this point briefly by stating that in California (1) the total consumption of gasoline has increased phenomenally in the twenty years ending 1948—because of the tremendously increasing number of automobiles registered; (2) the consumption of gasoline by individual consumers has increased materially during the same period—more trips, longer trips, greater use of car for business, etc.; (3) the consumption of gasoline is relatively little affected by changes in business conditions—consumers evidently finding it impracticable to reduce the use of the motorcar materially even when they are cutting other expenditures drastically; and (4) the consumption of gasoline by individual cars varies less with the seasons than in some of the eastern states. The data upon which these conclusions were based are, as we have said, for the State of California as a whole. Although the conclusions are based on statewide figures, it is felt that the consumption pattern for the Los Angeles area is very similar, if not precisely the same.

Elasticity of Demand

The most important aspect of demand, perhaps, is the relationship of the change in the amount of a product taken to a change in price, that is, price elasticity of demand.[15] Increase in the total

---

U. S. Govt. Printing Office, 1941], p. 77.) Thus, the consumption range for the United States is about 42 percentage points.

[14] The consumption pattern in many of the states is essentially the same as that of the United States as a whole (Ohio, Washington, Indiana, and Oklahoma seem to be in this category). However, Maine is atypical with a range of about 130 percentage points from January to August, and the consumption behavior for Florida is reversed—the consumption peak occurring in March and the low point in September (a range of 35 percentage points). (From Simon Kuznets *Seasonal Variations in Industry and Trade* [New York: National Bureau of Economic Research, 1933], pp. 232–235.)

This seasonal variation in the amount of gasoline used in summer and winter has decreased greatly for the United States as a whole since 1920; that is, in the past thirty years the peaks and troughs in gasoline consumption have been ironed out to some extent. What is more, at present the oil industry (taking the United States as a whole) instead of having a heavy peak load in the summer as it did previously, now has a peak load in the winter due to the tremendous increase in the demand for the burning oils (middle distillates). For an excellent article, including charts, on this subject see Courtney C. Brown, "Supply of Oil Products for Peak Seasons Provided Most Economically from Storage," *National Petroleum News*, November 16, 1949, pp. 26–36.

[15] Another aspect of elasticity is "income elasticity," or the effect of a change in income on the amount of the commodity taken, assuming prices remain unchanged. Closely allied to this is income "sensitivity" which is the actual changes in expenditures which are associated with changes in consumers' income (and thus includes the price element). A recent study by the Department of Commerce (Clement Winston and Mabel A.

amount of goods or services that would be taken at lower prices may result from (1) increases in the amounts acquired by those already buying the product or service, (2) initial purchases by those not now in the market, or (3) a combination of these.

If the usefulness of the concept is to be maximized, elasticity of demand must be considered from the point of view of the individual firm as well as that of the industry. This means, of course, that it is necessary to consider not only the total response to price changes of all sellers but the changes in the patronage of a particular vendor within the market in response to the price changes of that one firm.[16] Thus, elasticity of generic demand might be very small (since the lower price would neither draw many additional buyers in or induce many of those now buying to buy more), while the elasticity of demand for the product of the firm is very great (since the lower price would attract some of those now patronizing a competitor).

Generally speaking, the demand schedule for the product of a particular firm is likely to be flatter than that for the product of the whole industry, assuming no reciprocal price action by rivals, because in addition to increases in amounts taken which would result from increased use and new users, enhanced sales are likely to result from shifts in patronage from one concern to another.

Elasticity of Demand for Generic Product. The evidence strongly suggests that the demand for gasoline in total is inelastic.[17] There are several reasons for this: (1) Gasoline has only one main use—therefore consumers cannot put the product to other uses when its price is low, thereby expanding consumption. (2) There are no practical substitutes for gasoline as a motor fuel—thus consumers cannot shift to other products when the price increases. (3) Gasoline is a product whose demand is derived—thus consumers are not likely

---

Smith, "Income Sensitivity of Consumption Expenditures," *Survey of Current Business,* January, 1950, pp. 17–20) indicates that the coefficient of income sensitivity for gasoline is 0.5 which means that a 10 per cent increase in income is associated with only a 5 per cent increase in expenditures for that product. Other products with the same or about the same sensitivity: drug preparations and sundries (0.6); tobacco products and smoking supplies (0.5); magazines, newspapers, and sheet music (0.5). Products with above-average coefficients: radios, phonographs, and similar merchandise (2.5); new and used cars (2.0); theater and opera admissions (1.9); jewelry and watches (1.8).

[16] The impact of one seller's price change on the sales of another is known as "cross elasticity."

[17] That is, the percentage response is less than proportional to the percentage change in price.

to use more merely because the price is low. (4) Gasoline is jointly demanded with other products—so that its purchase accounts for only a part of the transportation expenses; thus a lower price is not likely to induce greater consumption.[18]

The suggestion that total demand for gasoline is inelastic is supported by at least one study designed to measure demand elasticity for gasoline. A large eastern petroleum concern (which requested to remain anonymous) made a statistical analysis of the industrywide demand for gasoline at retail in the United States, using the method of the late Professor Henry Schultz.[19] Thus an attempt was made to measure price-quality relationships after adjustments intended ". . . to remove the influence of cyclical and secular changes in the level of prices and incomes from the price figures, and likewise to adjust the consumption data for changes in the number of vehicles." The conclusion reached in this study was that ". . . the response of consumers of gasoline at retail to an industrywide change in the price of gasoline at retail is comparatively slight." That is, the industrywide demand for gasoline is highly inelastic. More specifically, "a 10 per cent change in the average retail price would result in something like a 1.3 per cent change in the quantity taken by consumers. A price cut of around 30 per cent would be necessary to stimulate an increase in the amount taken by consumers equivalent to the 4 per cent secular increase in gasoline consumption, which occurred between 1930 and 1940." This inelasticity of demand for gasoline within a reasonable price range is well recognized by government authorities, by inference at least, as evidenced by the heavy tax on gasoline sales.[20]

---

[18] The cost of gasoline used by the moderate-income family was estimated to be $104.40 (9,000 miles at 15 miles to the gallon times 17.4 cents [price excluding taxes]) in Los Angeles based on September, 1948 prices. This is about 20 per cent of the total upkeep cost of an automobile but is only 2.3 per cent of the total budget for the family ($104.40 out of $4,566.64). Thus, the total expenditure for gasoline is very small as compared with the consumer's total expenditures. (Gloria S. Goldberg, *Haynes Foundation Budget for Moderate Income Families* [The Haynes Foundation, Los Angeles, California, 1949].)

[19] Henry Schultz, *The Theory and Measurement of Demand* (Chicago: The University of Chicago Press, 1938).

[20] Professor Lincoln Clark of the University of Tennessee made a study of the elasticity of the demand for gasoline in his own state. His findings suggest a substantial degree of elasticity in the demand for gasoline in Tennessee. However, the demand for the motor fuel offered in one state might have a substantial degree of elasticity if alternative supplies are available to large numbers of the population in a neighboring state at

Elasticity of Demand for Product of Individual Firm. While generic demand for gasoline evidently is inelastic, the demand for the product of one seller may be *very* elastic. The reason for this, as was mentioned previously, is that elasticity of demand for the firm's product is not dependent alone on a variation in the number of users and/or in the amount of the product used by existing consumers. It depends also on shifts in patronage among rivals. Thus, a price cutter gains most of his larger volume not from any increase in the total amount of gasoline used, but in a shift of consumer patronage from rivals to himself.[21]

The demand for any one seller's product, then, is more responsive to price changes in terms of amounts taken than for the product as a whole. But the demand for the products of some individual sellers is likely to be more elastic than the demand for the products of others. To illustrate: If Standard Oil Company were to offer its well and favorably known product at its well-located, clean, easy-to-enter stations at lower than most prices, it would very likely expand sales greatly at the expense of rivals. On the other hand, if a company selling a little-known product and operating a dirty, unattractive, poorly located station were to offer gasoline at a cut price it might enjoy no advantage at all. Thus, the demand for the product of the seller who is well and favorably known is likely to be more elastic than that of vendors who are not.[22]

Refinements in Elasticity Concept. Several refinements of the subject of demand elasticity as applied to gasoline should be introduced at this point:

1. Technically, elasticity of demand is a timeless concept, but

---

a much lower price (as a result of a difference in gasoline taxes, for example, as in this instance). See Lincoln Clark, "The Elasticity of Demand for Tennessee Gasoline," *The Journal of Marketing*, April, 1951, pp. 399–414.

[21] Elasticity of demand of commercial accounts for the product of an individual seller is even greater. A 0.5 cent variation in price will gain or lose large accounts over night, hence competition here is extremely vigorous since consumers in this instance buy judiciously and are well-informed concerning competitive offerings.

[22] Generally speaking, the degree of demand elasticity of a firm's product is likely to be greater below the present price (but probably not above it) if the product of the firm is well and favorably known—assuming, of course, that competitors' prices remain unchanged. The reason for this is that (a) a preference already exists for the well and favorably known brand, even without a price concession and (b) no doubts about product quality are created by a reduction in price of such an item.

realistic market analysis demands consideration of two aspects of time in relation to demand elasticity.

(a) The first proposition, stated simply, is: The demand for many products and services is more elastic when allowance is made for consumer adjustments to a changed price situation[23] than when only the immediate response to a price change is considered. This principle (unlike its application in connection with some products, e.g., phonograph records) has little validity with respect to the *generic* demand for gasoline. It may, however, have an important application in the demand for the gasoline of any one seller. That is to say, although no more gasoline in total is likely to be sold after allowing for adjustments which may take place over time, an individual price cutter with an acceptable product-service may reasonably expect a considerably greater response to a price change in time than that which would occur immediately.[24] Conversely, an individual seller who raises his price will likely experience a delayed reaction to the upward change (assuming others do not meet the increase). This proposition seems to be borne out by the data obtained from the market place in connection with this study. The evidence suggests that the full impact of a price cut by an individual seller is not felt for some time—that the initial response is much less than that experienced by the seller after several weeks or even months.

(b) The second proposition is that different rates of elasticity of demand prevail in different periods of the business cycle; more specifically, that elasticity diminishes as prosperity replaces depression.[25] Although there is no evidence supporting this principle as it applies to generic demand (and, moreover, it does not seem to stand the test of logical analysis), it appears to possess a considerable degree of validity when applied to the demand for a particular

---

[23] Time for completely absorbing the knowledge of a change in price, for altering expenditure patterns, for arranging for concluding existing commitments, and so on.

[24] This difference between the immediate response to a change in price and that prevailing over time may be quite the opposite from that described, i.e., a greater immediate response may occur than that which will be forthcoming in time. The authors surmise that this is what happens in the milk industry. Unquestionably *some* consumers of gasoline would respond to a price cut at first, but find continued patronage of the price-cutting station inconvenient or unnecessary budgetwise. The point is, however, that such consumers are probably not numerous in the gasoline field.

[25] R. F. Harrod, *The Trade Cycle* (London: Oxford University Press, 1936), p. 21.

seller's product-service.[26] Not only is it logical to assume that consumers are more bargain-conscious in depression times than in
prosperous times, but there is evidence lending support to the view
that consumers are more responsive to price concessions by individual sellers in "bad" than in "good" times.

The best such evidence is derived from Edmund P. Learned's
study of the Ohio gasoline market,[27] conducted in coöperation with
the Standard Oil Company (Ohio). In this study the author (1)
demonstrates the increase in impact of rivals' price cuts on company
outlets in 1937 (depression time) as against 1939 (relative prosperity), and (2) reports on the results of consumer surveys. When
questioned about their reasons for patronage of service stations,
consumers mentioned prices more often in times of depressed business conditions than in prosperous times.

2. In most discussions of demand elasticity it is assumed—if,
indeed, the writers consider the matter at all—that buyers are fully
informed concerning price adjustments made by sellers. Actually,
consumers may not be informed on such matters at all. As elasticity
of demand is conditioned by response of consumer-buyers to price
changes, it necessarily follows that the amount of information consumers have concerning price changes will affect elasticity.[28]

Technically, promotional efforts increase the rate of demand
elasticity for the individual seller's product. The dissemination of
information acts on upward as well as downward price adjustments.
Thus, if an unannounced price rise is posted by one firm, the amount
of negative response would be negligible as compared with that accompanying a publicized increase.[29] Consequently, display of price

---

[26] See Cassady, in *Theory in Marketing, op. cit.,* pp. 204 to 206.

[27] Edmund P. Learned, "Pricing of Gasoline: A Case Study," *Harvard Business Review,*
November, 1948, p. 741.

[28] However, product quality must be known or assumed in order to establish the
validity of a downward adjustment; this is the reason for the use of comparative prices
in special promotions in some fields. Actually, if consumers are informed about price
changes but are also informed that the low-priced offering is of inferior quality, the
responsiveness to the reduction might be nullified.

[29] The impact of publicity on elasticity has some peculiar angles. Partial findings in
recent price-quantity experiments made in Los Angeles on the sale of fresh vegetables
at retail (William M. Borton, "Reduce Prices, Increase Sales—Sometimes!", *Super
Market Merchandising,* October, 1949, pp. 84–85) are as follows: ". . . a price reduction
of 3 cents resulted in an average increase of 25 per cent in sales. But where a 3-cent
lower price was *featured,* average sales increased 301 per cent! A price raise alone
of 3 cents resulted in an average reduction in sales by 53 per cent. But [and this is

signs is important to the success of aggressive price competitors in the gasoline field, since they tend to intensify the response to the price cut.

3. Differences in income are not likely to affect much the elasticity of demand for the generic product from area to area; but the elasticity for the gasoline of any one seller (assuming prices among competitors remain the same) may be much higher in one place than another. That is to say, even in lower-income areas consumer-buyers may purchase little if any more gasoline because the price declines,[30] but they very likely will take greater advantage than their counterparts in higher-income areas of the offerings of price cutters. This may apply regionally, as well as from neighborhood to neighborhood within a metropolitan community. This probably explains in large part the existence of price cutters in some communities and their absence in others.

4. A seller operating at the retail level retains only a fraction of his sales dollar as margin (from which operating expenses and net profit must be provided), the balance going to the supplier in payment for merchandise. Consequently, the dropping of a price might result in substantially enhanced dollar volume, thus indicating a certain degree of demand elasticity, but at the same time result in substantial relative loss, even assuming that operating expenses are not affected.

Therefore, in the retail field, in order to gain by a cut in price, the increase in amount taken has to be considerably greater than is indicated by the elasticity of demand.[31] This is so because the

---

the startling fact] when a 3-cent higher price was featured, average sales *increased* 33 per cent."

The foregoing seems to suggest that when an item is publicized (1) some *think* the price is reduced and hence purchase, and (2) some have their interest awakened and buy regardless of the price.

[30] On the other hand, the total demand for the heavy residual product of petroleum refining which is used for fuel is likely to be much more elastic in eastern industrial areas where it may be substituted for other fuels when price is relatively low, than in West Coast communities where substitution is not likely because of the heavy reliance on electric power and gas.

[31] To take an example: A retailer operating on a 4-cent margin sells 10,000 gallons of gasoline at 25 cents. Wishing to induce additional patronage, he drops the price to 24 cents (a 4 per cent reduction). As a result, sales increase by 8 per cent (to 10,800 gallons). His sales volume which was $2,500 before, now is $2,592; thus, whereas before the amount he was able to retain as gross margin was $400 (10,000 times 4 cents), it now is $324 (10,800 times 3 cents), a substantial reduction. Actually, the retailer

amount of revenue the retailer *retains* (dollar gross margin) is the significant item, and not his total sales revenue—the bulk of which goes to the supplier in payment for the goods to be sold. The key factor, therefore, is not the effect of a price change on aggregate sales, but on dollar gross margin.

It should be emphasized, then, that the usual demand-elasticity analysis is inadequate in coping with the price-quantity relationship of a retail operation. That is, the attention of the business economist in such an operation should be centered not on differences in gross *revenue* caused by changes in the amount taken in response to changes in price, but on differences in the *dollar margin* caused by such changes. The notion that price reductions would be profitable in cases of elasticities of anything greater than 1 [32] is certainly erroneous in retail operations; actually, elasticities must be several (and often many) times greater than 1 if the retail vendor is to gain by the price reduction. Indeed, when a reduction reaches the invoice cost (thus wiping out the margin), even infinitely elastic demand conditions would be of no avail in making up the loss in unit margin.

Choice of Retail Suppliers

Thus far consideration has been given to the actual amount of gasoline consumed and to demand elasticity. The present section considers factors which motivate consumer-buyers in the choice of suppliers. In this, the analysis goes beyond the amount of the product taken (either actually or theoretically) and attempts to probe the question of the choice of vendors by consumers and the reasons underlying such choice.

Spatial Aspect of Demand for Gasoline. The demand for gasoline at retail must be related to a particular place in order to be completely meaningful. While we can speak of the demand for gasoline of a sizable area in general terms, individual consumer requirements must be in terms of specific locations within the major area. Therefore, the demand for gasoline is in a real sense unique in each

---

would have to sell 13,334 gallons at the 3-cent margin in order to do as well as before, even assuming that operating costs were not enhanced by the increased volume. That is, the rate of elasticity would have to be 8-plus if the seller were to break even on a one-cent price cut.

[32] See above, p. 25, n. 31.

neighborhood. Hence, the competition of more distant sellers is at best only indirect.[33]

A service-station "market area" may be defined as that area from which the station draws the bulk of its customers. Obviously these areas differ, depending on the location of the station and the policies of the vendor; for example, a superstation located on a busy thoroughfare, operating on a cut-price basis, will draw its customers from a much wider area than a small station located in a neighborhood community selling "at market." The boundaries of a market area of a station are limited not only by distance, but by artificial barriers as well.

While the choice of suppliers by gasoline consumers is largely local, service-station market areas are not mutually exclusive but may be pictured as a group of overlapping circles; hence each customer's market is affected to some degree by the policies of the others. This effect might extend for a considerable distance by wavelike transmission from vendor to vendor until the effect is dissipated. Indeed, in time, effects might be transmitted by this peripheral rivalry so as to extend finally over a whole metropolitan area. This would, however, depend on the size and operating policies of the vendor and the prevailing business conditions.

Patronage Motives. Generally speaking, consumer-buyers are not indifferent in their choice of suppliers of gasoline, although in many instances, perhaps, there will be more than one acceptable offering. Many studies have been made (mostly by oil companies) which attempt to isolate the factors that motivate consumers in their choice of service stations. The following factors are the result of a consensus of a number of such consumer studies:

1. *Convenient location.* This factor seems to be all-important to most consumers, but usually determines the general area within which the specific choice will be made rather than the selection of a specific station. The studies indicate that convenience of those buying in their own community (in contradistinction to those buying on tour) [34] is in relation to the home rather than to the place where the consumer-buyer works.[35]

---

[33] See below, chap. vii, pp. 90–91.

[34] Obviously, locational requirements for those on tour are quite different. The station must be located on the highway over which the tourist is traveling.

[35] No figures are available here, but according to these studies motorists patronize stations in this order: (1) those near home, (2) those passed going to and from work and (3) those near work.

2. *Amount and quality of service.* While a large majority of gasoline consumers seem to desire efficient, courteous, prompt, and complete service, there is a considerable number in this market who actually prefer to deal with serviceless outlets.

3. *Brand of gasoline.* Brand is an important motivating factor among those patronizing service stations in their home communities.[36] It is likely to assume even more importance when the consumers are on tour.[37]

4. *Personality and courtesy of gasoline station attendants.* This factor is undoubtedly of considerable weight in motivating patronage of gasoline stations but it is likely to be more important in retaining than in attracting patronage.[38]

5. *Ease of driving in and out of station.* This factor, which includes the *apparent* ease of getting in and out of a station, explains the fact that most stations are located at corners rather than in the middle of the block.[39] There is reason to believe that women, particularly, are influenced by ease (or apparent ease) of entrance and exit.

6. *Appearance of station, cleanliness of facilities.* These factors, while of some importance to those patrons living in the community, become even more important to those touring.

7. *Possession of a credit card.* While the bulk of people pay cash for gasoline,[40] some buy on credit, hence are influenced to some extent in their choice by the availability of such credit.

[36] Actually, according to an economist of one of the major companies, the consumer is not brand conscious as among major-company offerings; it is more a matter of the goodwill of the retail operator from whom he is accustomed to purchase his needs. Therefore, the company has to concentrate on selecting its operators with care—that being one of its main ways of competing at the retail level.

[37] Consumer studies indicate that major-company dealers are patronized in preference to independent stations by a much larger percentage of consumers who are touring than those remaining at home.

[38] The tendency of consumers to prefer to trade at the same station is indicated by the following figures from a study of buying habits (*Los Angeles Times*, "Continuing Home Audit Los Angeles County").

	1947		1948	
Regular patron of one or several dealers	Jan.	June	Jan.	June
Usually buy at same station..........	75.0	71.1	73.5	70.2
Usually buy at different station.......	24.6	28.0	25.2	28.5
Don't know......................	0.4	0.9	1.3	1.3
Total........................	100.0	100.0	100.0	100.0

[39] Patronage of stations on the right hand (driver's) side is much greater than on the opposite side. Indeed, patronage of stations on the near right hand corner is, other things being equal, likely to be greater than patronage on the far corner.

[40] According to the survey made by Alfred Politz in 1947 (*op. cit.*) only 24.2 per cent of the Los Angeles consumer-buyers had credit cards; 77.0 per cent paid cash while 8.1 per cent ran charge accounts. (Multiple answers result in a total of over 100 per cent.)

8. *Low price.* Low price usually is mentioned least in studies designed to probe factors motivating patronage.[41]

While such studies throw considerable light on consumer motivation, the mere listing of patronage motives, no matter how sound they may be, is inadequate in explaining fully the basis of choice. Therefore, most such studies are unreliable for several reasons:

1. They do not differentiate between the motives governing patronage of a particular station and those merely determining the general type of station patronized. Thus, the reasons for patronizing a Standard Oil Company station, for example, as distinguished from any number of other major-company outlets, similarly situated, are never adequately isolated.

2. They place too much reliance on each factor as an entity, hence do not show sufficient awareness of the complex nature of actual choices created by combinations of several motivating factors.

3. They are not properly designed to overcome biases of getting at the effect of certain basic motives such as low price. Thus, price considerations are likely to be underestimated in consumer surveys (because of the possible inference of parsimony on the part of the consumer-buyer who mentions price) unless the information is derived indirectly through so-called depth interviews.[42]

It should be obvious, therefore, that a considerable refinement of analytical techniques is necessary if a clear picture of motivational factors governing service-station patronage is to be obtained. Patronage motives should be classified on a basis of (1) those governing

---

[41] However, a recent public-opinion study indicates that more than a third of the respondents feel that gasoline prices are high (Opinion Research Corp., Princeton, New Jersey, as reported in *National Petroleum News,* October 19, 1949, p. 48). As one might expect, such opinions will vary with business conditions. Following is a table comparing figures for 1949 and 1946.

Gasoline prices	1949	1946
	(per cent)	(per cent)
High..........................	37	12
About right....................	52	66
Low...........................	4	13
No opinion....................	7	9
Total......................	100	100

[42] The informal and intensive probing by an expert interviewer into basic underlying consumer motivations and the free response by interviewees.

the type of station which will be patronized (qualifying factors), and (2) those which govern the purchase at the particular station (selective factors). That is, certain basic factors, such as convenient location in relation to the home, might *qualify* the outlet for inclusion among those from which *selection* is made on a basis of some differentiating characteristic, such as attractive facilities.

The following table (provided for illustrative purposes only) classifies the various factors on this two-way basis:[43]

Basic or qualifying motive governing the *type* of station which will be patronized. To be included among those from which selection is made, one or a combination of the following factors must apply to the stations:	Selective motives governing the purchase in a *particular* station. Specific selection made on some one or a combination of the following factors:
(1) Convenient location	(1) Ease of entrance
(2) Reputation for efficient service	(2) Extraordinary service (including minor repairs)
(3) Acceptable brand	(3) Preference for a particular brand
(4) Generally acceptable price	(4) Concessions from market price
(5) Clean and attractive facilities	(5) Personality of attendants
(6) Availability of credit	(6) Possession of credit card by consumer
(7) General reputation of company represented	(7) Urgent need of product or service

Two points should be made here:

1. The selective motives in the second column should not be related to any particular qualifying motive merely because they carry the same number. Thus, while convenience may qualify a station for a certain consumer, ease of entrance may have no influence in the final selection at all, but rather, possession of a credit card may be the deciding factor.

2. Even when factors motivating gasoline-station patronage are properly classified as indicated, a mere listing of them suggests a much too neat explanation of actual market behavior. For example, it implies that consumers are motivated by only one of the factors listed. Actually, as mentioned earlier, the market for gasoline is made up of various groups of consumers with many and differing combinations of motives. Indeed, a certain combination of *basic* or qualifying factors may provide sufficient motivating force to prompt patronage of a particular station.[44]

---

[43] This classification, but not the specific scheme, was suggested by Professor W. F. Brown (see below, p. 31, n. 47.)

[44] To illustrate, one important qualifying factor influencing gasoline patronage is convenience of location, but a substantial group (considerably more than one-half in most markets undoubtedly) indicate a preference for one or more of the major brands

The complexity of the situation is intensified by the fact that motor-fuel consumers respond differently to the various offerings depending upon whether they are at home or on tour.[45] Those on a trip rely more heavily on major brands and attach more importance to clean stations; at the same time, location requirements differ entirely.

It should be obvious, therefore, that (1) scores of different combinations of motivating factors prevail,[46] and that actually the market is made up of a large number of subgroups which react quite differently to the offerings of sellers, and (2) that even gasoline outlets which are close to one another are to a considerable degree noncompeting, that is, that normally the service, brand, and attractiveness of facilities of one seller may appeal to one group but not to another, and that, therefore, two stations only one hundred feet apart, with different (and to some extent, diametrically opposed) characteristics, may both thrive. Further probing of motivating factors, therefore, is required, but this is beyond the scope of the present study.[47]

Who Makes the Purchasing Decision?

So far we have considered three aspects of demand for gasoline: (1) consumption behavior, (2) relationship of price to the amount

---

of gasoline as well. These two basic factors may be enough to govern the selection of a particular station by some individuals. However, given only two factors, the market is divided spatially into a large number of submarkets of varying combinations of selective factors, such as ease of entrance, the personality of attendants, or price concessions, which may underlie the choice of many consumers.

[45] That the nature of the activity in which the consumer is engaged at the time of purchase influences his reaction to the offerings of different sellers is illustrated by data from the Politz study (*op. cit.*). As was mentioned earlier, personality of attendant, convenient location, and service given were the most important reasons for patronizing particular stations when at home; on the other hand, appearance of station, brand of gasoline, and reputation for clean rest rooms were the important factors when touring.

[46] To illustrate, there are those who demand a particular brand (or brands) at a clean, conveniently located station; those who are indifferent to brand, but choose on a basis of price combined with a location convenient to the home; those who desire full service (including credit) and a well-known brand of gasoline at a station near work; those to whom location is not important, who have no brand loyalty, and who do not wish service, but who do buy on a basis of price.

[47] Professor William F. Brown of the University of California, Los Angeles, has been engaged for some time in studies of consumer motivation based on painstaking depth interviews, including factors influencing the choice of gasoline stations. That is, the interviewer encourages the interviewed person to recall the circumstances of a specific purchase and report all circumstances which had an influence on the selection.

taken, and (3) consumer motivation underlying service-station patronage. One final aspect of demand analysis (seldom considered by economists) is the attempt to pin point demand for gasoline by determining the class of individuals who make the purchasing decision.

This goes even beyond finding out who actually makes the purchase since those buying may not make the decision as to what is to be bought. Just as a purchasing agent of a company often buys certain brands of products only because they are specified by the plant engineer, the consumer-buyer of gasoline may select a brand only at the instruction of some other member of the family.

The following figures throw some light on this matter:

	Per Cent of Patrons in		
	June 1947	Jan. 1948	June 1948
Person in family governing choice of brand:[a]			
Housewife never buys....................	50.5	47.0	45.8
Man recommends brand (even though woman buys)..........................	30.3	35.6	28.5
Housewife chooses.......................	19.2	17.4	25.7

[a] From the *Los Angeles Times*, "Continuing Home Audit Los Angeles County."

Several significant inferences may be drawn from the foregoing table on a basis of the figures for June, 1948:

1. More than 45 per cent of the families purchasing gasoline in the Los Angeles market are represented by someone other than the housewife (presumably largely the man of the house).

2. Close to 30 per cent of the patrons are women purchasers, but presumably the man of the house influences the *selection* of the brand.

3. In only about 25 per cent of the instances choice of brand is made by the housewife.

Thus the woman of the house has relatively little influence in selecting the brand of gasoline (and very possibly the station from which it is bought). Rather, it appears that the man of the house does the selecting. Generally speaking, then, the competitive efforts of vendors should be mainly, although not exclusively, directed toward him. In the large majority of instances his decision will determine the choice of offerings. This is of importance to sellers in their attempt to satisfy demand but it is of particular importance in their efforts to manipulate demand. It has a bearing on the choice of media to be employed, the kind of appeal to be used, the pre- ferred position in the medium, if any, and so forth. While the evidence suggests that men do seem to have a greater influence in the selection of brands of gasoline than women, this does not mean that women have no influence in this direction. Indeed, some sellers might make great gains by specially catering to the group of women which not only buy gasoline but decide on the brand of gasoline to purchase. Such effort might result in increasing the influence of housewives in selecting sources of supply of motor fuel.

IV

SUPPLY OF GASOLINE

Technically, "supply" of a product or service is a schedule of the amounts that would be offered at various prices in a particular market at any one time. Gasoline is a commodity which is produced jointly[1] with other petroleum products (fuel oil, gas oil, liquefied gas, asphalt, lubricating oils, distillates, kerosene, etc.) from crude oil. The commodity is freely reproducible under cost conditions which do not seem to vary much on a basis of size of plant.[2] It would

---

[1] Gasoline is a joint product in the sense that one productive process gives rise to two or more finished goods or materials.

[2] The available evidence suggests that the efficiency of refineries varies greatly among plants, but that small refineries may be just as efficient as large ones. One of the T.N.E.C. studies (Monograph No. 13, *Relative Efficiency of Large, Medium-sized, and Small Business*, p. 42) reported, for example, that out of 22 California non-lubricant refineries covered in 1929, and 23 in 1930, the 4 having the lowest costs were medium-sized or small. And of the 6 lubricant refineries covered in 1929, and of the 7 in 1930, the 2 lowest-cost refineries of the group were small and medium-sized, respectively. Much of the same situation seems to have prevailed elsewhere (particularly the Atlantic coast, and interior states). See also data on rates of return on capital invested in refineries, *ibid.*, p. 80, where the next to the smallest concern (in terms of investment in 1922) was the most profitable.

This condition may have changed considerably since the development of the cracking process, although there is substantial evidence suggesting that the small refinery may be able to operate efficiently enough to compete with the large refinery. One of the small operators indicates that while crude costs his company a little more than it does large refiners (5 to 10 cents a barrel) and its labor costs are somewhat higher (since one

34

appear that the supply of gasoline is highly elastic within a rather wide price range (in the sense that very little increase in price is required to call forth increasing amounts of the product).

Gasoline is produced from a raw material which is, in short-run terms at least, plentiful.[3] The refined product is bulky but readily transportable, although the cost of transportation may have a restrictive effect on intermarket movements except when accomplished by mass means, e.g., pipe line or tanker.[4]

The commodity is storable under proper conditions. However, as was mentioned earlier, gasoline ordinarily is not delivered to the customers' homes but moves forward from the point of production only to especially equipped dispensaries at convenient distribution

---

man can watch a 5,000-barrel still just as well as one of 1,000-barrel capacity), its overhead costs are much lower. Another feels that manufacturing costs per barrel of gasoline are about the same as the majors', but his crude costs are about 10 cents per barrel more. He, too, feels that low overhead is a sufficient offset to any direct cost disadvantage with which small refiners may be faced. This point of view is shared by still another independent-company executive. On the other hand, one independent-company official feels that no small refinery without cracking facilities can possibly compete in today's market, so that it is better for the small companies to make supply arrangements than to try to operate refineries. In between these two views is one expressed by another small-company officer, who sees the small refinery as less efficient than the large one but argues that since the refinery margin is wide, the small refiner is still able to compete effectively. It is a striking fact, of course, that small refineries *are* competing! This suggests that small concerns may be able to operate as efficiently as large ones, but that costs may vary materially from plant to plant, depending on (1) the efficiency of the management and (2) the intensity of use of the facilities.

[3] There are, of course, ultimate, indeed foreseeable, limits to the supply of crude. The U. S. Bureau of Mines has been experimenting in Rifle, Colorado, on the development of a means of extracting petroleum from an almost inexhaustible raw material —oil shale. The raw material is burned, with the result that vapors condense and form a petroleumlike substance. (*Life,* July 18, 1949.) The latest reports indicate that success has been achieved in the production of crude from shale and that the cost of the new process ($2.25–$2.50 per barrel) is almost if not quite as low as the price of natural petroleum (around $2.50 in mid-1949). (*Los Angeles Times,* September 15, 1949.) On the other hand, it is argued by industry representatives that the U. S. Bureau of Mines figures may be misleading since they do not indicate which cost items have been included. Even assuming that the extraction of the crude oil is a *fait accompli,* the refining process has still to be perfected—reportedly the product is somewhat heavy in sulphur and nitrogen; hence this source which is of tremendous importance potentially is neither necessary nor available at the moment. (*National Petroleum News,* July 6, 1949, p. 12.)

[4] Profitable shipments of California gasoline to the Atlantic coast were recently reported in the local press, although they have been admittedly rare and had the character of distress measures to rid the local market of surpluses. (*Los Angeles Times,* June 23, 1950.)

points to which customers must come from time to time as they require supplies. This means, of course, that supplies must be made available at numerous points conveniently located to consumer homes.

Supply of Crude

The basic commodity of which gasoline is at present made is crude oil. California crude is found mainly in three areas—the San Joaquin Valley (which produced 46.8 per cent in 1947), the Los Angeles area (36.4 per cent) and the coastal area (16.8 per cent).[5] The bulk of the state's crude, then, comes from the valley and the Los Angeles areas. Los Angeles refineries obtain their crude supplies mainly from the local area.

While most companies operating refineries have crude-production facilities, few of the refiners produce enough crude to satisfy their own requirements completely.[6] Although a substantial amount comes from major-company wells, California crude orginates from the wells of many hundreds of producers.[7] These producers sell to refiners at buyer-set posted prices which vary with the specific gravity of the crude supplied. Reportedly, crude oil prices in California are

---

[5] Based on data in the *Petroleum World Annual Review, 1948,* pp. 130–131.

[6] Professor Bain states ". . . with the exception of Shell, which seems self-sufficient, the rank of the companies as buyers is roughly the same as their rank as refiners, but . . . the degree of their dependence varies considerably. . . . Thus, Standard purchases about 30 per cent of all the crude sold, Union and Richfield about 10 per cent each, General about 7.5 per cent, Tidewater and Texas about 4 per cent each, and Shell none." (Joe S. Bain, *The Economics of the Pacific Coast Petroleum Industry, Part 1: Market Structure* [Berkeley and Los Angeles: University of California Press, 1944], p. 53.)

[7] The region and type of company from which California crude originated in 1947 were as follows:

Type of firm[a]	Region		
	Los Angeles	San Joaquin Valley	Coastal area
	(per cent)	(per cent)	(per cent)
Major companies..........................	42.4	49.3	62.4
Principal minor companies..................	36.4	30.6	23.7
All other producers (over 1,200).............	21.2	20.1	13.9
	100.0	100.0	100.0

[a] Based on data in the *Petroleum World Annual Review, 1948,* pp. 130–131.

set by a leader and are concurred in by other concerns which operate refineries.[8]

Crude oil is by no means homogeneous. Generally speaking, much of the California crude is very heavy, with the result that the gasoline yield is relatively low by ordinary refining methods. Small refineries of the non-cracking type prefer lighter crudes which yield a larger percentage of gasoline by simpler refining methods. This lighter crude often is scarce and may bring a premium price, even when oil is plentiful.

The average gasoline yield from crude produced in California was 37 per cent in 1940, including that derived from the cracking process; this was considerably below the national average of approximately 44 per cent[9] (1938). It might be mentioned at this point that yields for the nation have increased tremendously over a period of twenty to twenty-five years.[10] The average yield for California is said to have increased to approximately 40 per cent currently. Because of (1) the prodigious demand for gasoline in California and the West generally and (2) the resulting large production of residual fuel oils during the gasoline refining process, definite steps have been taken by various companies recently to install facilities which will increase the yield even more.[11]

---

[8] According to Bain: "The Standard Oil Company of California seems to be the principal price leader, although leadership may be shared with Union." Joe S. Bain, *op. cit.*, Part 2: *Price Behavior and Competition* [Berkeley and Los Angeles: University of California Press, 1945], p. 114.

[9] The national and California yields were as follows in 1938 and 1940, respectively:

	National (1938)	California (1940)
	(per cent)	(per cent)
Gasoline[a]...................	44.3	37.0
Residual fuel oil..................	25.3	37.8
Gas oil and distillate fuel oil.........	13.0	15.1
Kerosene.......................	5.5	1.8
Lubricants......................	2.6	1.9
Other (including asphalt, road oil, liquefied gas, wax, coke, still gas)....	9.3	6.4

[a] From Joe S. Bain, *op. cit.*, Part 1: p. 36.

[10] Taking the nation as a whole, the yield of gasoline from crude increased from 26.1 per cent in 1920 to 43.1 per cent in 1940. (U. S. Bureau of the Census, *Statistical Abstract of the United States: 1948* [Washington, D. C., 1948], p. 773.)

[11] For example, General Petroleum announced in mid-1949 that it had begun construction of another "coker" in this area to convert fuel oil into other more salable products.

There is no compulsory oil-production limitation (conservation) program in California at present, as there is in Texas.[12] However, California producers operate under a voluntary conservation scheme. It is reportedly not based on market demand, but on such physical factors related to conservation of resources as the avoidance of un-economical drilling, preservation of proper gas and oil pressures, and others. This scheme, it is claimed, has little restrictive effect on the production of crude in this state.[13] Presumably, therefore, the amount of oil coming to the market in California, and therefore in Los Angeles, is largely determined by (1) the amount vendors can and will deliver at the price posted and (2) the amount buyers can and will accept at the price. Thus, price is the regulator of production and consumption.[14]

Production of Refined Gasoline

While there are many hundreds of producers of crude oil in the area under consideration, the number of refiners is relatively small. Table 1, adapted from U. S. Bureau of Mines reports, gives the num-

---

Such a unit uses heavy fuel oil as a charging stock, with reported yields of 20 per cent gasoline, 50 per cent gas oil (which itself can be made into products which are in active demand) and a residual of coke. Union Oil had reportedly let contracts for a very large expansion along the same line. (*Los Angeles Evening Herald & Express,* July 28, 1949.) Other large producers were in the process of modernizing their equipment to achieve some semblance of marketing balance between gasoline and residuals. (*National Petroleum News,* June 8, 1949, p. 13.)

[12] The Texas law, among other things, prohibits waste, and Article 6014 defines as waste the production of oil in excess of the reasonable market demand. (*Conservation of Oil and Gas: A Legal History, 1948,* edited by Blake M. Murphy [Chicago: Section of Mineral Law, American Bar Association, 1949], pp. 467–468.)

In early January, 1950 it was announced in the Los Angeles press that "the opening gun in a campaign to adopt in California an oil conservation and control measure similar to that in Texas has been fired by the Oil Producers' Agency of California." The article went on to say: "The present critical situation in the balance of supply and demand of petroleum products in this state appears to be the real factor behind the move." (*Los Angeles Evening Herald & Express,* January 5, 1950.)

[13] But the Department of Justice seems to have other ideas on this matter. See *Complaint, United States v. Standard Oil Company of California, et al.,* (Civil No. 11584-C, S. D. Cal., May 12, 1950) esp. pp. 12–15.

[14] The use of restrictive devices in the oil industry, however, is no panacea, for at least two reasons: (1) the end products of petroleum are jointly produced, with the result that when one (e.g., gasoline) is produced in the amount required by consumers, another (e.g., fuel oil) might be greatly overproduced in terms of market requirements; and (2) when a restriction scheme is prosecuted on an individual-state basis, the state having the program carries, in part at least, the burden of holding up prices for the rest—thus individual producers in a noncontrol state gain at the expense of producers in a control state.

ber, location, and capacity of gasoline-producing facilities in the Pacific Coast territory—including the states of Arizona, California, Nevada, Oregon, and Washington. These data show, for one thing, that almost all of the refining activity in the Pacific Coast territory is in California (99.5 per cent). They show, moreover, that a substantial portion of the state's gasoline-producing facilities is in the Los Angeles area (approximately 58 per cent of the refining capacity, 68

TABLE 1

NUMBER OF PETROLEUM REFINERIES, CRACKING PLANTS, AND NATURAL GASOLINE PLANTS
IN THE PACIFIC COAST REGION, CALIFORNIA, AND THE LOS ANGELES AREA,
AND CAPACITY OF THE CALIFORNIA AND LOS ANGELES PLANTS
AS PER CENT OF TOTAL PACIFIC COAST CAPACITY,
1929, 1939, AND 1949

	1929		1939		1949	
	Number of plants	Per cent of Pacific Coast capacity	Number of plants	Per cent of Pacific Coast capacity	Number of plants	Per cent of Pacific Coast capacity
Pacific Coast						
Petroleum refineries[a].......	53	100.0	58	100.0	43	100.0
Cracking plants..........	12	100.0	19	100.0	32	100.0
Natural gasoline plants.....	137	100.0	103	100.0	74	100.0
California						
Petroleum refineries[a].......	52	99.9	58	100.0	42	99.5
Cracking plants..........	12	100.0	19	100.0	31	99.5
Natural gasoline plants.....	137	100.0	103	100.0	74	100.0
Los Angeles area						
Petroleum refineries[a].......	28	64.3	37	62.6	23	57.5
Cracking plants..........	8	66.1	12	58.7	21	67.6
Natural gasoline plants.....	102	72.9	54	52.0	36	54.2

[a]Not including those designated as asphalt plants only.
Source: Original data obtained from U. S. Bureau of Mines, *Petroleum Refineries, Cracking Plants and Natural Gasoline Plants on the Pacific Coast, January 1, 1929;* U. S. Bureau of Mines, *Petroleum Refineries, Cracking Plants and Natural Gasoline Plants on the Pacific Coast, January 1, 1939;* and U. S. Bureau of Mines, *Petroleum Refineries, Cracking Plants, Natural Gasoline Plants and Cycle Plants in District Five, January 1, 1949.*

per cent of the cracked-gasoline capacity, and 54 per cent of the natural-gasoline capacity). There has been a trend toward a smaller percentage of refining capacity in the Los Angeles area relative to that of the state, but the percentage of cracking capacity in this area has been maintained from 1929 to 1949. Los Angeles is likely to hold its own in gasoline production, despite some reduction in the percentage of the region's refining capacity located in this area.

While no figures are available on the amount of gasoline produced by the companies in the Los Angeles area, rough approximation of the amount can be derived by applying facility-capacity percentages to known U. S. Bureau of Mines gasoline-production figures for the territory as a whole. Such a computation shows that in 1948 the Los Angeles area produced an estimated 3,031,000,000 gallons of gasoline.[15] It will be recalled that this area used an estimated 1,188,725,-000 gallons in that year; it would appear from this that it "exported," either to other areas within the state or to other states and countries, about 1,843,000,000 gallons, or about 60 per cent of the total quantity produced. While these figures are approximations,[16] there is no question that the Los Angeles basin is a surplus gasoline producing area —a point of considerable importance in evaluating the competitive situation.[17] It may be added that unlike some surplus areas for some commodities,[18] the bulk of the gasoline used in the Los Angeles area is produced in this area.[19]

Division of Refining Facilities between Majors and Independents. One further aspect of refining should be presented at this point— namely, the division of the control of the gasoline refining facilities between major and independent companies. The following figures for 1929, 1939, and 1949 illustrate this situation in the Los Angeles area:[20]

---

[15] This estimate was arrived at by applying the percentage of the state's refining capacity located in the Los Angeles basin to the total amount of gasoline produced in California during 1948 (as reported by the U. S. Bureau of Mines). The actual figures are: 57.5 (per cent) times 5,271,378,000 gallons = 3,031,042,000.

[16] The authors endeavored to obtain an estimate from various representatives of the industry on the percentage of the state's gasoline production originating in the Los Angeles basin but found that apparently no one has attempted to establish such a relationship. It was suggested, however, that the best basis for computing an estimate would be the capacity of crude oil refining facilities. It should be noted that finished gasoline includes the yields of crude oil refineries, cracked gasoline plants, and a part of the output of natural gasoline plants. To the extent that the capacities of cracking facilities and natural gasoline plants vary from one section of the state to another, the proportion of gasoline produced would be affected. In addition, the yield of gasoline from the crude oil varies with the quality of the crude as well as with the type of refining equipment used.

[17] This is true in theory at least. For one thing, all the sellers in this market are potential sources of supply for buyers in this area, while only a relatively few vendors sell in deficit areas. For another, the product is available here and can be acquired in this market on a "quick-deal" basis "at the rack" by aggressive retailers.

[18] In some surplus situations, because of seasonal demands or differences in quality, the area might import large quantities of goods for its own use.

[19] But see below, p. 46, n. 24.

[20] Original data obtained from: U. S. Bureau of Mines, *Petroleum Refineries, Crack-ing Plants and Natural Gasoline Plants on the Pacific Coast, January 1, 1929;* U. S. Bureau of Mines, *Petroleum Refineries, Cracking Plants and Natural Gasoline Plants*

	1929		1939		1949	
	Number	Per cent of capacity	Number	Per cent of capacity	Number	Per cent of capacity
Major-company plants						
Petroleum refineries........	9	68.9	7	72.8	10	83.8[a]
Cracking plants...........	6	87.3	8	87.1	15	92.5
Natural gasoline plants.....	50	51.8	28	58.1	23	65.4
Independent-company plants						
Petroleum refineries........	19	31.1	30	27.2	13	16.2
Cracking plants...........	2	12.7	4	12.9	6	7.5
Natural gasoline plants.....	52	48.2	26	41.9	13	34.6

[a] This figure includes two subsidiary-company plants, amounting to 1.4 per cent of the total capacity for the area.

These data indicate that the bulk of gasoline-producing capacity is controlled by major companies. Thus, over 80 per cent of the petroleum-refining capacity, over 90 per cent of cracking-plant capacity and approximately 65 per cent of natural-gasoline capacity of the Los Angeles area is major-company controlled. Moreover, the trend since 1929 has been toward more, rather than less, concentration. This trend toward major-company control of refinery operations may be intensified even more by the recent moves of the large concerns to attack the problem of imbalance between the lighter hydrocarbons and the heavy residuals by providing facilities designed to increase the yields of the former.

It should be borne in mind, however, that independent facilities *do* exist in this area, a point of considerable importance in determining the type of retail competitive structure that is found here. It should also be remembered that (1) assuming the major companies are in competition with one another, they may not behave as monopolists in their dealings with buyers (especially when the product is plentiful) and (2) gasoline is a commodity that is readily transportable in bulk, and thus supplies may be brought in from other producing areas, if that seems advisable.[21] Hence supplies are available in this market for those requiring them.

---

on the Pacific Coast, January 1, 1939; U. S. Bureau of Mines, *Petroleum Refineries, Cracking Plants, Natural Gasoline Plants and Cycle Plants in District Five, January 1, 1949.*

[21] In fact this was done by Eagle Oil & Refining Company when the company's contract with Standard Oil Company was concluded in 1949. (See below, p. 46, n. 24.)

Stocks an Important Supply Factor

The most critical factor in the supply picture, from the point of view of competition, is not the amount of product refined at any particular time but the stocks of gasoline on hand. Figure 4 shows the volume of stocks of gasoline held by California companies from 1932 to 1948, in relation to gasoline production figures which are provided for perspective purposes. The point here is that when total storage facilities for gasoline (finished and unfinished) are filled to capacity, the product must be moved into the market, even if a sacrifice in price must be made.

Figure 4 has several interesting aspects:

1. Gasoline stocks have a distinct seasonal element. Generally speaking, stocks are at their peak around March, and then typically decline throughout the spring and summer months until fall, when they start accumulating again.

2. Levels of stocks fluctuate for various reasons, in addition to normal imbalance between supply and demand. The highest peak (March, 1943) was reached at a period during World War II when production facilities were being taxed to turn out the product for defense purposes but before the government was ready to draw on these stocks for the big military campaigns ahead. The latest trough (late 1948) was due to strike conditions combined with the normal seasonal decline of that year.

3. Evidently there is no "normal" stock figure; the question is simply one of observing to what extent, if at all, stocks are "backing up" instead of moving out into distribution channels.

There can be little doubt that the volume of gasoline stocks has an effect on competitive activity and therefore on the price structure. In fact, those close to the market feel that the "sloppy" supply conditions during the late 1940's were a major factor in the weakening of the price structure at that time. The stock situation was considered critical because the amount of gasoline in storage had been steadily climbing toward the all-time peak reached in April 1943—25,000,000 barrels;[22] this, despite depletion of the stocks caused by the strike in late 1948. The point here is, that present production

---

[22] 25 million barrels of gasoline = 1,050,000,000 gallons.

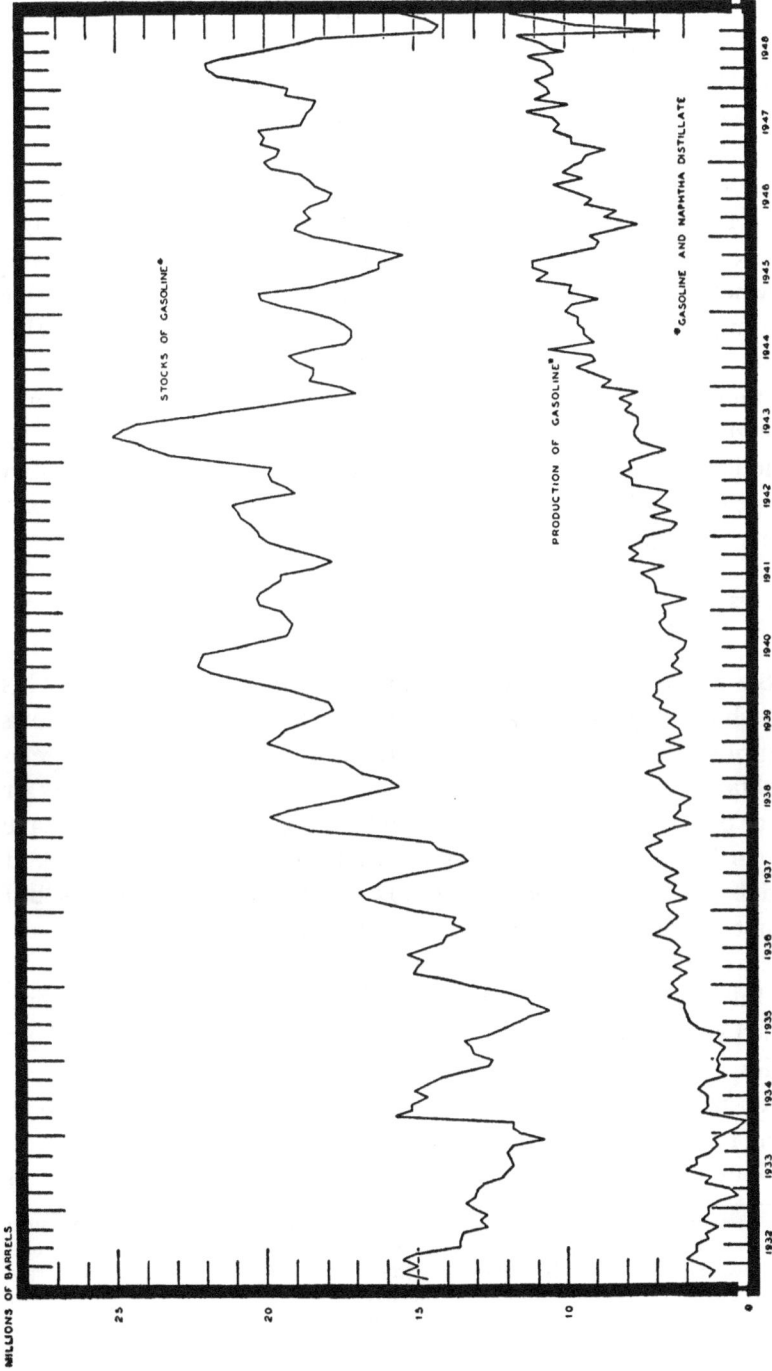

Fig. 4. Stocks of gasoline and naphtha distillates by California companies, and production of gasoline and naphtha distillates in the Pacific Coast territory, 1932–1948. From *Petroleum World Annual Review*, 1935–1949.

capacity tends toward the building of large stocks, which has an important influence on the thinking of competitors.

While it is undoubtedly true that stocks have an important bearing on the intensiveness of competition (buyers at times aggressively seeking supplies, and suppliers at other times aggressively seeking markets), stocks are not the only influencing factor. Indeed, it is a puzzling fact that there was little evidence of large surplus stocks in 1935 during one of the worst price disturbances in this area. Moreover, even when "sloppy" conditions prevail, intensive price-competitive conditions are not found in all markets but only in certain areas. This suggests the importance of two other factors: (1) the weakening or strengthening of demand through changes in population and income (although this should eventually affect the volume of stocks, assuming production is not adjusted to such a situation) and (2) the number and type of suppliers and retail outlets operating in the market (particularly the *type*).[23]

Sources of Gasoline at the Wholesale Level in the Los Angeles Market

Table 2, the authors feel, is quite a unique presentation. This table, which required a great amount of field investigation, shows the supplier companies from which retail dealers in the Los Angeles area obtained their gasoline requirements. These suppliers may or may not operate refineries; even if they do they may or may not have relied entirely on such facilities for their requirements in 1948. It should be noted that some suppliers owned refinery facilities but were not operating them at the time the study was made.

Several conclusions may be drawn from the data in table 2:

1. Only 18 of the 35 suppliers listed for the area, or 51 per cent, provided even a part of their requirements from their own refining facilities.

2. All majors operated refineries which provided most of their gasoline requirements in the Los Angeles area.

3. None of the subsidiaries, and only slightly over 45 per cent of

---

[23] The presence of aggressive competitors is an important factor. Indeed, once such competitors are established, overstocking is not a requisite to intensive price competition, because each seller is striving for the custom of consumer-buyers who care nothing about short or long supplies of the basic commodity, but are influenced by the relative values offered by the various alternative sources of supply at the retail level.

TABLE 2

FIRMS WHICH SUPPLIED GASOLINE TO RETAIL OUTLETS IN THE LOS ANGELES MARKET AND SOURCES FROM WHICH PRODUCT ORIGINATED, 1948

	Origin of gasoline			Origin of gasoline	
	Own refinery	Other sources		Own refinery	Other sources
Major companies			**Independent companies** (*cont.*)		
General Petroleum Corp.[a]	X	—	East-West Distribs.[l]	—	Hancock
Richfield Oil Corp.[b]	X	—	Fletcher Oil Co.	X	—
Shell Oil Co., Inc.	X	—	Hancock Oil Co. of Calif.	—	General Petr.[m]
Standard Oil Co. of Calif.	X	—			
The Texas Co.	X	—	Harbor Refining Co.	—	General Petr.
Tide Water Assoc. Oil Co.	X	Wilshire Oil[o]	Kern Oil Co., Ltd.	—	Wilshire[n]
Union Oil Co. of Calif.	X	—	Macmillan Petrol. Corp.	—	Shell[o]
			McCallen Refining Co.	X	—
Subsidiary companies			Mohawk Petroleum Co.	—	Richfield
Rio Grande Oil Co.	—	Richfield	Newhall Refining Co.	X	—
Seaside Oil Co.[d]	—	Associated	Olympic Refining Co.	—	General Petr.
Signal Oil Co.	—	Standard Oil[e]	Pathfinder Petroleum Co.	—	General Petr.
The Petrol Corp.[f]	—	Standard Oil	Signal Oil & Gas Co.[p]	—	Standard Oil
Independent companies			Socal Oil & Refining Co.	X	—
Baker Sales Co.	—	Various indep's.[g]	Sunland Refining Corp.	—	General Petr.
Ben Hur Refining Corp.	X[h]	Shell, Sunset, etc.	Sunset Oil Co.[q]	X	Associated
Calstate Refining Co.	X	Century	The Rothschild Oil Co.	X	—
Century Oil Co.[i]	X	Calstate	Time Oil Co.	—	Hancock and others
Douglas Oil Co. of Calif.	X[j]	Shell, principally			
Eagle Oil & Refin. Co., Inc. ...	—	Standard Oil[k]	Wilshire Oil Co., Inc.	X	—

[a] Wholly-owned subsidiary of Socony-Vacuum Oil Company Inc.
[b] Subsidiary of the Sinclair Oil Corporation and Cities Service Company.
[c] Wilshire has an exchange agreement with Associated to furnish Associated with some of its requirements in southern California, while Wilshire draws from Associated in the San Francisco Bay area.
[d] Seaside operates a refinery in Santa Barbara which is its source of supply in that area, but in the Los Angeles area it draws from Associated.
[e] Standard Oil Company of California.
[f] The Petrol Corporation has been a wholly-owned subsidiary of Standard Oil Company of California since January 14, 1948. The Petrol stations were subsequently converted to Chevron and Signal Oil Company outlets.
[g] Signal Oil & Gas, Ben Hur, Sunset, McCallen, etc.
[h] Refinery reported used for refining purposes only during the months of September and October 1948; blending operations were carried on for the entire year.
[i] Calstate and Century jointly controlled by one individual who is president of both concerns.
[j] Douglas produces very little gasoline in the Los Angeles basin as compared with its sales in the area (about 20 per cent of its requirements).
[k] As of July 1, 1949, when its contract with Standard Oil expired, Eagle began to seek out other sources and now obtains none of its requirements from Standard.
[l] Formerly operated a refinery, now dismantled and sold. Presently operate as distributors under name East-West Distributors.
[m] Exchange deal reportedly very favorable to Hancock because of Hancock's exceptional crude supplies.
[n] From Associated via Wilshire.
[o] Macmillan turns over gasoline partially processed to Shell in exchange for its finished product.
[p] Acquired by Standard Oil of California in August, 1947. (Not to be confused with the Signal Oil Company listed above.)
[q] After considerable period of time and several false starts, Eagle Oil recently acquired the controlling interest in Sunset Oil Co. including its terminal facilities and refinery.

Source: Field investigations by the authors.

the independents, operated refining facilities; the rest depended on major companies for their supplies.[24]

4. The ultimate source of supply of gasoline may be twice removed from the immediate source; that is, an independent company (e.g., Hancock) might be given as the source of supply for another (e.g., Time Oil Company) but the ultimate source may be one of the majors (e.g., General Petroleum).

It may be seen from this that (1) not all suppliers have refining facilities but purchase their requirements from those having such facilities, (2) some companies with refining facilities produce only a part of their requirements and acquire the rest elsewhere, and (3)

---

[24] Until mid-1949 the Eagle Oil & Refining Company, an aggressive independent-supplier company in this area, was purchasing its gasoline on a contract with Standard Oil Company of California. The contract had been consummated in 1945 when it appeared that gasoline was going to be in oversupply; the contract was reputedly very favorable to Eagle. According to the terms of this agreement, the price to be paid was on an "escalator" basis (a certain amount below the posted tankwagon quotation and fluctuating with it); reportedly, Eagle Oil was required to maintain the retail price. Eagle was allowed to rebrand the gasoline acquired from Standard Oil; the product was accordingly sold under the *Golden Eagle* brand.

It is reported that Standard Oil was unhappy about the arrangement for two reasons: (1) The threatened surplus did not develop in this market as soon as was expected, hence the company could have sold its supplies at considerably higher prices. (2) The Eagle Oil Company became one of the most aggressive price competitors in the Los Angeles market.

In late June, 1949, when the contract termination date arrived, Standard Oil announced that it would not renew under the old terms, although reportedly the company was willing to serve Eagle at a higher price (1.85 cents above the old quotation, according to the *National Petroleum News*, August 3, 1949, p. 15). Eagle evidently started looking elsewhere for its supplies and the company's efforts in this direction created quite a flurry in the market. One large retail distributor reported that he had been buying from Sunset Oil Company until the termination of the Standard Oil-Eagle Oil contract, and when Eagle was forced to scurry for gasoline supplies he was no longer able to obtain the necessary amount of gasoline from Sunset and had to go elsewhere and pay a higher price.

Eagle Oil & Refining Company sought a court order to force Standard Oil to continue to serve it on the grounds that the cutting off of its supplies by Standard Oil was part of a conspiracy and in violation of the antitrust laws. Eagle obtained a temporary restraining order in mid-July, 1949, requiring continuation of service by Standard pending a hearing as to whether a temporary injunction should be granted. A decree quashing Eagle Oil Company's request for an order to compel Standard Oil to continue to sell the company gasoline was handed down in mid-August, 1949. Eagle temporarily solved its problem by "importing" at least a part of its requirements (its total needs at that time were reportedly 10 to 12 million gallons per month) from Texas (*National Petroleum News*, August 17, 1949), and purchasing the balance from various local sources including Tide Water Associated and others. In March, 1950, it was announced that Eagle had acquired the controlling interest in Sunset Oil Company, including its marine terminal (which would facilitate intermarket operations), a refinery, crude oil holdings, and retail outlets (*Los Angeles Times*, March 22, 1950).

the bulk of gasoline sold in the Los Angeles area originates with major company refineries. However, there are many alternative sources of supply of gasoline in this market, which is of significance as a competitive factor in retail gasoline distribution.

Just one more comment on this subject: Gasoline may be purchased outright on some contractual basis, either by a retailer for direct sale to the consumer, or by supplier companies for sale to retailers. In addition, it may be (1) acquired in exchange for crude, or (2) obtained in one area in exchange for gasoline to be delivered in another.[25] The following are examples of arrangements which exist in the Los Angeles area:

1. The straight sale of gasoline by one supplier to another on a contractual basis, as for example the Standard Oil-Eagle Oil & Refining Company contract (now concluded) and the General Petroleum-Olympic Refining Company arrangement.

2. The exchange of petroleum for gasoline, as for example the Harbor Refining Company-General Petroleum agreement, whereby Harbor provides the crude to General Petroleum and receives gasoline in return.[26] The former reportedly retains ownership of the product at all times and, in effect, pays General Petroleum a processing charge. In a similar but slightly more involved agreement Kern Oil Company supplies crude to Associated and in return receives

---

[25] With all the trading in gasoline going on in this market one might expect that brokers would be a factor. By brokers we mean functionaries who arrange transfers of title but do not accept title to the merchandise whose sale they have arranged. Actually, the authors have been able to find few instances of any suppliers or large retailers in this area using the services of a broker. Although we have not been able to get very much information from the field on this matter, it would seem that because of the small number of suppliers and large buyers, and the fact that each seems to coöperate with the other in passing on supply information, intermediaries are not necessary in the seeking out of supplies by buyers or the finding of buyers by vendors. We feel safe in saying that there are no functionaries who employ *all* of their time and facilities in brokerage operations in the gasoline field. However, individuals who normally deal in gasoline at wholesale on their own account might from time to time arrange transfers of title for a fee, although we have not discovered any actual cases. Moreover, it appears that brokers operate in the crude petroleum field (and possibly in unfinished gasolines, and in certain refined petroleum products), especially for export.

[26] According to one independent producer, the best of these arrangements is the Hancock-General Petroleum contract, in which Hancock supplies crude petroleum and General Petroleum furnishes Hancock with its gasoline requirements. This agreement reportedly was entered into because of General Petroleum's desire to share in Hancock's large supply of crude. Rumor has it that Hancock obtains gasoline actually below General Petroleum's cost, which in effect amounts to a bonus on the crude.

supplies of gasoline from the Wilshire Oil Company plant. This plant is conveniently located to the Whittier-Pico area, where most of the Kern Company's retail business in the Los Angeles area is concentrated.

3. The straight exchange of finished product as in the Mohawk-Richfield arrangement whereby Mohawk draws on Richfield for gasoline in the Los Angeles area and Richfield draws on Mohawk for gasoline in the Bakersfield area.[27]

Supply at the Retail Level

We now turn to the source of supply from the point of view of the ultimate consumer. Gasoline is of course offered at retail in combination with other related products and with a considerable number of free services, including windshield cleaning, tire inspection, and the like.[28] The importance of the spatial factor is intensified at the retail level, because the product-service is a repeat-purchase item; facilities must therefore be available at various points within a rather narrowly confined geographical area, so that it will be possible to secure the product-service at the time and place of the consumers' needs.[29] The

---

[27] According to an executive of one of the companies, the Richfield-Mohawk agreement was made some years before World War II. At the time it was made, Richfield was selling about 2 million gallons in the San Joaquin Valley area, and Mohawk about the same amount in the Los Angeles area, so the exchange agreement resulted in a saving of a considerable sum in hauling fees.

[28] Sales made in earlier stages of distribution often include service elements also, although sometimes such sales involve little if any service, that is, when the commodity is sold f.o.b. refinery ("at the rack") for cash. Services offered at the wholesale level might take the form of convenient delivery, extended credit terms, providing improvements in the retailer-buyer's facilities, and others.

[29] A recent study analyzes the problem of how many filling stations would be necessary to perform certain basic functions at specified levels of adequacy. The assumption is made that the three basic functions of the service station are (1) to supply the needs of the motorist, (2) to yield a satisfactory money profit to the operator, and (3) to add value to the community. The author concludes: "If the criterion of adequacy is to maximize the profits of individual station operators, anything more than approximately 2,000 stations [for the United States] would have been too many in 1946. Correspondingly, if the criterion of adequacy is to pump a given quantity of gasoline over a given period of time, through as few pumps as possible, without regard to what the consumer wants from the retailer other than the physical product gasoline, then anything more than 1,900 or 2,000 stations in 1946 would have been hard to justify. On the other hand, four million or even five million stations might have been necessary to provide gasoline plus maximum convenience of consumers. . . . In a society organized to give the consumer as little service as possible and to squeeze out of him as high a profit as possible for the station from which he buys, the number operating in 1946

quantity of gasoline available at retail locations normally has little significance since these outlets act only as channels through which the product is transmitted (although the capacities of these distribution facilities might well be a supply factor). Thus, the emphasis here is on the number, location, and nature of retail facilities through which the product-service becomes available to consumer-buyers rather than on the supply of the basic product available.

Table 3 shows the number of service stations in the Los Angeles area, and the percentages of the total number, classified by individual suppliers and types of firms. According to these data some 6,800 stations existed in the area in 1947. They distributed the products of some 35 suppliers under scores of brand names. In 1947, 53.6 per cent of the gasoline outlets carried the products of major companies, 11.2 per cent carried subsidiary-company products, 34.0 per cent carried the products of independent companies, and 1.2 per cent were classified as retailer-rebranders. (This latter figure probably has increased considerably since 1947.) Thus, the area as a whole is represented by a considerable number of suppliers selling through a large number of outlets of various types.

The figures in table 3 leave much to be desired since they are for the Los Angeles area as a whole and not classified by submarkets. This latter is important in evaluating the adequacy of retail facilities from the standpoint of service to the consumer. Therefore, table 4 is provided to present data showing the number of service stations by types of suppliers in the 48 subareas composing the Los Angeles market. From this one may note that with only one exception major companies, subsidiaries, and independents are represented in all 48 subareas. The data in table 4 suggest that (1) generally speaking the Los Angeles area is well supplied with service-station facilities in all subareas (although not necessarily in every neighborhood *within* each of the subareas) and (2) all types of service are available to consumers since major, subsidiary, and independent stations exist in substantial

---

was excessively large. The number of stations fell very far short indeed, however, of what would be required for a consumer's paradise where everything possible was done to reduce the energy and foresight he must himself exercise if he is always to have gasoline for his automobile tank exactly where and when he wants it with no more than a few moments delay." (Richard D. Lundy, "How Many Service Stations Are Too Many," in *Theory in Marketing, op. cit.,* pp. 321–333.)

TABLE 3

NUMBERS AND PERCENTAGES OF SERVICE STATIONS IN THE LOS ANGELES AREA,
BY TYPES OF SUPPLIERS AND BY INDIVIDUAL COMPANIES, 1947

Company	Number of stations	Per cent of total	Company	Number of stations	Per cent of total
Majors			Independents, (cont.)		
General Petroleum Corp....	783	11.50	Harbor Refining Co.......	130	1.91
Standard Oil Co. of Cali-			Rothschild Oil Co.........	97	1.43
fornia..................	609	8.95	Kern Oil Co., Ltd........	88	1.29
The Texas Co............	531	7.80	Caminol Co.............	81	1.19
Union Oil Co. of California.	513	7.54	Century Oil Co..........	73	1.07
Richfield Oil Corp........	469	6.89	Pathfinder Petroleum Co..	69	1.01
Shell Oil Co., Inc.........	442	6.50	Mohawk Petroleum Co....	46	.68
Tide Water Associated Oil			Newhall Refining Co......	42	.62
Co...................	301	4.42	Olympic Refining Co......	31	.46
			Socal Oil & Refining Co...	31	.46
Total majors...........	3,648	53.60	Sunland Refining Corp....	15	.22
			Exeter Oil Co., Ltd.......	15	.22
Subsidiaries			Operators' Oil & Refining		
Signal Oil Co. (Standard			Co...................	12	.18
Oil)..................	331	4.86	W. G. Krieger, Inc........	10	.15
The Petrol Corp.ᵃ (Stand-			Ben Hur Refining Corp....	10	.15
ard Oil)...............	197	2.89	East-West Distributors ...	9	.13
Rio Grande Oil Co.			Calstate Refining Co......	5	.07
(Richfield).............	133	1.95			
Seaside Oil Co. (Tide Water			Total independents	2,310	33.97
Assoc.)................	105	1.54			
			Retailer-rebranders		
Total subsidiaries........	766	11.24	Parks...................	10	.15
			Hane Bros...............	5	.07
Independents			Sears, Roebuck & Co......	4	.06
Sunset Oil Co............	292	4.29	Mark Bloome...........	4	.06
Wilshire Oil Co., Inc.......	283	4.16	Craig Oil Co............	1	.01
Eagle Oil & Refining Com-			Miscellaneous...........	57	.84
pany, Inc..............	235	3.45			
Hancock Oil Co. of Cali-			Total retailer-rebranders.	81	1.19
fornia.................	212	3.12			
Douglas Oil Co. of California	212	3.12			
Fletcher Oil Co...........	174	2.56	GRAND TOTAL...........	6,805	100.00
Macmillan Petroleum Corp.	138	2.03			

ᵃ Petrol did not become a subsidiary of Standard Oil until January 1948 (see footnote (ᶠ), table 2).
Source: *Service Station Route List*, Hearst Publications, Inc. (*Los Angeles Examiner* Dept.), 1947, supplemented by field investigation in June, 1949, to determine brands handled by those outlets for which complete information was not available.

numbers in all subareas except one. This general availability of numerous outlets of different types, well distributed from the standpoint
of consumer requirements, has an important bearing on the nature
of competition in the Los Angeles market.

TABLE 4

NUMBERS OF SERVICE STATIONS IN THE FORTY-EIGHT SUBMARKETS OF THE LOS ANGELES
AREA, CLASSIFIED BY TYPES OF COMPANIES REPRESENTED, 1947

No.	Submarkets Location	Major companies	Subsidiary companies	Independent[a] companies	Total
	Downtown	132	21	30	183
1	Westlake	85	10	43	138
2	Elysian Park	53	9	38	100
3	Glendale	190	27	111	328
4	Burbank	65	26	46	137
5	San Fernando	37	4	35	76
6	Valley	80	24	51	154
7	North Hollywood	61	17	42	117
8	Hollywood	165	15	77	256
9	Wilshire Center	126	8	35	169
10	Miracle Mile	101	16	31	142
11	West Hollywood	61	14	24	99
12	Beverly Hills	75	12	23	110
13	Westwood	44	5	3	52
14	Santa Monica	155	41	72	268
15	Culver City	42	11	35	88
16	Washington-Jefferson	89	20	74	183
17	Crenshaw-Santa Monica	103	17	64	183
18	Inglewood	76	10	59	145
19	Westchester	8	—	3	11
20	Manhattan-Redondo	48	11	24	83
21	Torrance	31	7	24	62
22	Morningside-Gardena	82	25	102	209
23	South Downtown	62	9	35	106
24	South Central	123	41	155	319
25	Compton	66	17	80	163
26	Dominguez	6	7	6	19
27	Wilmington-San Pedro	70	14	33	114
28	Long Beach	209	55	157	413
29	Downey	43	12	45	100
30	Huntington-So. Gate	89	29	97	215
31	Vernon-Maywood	54	18	41	113
32	Lincoln-Heights	33	10	26	69
33	South Gate	48	13	30	91
34	Pasadena	182	25	82	288
35	Foothills	61	13	28	102
36	Pomona	94	30	45	169
37	Baldwin-Covina	22	6	26	54
38	El Monte	48	10	49	107
39	Alhambra	99	27	74	200
40	Boyle Heights	68	19	48	135
41	Belvedere	46	10	60	116
42	Montebello	17	5	23	45
43	Whittier	50	2	36	88
44	Fullerton	46	3	21	70
45	Anaheim	146	9	43	198
46	Santa Ana	69	17	51	137
47	Orange Coast	88	15	54	157
	Totals	3,648	766	2,391	6,805

[a] Including retailer-rebranders.

Source: *Service Station Route List*, Hearst Publications, Inc. (*The Los Angeles Examiner* Dept.), 1947, supplemented by field investigation in June, 1949, to determine brands distributed by outlets for which complete

Integration in Production and Distribution

We have referred in previous sections of this chapter to supply at various levels of production and distribution. The question now arises as to the continuity of ownership control by individual oil companies from the production of the crude product to the placing of the finished commodity in the hands of the consumer. Actually this question has two sides: (1) the extent of any integration which may prevail and (2) the type of such integration.

Extent of Integration. Vertical combination in gasoline production and distribution varies considerably among companies. The following is an attempt to classify integration by the type of concern.

1. The major suppliers operating in the Los Angeles area typically produce some of the crude they use, and carry on a large part of the transportation and jobbing (wholesaling) operations themselves; but, with one main exception, they distribute little of their products through their own retail outlets.

2. Subsidiary companies may, and often do, produce crude petroleum and may even control some transportation and wholesale marketing facilities; but typically they do not operate refineries or service stations.

3. Independent supplier companies may, or may not, control the source of their crude petroleum, operate refineries, and conduct their own wholesale marketing operations; but they typically do not own transportation facilities and do not operate their own service stations.

One may infer from the foregoing that: (1) In the Los Angeles area complete integration does not exist in the sense of the operation of oil wells, transportation facilities, and refineries on a self-sufficient basis, and the complete distribution of the product to the consuming public through company-owned stations.[30] (2) There is, however, a considerable degree of integration, especially among major companies in the sense of partial control of crude sources, ownership of refineries, and the operation of marketing facilities up to, but not

---

[30] Various methods are used in the wholesale distribution of gasoline: (1) Complete company ownership and operation of wholesale distribution (jobbing) facilities (e.g., major companies, at least in the more populous areas). (2) Company ownership but distributor-operated distribution facilities (e.g., some of the smaller companies, generally, and major companies in outlying areas). (3) Distributor ownership and operation of facilities (e.g., most of the smaller companies and some major companies in rural areas).

including, the retail level. (3) A substantial segment of the industry —including subsidiary and independent companies—is still either unintegrated or integrated to only a minor extent.[31]

We may conclude, therefore, that typically a substantial degree of, but by no means complete, integration prevails in this industry, but that it stops short of the retail level;[32] and that with only one important exception (Standard Oil of California)[33] the actual operation of gasoline service stations is a nonintegrated activity in the Los Angeles market.

[31] Atypically, Rothschild Oil Company owns a considerable number of crude oil holdings, and operates its own refinery from which it serves several company-operated self-serve stations as well as its approximately two hundred uncontrolled service-station accounts.

[32] Although, admittedly, close control of retailer policies through lease or contractual arrangements may prevail.

An important change occurred during the years 1929–1939 from company-operated toward dealer-operated stations; this latter type of operation was known as the "Iowa plan." Evidence of this change is found in the United States figures for chains and independent service stations:

United States	Per cent of total sales	
	1939	1929
Independents...................	88.4	66.0
Chains.......................	10.2	33.8
Other types..................	1.4	0.2
	100.0	100.0

The decline in company-operated stations during these ten years was much less striking in Los Angeles than the United States as a whole, as evidenced by the following data:

Los Angeles	Per cent of total sales	
	1939	1929
Independents...................	79.7	71.8
Chains.......................	20.3	28.2
Other types..................	—	—
	100.0	100.0

The above figures are from the *Sixteenth Census of the United States 1940, Census of Business, Retail Trade: 1939—Types of Operation*, pp. 6 and 17. The figures for chain operation do not represent company operation exclusively but include numerous small independent companies which operate four or more stations.

[33] This company distributes the bulk of its products through dealers rather than company-operated stations, however.

Type of Integration. It appears that integration in the gasoline field has been largely if not entirely of the "forward" type thus far, i.e., the integration movement seems to have proceeded from crude production through refining operations to market distribution, rather than conversely.[34] This seems to suggest the growing importance of the struggle for markets over the years. However, as was noted previously, this trend was reversed in part a few years ago when many of the companies operating service stations shifted to some sort of leasing scheme.

While backward integration (from the retail level to wholesale distribution to refining, at least) has not developed to any great extent in this area thus far, it may be that some such development will be forthcoming, especially if the aggressive mass distributors run into any difficulty in obtaining supplies of gasoline. The move by retailers to acquire refinery facilities would be theoretically possible either as an individual company development or as a coöperative venture. Such a tendency would not be inevitable, however, even assuming a "squeeze" by major suppliers, because of the existence of what may be considered better alternatives, such as importing gasoline from some other producing center.

---

[34] However, Rothschild Oil Company is an example of backward integration. The company started, reportedly, some time in 1934 with a small delivery truck, gradually developed until it now owns a refinery, and by mid-1950 was active in the Placerita Canyon drilling operation.

V

THE QUALITY OF GASOLINE
IN THE LOS ANGELES MARKET

A full understanding of the supply of a commodity requires not only analysis of the quantity of product available but also of the quality. Without some knowledge of product quality, quantitative analysis would not be complete, since it would have no specific referent. Thus, when considering the competitive offerings of individual sellers, statements of quantity without reference to quality are meaningless.

We are not concerned at the moment with what consumers think of the various offerings; we are concerned with the physical aspect of the product. Fortunately, (1) gasoline is susceptible to rather precise grading and (2) a substantial amount of data concerning the quality of the product in this market is available from government publications and commercial sources.

Nature of Quality Tests

The two principal tests[1] used in determining the quality of gaso-

---

[1] The State of California provides minimum standards for gasoline quality by statutory definition, largely on the basis of distillation limits. Despite the fact that this law was passed some years ago, these standards are high enough to be effective in

line are the distillation range and the octane rating. Other criteria used in the rating of gasoline quality are sulphur content, vapor pressure, gum content, and gravity A.P.I.[2]

Principal Tests. (1) Distillation Range.—These points indicate the temperature at which evaporation starts (initial boiling point) and at which 10 per cent, 50 per cent, and 90 per cent of the product evaporates. The end point is reached when all of the product has evaporated, with the exception of a small residue. The initial boiling point should not be too high, 100 degrees Fahrenheit or so, because if it is too far above this point the gasoline loses its starting quality. A high end point increases crank-case dilution and engine deposits (the higher the end point, the greater the temperature needed for complete combustion); at the same time too low an end point means the sacrifice of power and mileage. It is, therefore, a matter of proper balance: the refiner must obtain all the power possible without causing too much crank-case dilution and engine deposits. Fuels with end points in the range of 350 to 400 degrees are commonly considered to be cleaner burning with less carbon deposits and crank-case dilu-

---

preventing the sale of low-grade motor fuels. Thus, "gasoline" as defined in the statute means ". . . any liquid petroleum product which conforms to the following specifications: (A) [Freedom from water and suspended matter] It shall be free from water and suspended matter. (B) [Discoloration] A clean copper strip shall not show more than extremely slight discoloration when submerged in the gasoline for three hours, at 122 degrees Fahrenheit, . . . (C) [Distillation limits] It shall distill, within the following limits, . . . using the low distillation thermometer: 1. When the thermometer reads 167 degrees Fahrenheit, not less than 10 percent shall be evaporated. 2. When the thermometer reads 284 degrees Fahrenheit, not less than 50 percent shall be evaporated. 3. When the thermometer reads 392 degrees Fahrenheit, not less than 90 percent shall be evaporated. 4. The end point shall not be higher than 437 degrees Fahrenheit. 5. At least 95 percent shall be recovered as distillate in the receiver from the distillation. 6. The distillation residue shall not exceed 2 percent." (*Business and Professions Code of California,* Art. 4, Sec. 20780.)

Actually, according to one official of the Bureau of Weights and Measures (the policing agency), most automobiles would operate satisfactorily on gasoline which barely meets the standards imposed, except perhaps for a possible ping because of a low octane rating. The bureau has little to do with the latter; however, if there is a misleading advertisement containing reference to the octane rating, it can turn over the case to the proper authorities upon a misleading-advertising charge. (*Bus. and Prof. Code of Calif.,* Sec. 17500; also Section 5 of the Federal Trade Commission Act which covers misleading advertising in interstate commerce.) Thus, like some products (e.g. foods, drugs), and unlike others (e.g. hardware, shoes), gasoline must meet a minimum standard before it is offered for sale.

[2] These tests are not necessarily of minor significance in measuring the quality of gasoline. For example, sulphur content may not be very important as long as it tests within the normal limits, but it is quite important if it is above the "normal."

tion than those outside these limits.[3] The middle (50 per cent) point is an indication of the proper blending of the initial boiling point and the end point ratings to achieve efficient operation. The middle point should be around 240 degrees but may have considerable variation either way without greatly affecting performance.

(2) Octane Rating.—The purpose of octane tests is to determine the antiknock rating of the gasoline. Gasoline with higher octane ratings tends to be "ping free." Two methods are used, the motor method and the research method. The octane rating for regular-grade gasoline should be at least 75 by motor method, or 80 by research method; the octane rating for premium-grade gasoline should exceed 80 (motor) or 88 (research).[4]

Other Tests. (1) Sulphur Content.—Sulphur is an impurity. Gasoline containing too much of it may (a) be lacking in power (b) cause formation of sulphuric acid and consequently corrosion of exhaust pipes (especially when driving is intermittent and the engine does not have time to warm up sufficiently to blow the burned sulphur residue out of the exhaust pipe), and (c) have low "lead suscepti-

---

[3] One who is familiar with this test stated that the amount of gasoline that can be recovered from the crude product is dependent to a considerable extent on the end point desired. Most refiners consider an end point of 400 desirable. Gasoline quality, however, largely "follows the leader." For instance, it is reported that when one of the majors announced an aviation ethyl with an end point of 350, the other majors followed suit, putting their medium-grade product at 350 and keeping the "house brand" in the neighborhood of 400. This is approximately where the companies try to keep their end points at the present time.

[4] There is no consistent differential between the motor and research results. The booklet *What Is Octane Number?* (New York: Ethyl Corporation, 1947) pp. 4–5 states: "The American Society for Testing Materials (ASTM) Motor Method of rating motor fuels gave satisfactory results for many years. However, with the advent of newer refinery techniques, it was found that blends of the newer gasolines would often give better road performance than their laboratory octane number would indicate. As a result, a second method of test was developed called the CFR Research Method. Although, to date, no one test has been developed which will satisfactorily rate a gasoline for all the operating conditions that are experienced on the highway, these two methods of laboratory octane number determination are now in widespread use. Both tests are run in the same CFR engine, but under different sets of operating conditions. For most gasolines the conditions in the CFR Research Method of test are considered less severe than in the ASTM-CFR Motor Method of test. Accordingly, most gasolines will have a higher octane number by the Research Method of test than they will by the Motor Method.

"Fuel 'sensitivity' is defined as the Research rating minus the Motor Method rating. Within reasonable limits, gasolines having higher sensitivities will normally give better road performance, assuming the two fuels being compared have the same octane number by the ASTM Motor Method. The type of crude oil and the refining methods applied to it will influence the antiknock behavior of the gasoline."

bility," requiring more ethyl lead to reach a certain octane rating.[5]
Sulphur content limits of around 0.27 per cent in regular grade and
0.135 per cent in premium grade are considered reasonable in southern California, although higher ratings are not necessarily too critical.

(2) *Vapor Pressure.*—Vapor pressure affects the quick-starting
quality of the gasoline. The pressure must be high enough to insure
quick starting but low enough to avoid vapor lock. Therefore gasoline should test less than 10 pounds per square inch,[6] but preferably
not less than 7.

(3) *Gum Content.*—Gum is another impurity, hence undesirable.
The amount of gum in gasoline may result from storage rather than
the refining process. Gasoline may come from the refining plant with
little or no gum content; after storage for a period of time oxidation
may take place and form gum. Gasoline may test as high as 3 mg. of
gum per 100 cc. without great harm but the preferred rating is 1 mg.
per 100 cc.

(4) *Gravity° A.P.I.*[7]—This test is of little importance now.

Grades of Gasoline

Gasoline has been sold in the Los Angeles market, as in others, at
several different quality levels. However, while a third-grade[8] motor
fuel was offered in this market[9] prior to World War II, for some
years now gasoline has been offered almost exclusively, if not entirely,

---

[5] When the Ethyl Corporation first controlled the use of tetraethyl lead, it required
a maximum limit of 0.10 per cent sulphur content for premium-grade gasoline and
later changed the requirement to 0.25.

[6] In cold climate vapor pressure may go as high as 12 without danger, but in California it normally should be under 10.

[7] Standard set by the American Petroleum Institute.

[8] According to the results of tests published by the California Testing Laboratories,
Inc. for November, 1934 (California Testing Laboratories, Inc., *Gasoline in Southern
California 1934–1944*, [Los Angeles] 1944), the third-structure gasoline was distinctly
inferior to regular-quality gasoline. Specifically, the end point was considerably higher
and the octane rating was definitely lower.

[9] This move reportedly was introduced by majors during the intensive price-competitive conditions of the early 1930's and was at once a device for (a) catering to
both their quality and price customers, and (b) strongly implying that the quality
of gasoline sold by price-cutting independents was third grade (as it was). Thus,
General Petroleum had *Metro;* Richfield had *Rocor;* Shell had *Green Streak;* Standard
had *Flight;* Texas had *Indian* and *Calpet;* Tidewater had *White Gold* and Union had
White Magic.

at only two quality levels: regular quality ("house brand" so called) and premium quality.[10] The Ethyl Corporation claims that the octane rating of ethyl gasoline is at least five points higher than that of regular grade;[11] this seems to be borne out by the figures (see table 6).

There is some question as to whether the use of premium-quality gasoline provides any advantage to the motorist. The manufacturers of a few cars with exceptionally high compression ratios (e.g., Oldsmobile "90" and Cadillac) recommend its use, and some manufacturers say that it "may be used" (e.g., Buick "50" and "70"). A balanced view of the matter seems to be that for most motors the premium grade is not at all necessary, except possibly as an assurance against occasional "pinging." Despite this fact, premium-grade gasoline is used by approximately 60 per cent of the families in this market area according to the *Los Angeles Times* consumer studies.[12] (However, there is considerable variation in the proportion sold by particular stations.)

The relationship between the amount of regular-grade and premium-grade gasoline sold in this market is a result of (1) the current

---

[10] Premium-quality gasoline for one thing generally has a high antiknock rating, which is usually provided by the adding of tetraethyl lead (T.E.L.). According to one of the men in the Los Angeles office of the Ethyl Corporation, one eastern company for a number of years raised the octane number to a level satisfactory enough to permit it to compete in the market without the use of Ethyl. Finally, however, the economics of the proposition caught up with the company: recently it found that the use of the lead is the cheaper method of increasing octane rating.

Tetrathyl lead is supplied by two companies—the Ethyl Corporation and Dupont. Standard Oil, for example, buys lead from both Dupont and the Ethyl Corporation; Shell Oil and Tide Water Associated reported that they purchase from both these companies, also. No other sources of the lead are available according to all reports collected from the oil companies and from the Ethyl Corporation.

[11] Advertisement in *Life*, April 17, 1950, p. 1.

[12] The following is a percentage breakdown of answers to the question, "Does your family usually buy regular or Ethyl gasoline?":[a]

	Combined July–Sept. 1949	Combined Oct.–Dec. 1949
Regular....................	37.3	34.2
Ethyl......................	59.1	61.2
Both.......................	2.7	2.1
Don't know................	.9	2.5
Total....................	100.0	100.0

[a] *Los Angeles Times*, "Continuing Home Audit Los Angeles County."

cyclical situation (consumers are at present *able* to buy the more expensive fuel) and (2) the present price differential between premium grade and regular grade. (Consumers are *willing* to pay the premium for the higher-test product.) Less favorable conditions (e.g., in depression times) would undoubtedly result in a sharp shift away from the purchase of the premium-grade product.[13]

Evaluation of Quality in Los Angeles Area

As was mentioned earlier, data are available regarding the quality of gasoline sold in the Los Angeles area. These data are (1) the results of tests of gasoline samples taken in the Los Angeles area and in other areas and (2) the results of tests made of gasoline sold by the various suppliers within the Los Angeles area.

Quality in This Area Compared with Other Areas. The data in table 5 are the result of tests of regular-grade and premium-grade gasoline samples taken by the U. S. Bureau of Mines in southern California compared with the average for the United States in 1936 and 1948; the tests include: Gravity° A.P.I., distillation, Reid vapor pressure, gum content, tetraethyl lead content, sulphur content, and octane ratings by the motor method. Thus, figures are presented which make possible comparisons between (1) the market area under observation and the national average and (2) the market area under observation for 1936 and for 1948. (This comparison over time is not perfect because of a broadening of the area in the latter year.) [14]

A study of table 5 reveals that:

1. Although the difference is so slight as to be insignificant, the quality of gasoline sold in Los Angeles is, if anything, higher than the average of other cities included in the U. S. Bureau of Mines sample. Even though the gasoline in the area contains more sulphur than the national average according to the sample, it has a lower end point and a higher octane rating.

2. Gasoline has improved in quality in Los Angeles as well as in other areas in the United States over a period of years as is shown in table 5, although the quality of gasoline available to the consuming public suffered a temporary setback during World War II. The im-

---

[13] See section on the pricing of regular-grade and premium-grade gasoline in chapter xiii, pp. 205–206.

[14] The area covered in 1936 was Los Angeles only, but in 1948 the area for which samples were taken had been extended to include all of southern California.

TABLE 5

QUALITY OF GASOLINE SOLD IN LOS ANGELES COMPARED WITH THE AVERAGE QUALITY OF A NATIONAL SAMPLE, SUMMER, 1936, AND QUALITY OF GASOLINE SOLD IN SOUTHERN CALIFORNIA COMPARED WITH THE AVERAGE QUALITY OF A NATIONAL SAMPLE, SUMMER, 1948

	Gravity °A.P.I.	Distillation										Per cent resid. loss		R.V.P. lb.	Gum mg/100 ml.	T.E.L. ml./gal.	Sulphur per cent	Octane no. motor method
		I.B.P.	5	10	20	30	50	70	90	95	End point	resid.	loss					
Summer, 1936																		
Regular:																		
Los Angeles	57.9	98	...	150	182	209	255	298	355	(a)	403	0.9	2.1	...	...	...	0.14	70.3
Average of U.S.[b]	59.5	103	...	148	177	203	250	294	355	(a)	401	1.0	1.6	7.6	...	...	0.069	69.6
Premium:																		
Los Angeles	60.4	102	...	151	174	195	230	265	316	(a)	370	0.9	1.4	...	...	...	0.04	80.4
Average of U.S.[b]	61.0	107	...	149	172	194	231	271	325	(a)	384	1.0	1.4	7.1	...	...	0.044	77.2
Summer, 1948																		
Regular:																		
So. California	57.9	100	120	139	171	202	250	293	347	369	396	0.9	2.3	8.0	1.8	1.59	0.234	75.9
Average of U.S.[c]	60.2	99	120	138	166	192	238	283	343	369	401	0.9	1.5	8.0	2.4	1.58	0.099	75.2
Premium:																		
So. California	58.7	101	120	139	167	192	235	275	328	349	380	0.9	2.1	7.9	1.7	2.52	0.112	81.3
Average of U.S.[c]	60.5	101	121	136	161	184	228	273	335	362	396	1.0	1.4	8.0	2.7	1.99	0.078	79.5

a Data not available.
b Average of 22 cities in the United States.
c Average of 17 districts, representing 207 cities in the United States.
Source: United States Bureau of Mines, *Cooperative Fuel Research Motor-Gasoline Survey, Summer, 1936*, January, 1937, and *National Motor-Gasoline Survey, Summer, 1948*, December, 1948.

provement in gasoline quality has been largely a matter of higher anti-knock ratings;[15] these have increased in response to the need for higher-test gasoline as a result of an increase in the compression ratio of modern motors.[16] As a matter of fact, the improvement from 1936 to 1948 shown in the table is largely, although not entirely, confined to the regular-grade product.

Quality of Gasoline Among Suppliers in This Area. Assuming service and quality competition prevails among major sellers of gasoline, a strong tendency toward product homogeneity is likely to prevail among the offerings of the major companies operating in this area.[17] That is, although temporary differences might exist, individual major sellers would not tolerate continued product superiority by competitors if it were in their power to prevent it. Since no technical limitation prevails which would make such matching of quality impracticable, the gasolines of the major suppliers are likely to be much the same.

The argument that applies to the major-company product quality does not necessarily apply to independents. The latter often seek business on a cut-price basis, and it might be reasoned that they need not maintain the highest standards of quality. It should be pointed out, however, that (1) a considerable share (75 per cent, perhaps) of the gasoline sold by independent suppliers originates from major company refineries,[18] and (2) independent refiners may feel that their gasoline *must* match the quality level established by the various com-

---

[15] In fact, the quality declined in some respects (e.g., the increase in sulphur content).

[16] Actually it is hard to say which came first, the higher-test gasolines or the high-compression motors. One industry man states that the improvement in gasoline refining has come about more as a result of a search for methods to get more gasoline from a barrel of crude than as a result of attempts to produce a better motor fuel.

[17] General Petroleum, Richfield, Shell, Standard Oil, Texaco, Tide Water Associated, and Union.

[18] However, one person, supposedly expert in such matters, argues that different vendors have different specifications for different buyers, and in most cases stick to them closely. He indicated that, except in an urgent need, in which case gasoline purchased from another company might be the same as that sold by that company through its own dealers, there might be two separate gasolines with separate specifications, even though they originated from the same refinery. The authors attempted to check this view from every conceivable angle, and now conclude that this informant is in error; that usually when one company acquires gasoline from another company, even on a long-term contract, the product is almost of necessity precisely the same.

panies in order to offset the fact that the majors' product is well and favorably known.

But this abstract analysis is not conclusive. Table 6 shows average results of quality tests of gasoline sold in the Los Angeles market classified by grades of product and types of companies. These tests were discussed fully above and are largely, if not precisely, the same as those used by the U. S. Bureau of Mines. The tests covered 56 brands of gasoline of 27 different suppliers and were made in December, 1949.

Table 6 shows some differences in the average test results of the products of the majors, subsidiaries, and independents in this market; thus, the sulphur content is slightly higher, the octane rating fractionally lower, and (for the regular grade only) the gum content somewhat higher for the product of the independents as compared with that of the majors. The average results for the subsidiaries are essentially the same as for the independents. According to expert observers, none of these differences is large enough to be of any significance.

There are, of course, limitations to an analysis based on averages, since variations among individual companies may be obscured. An examination of the figures for the individual companies (not available for publication) reveals that the variations among the various brands of gasoline offered in the Los Angeles market at each quality level are small.[19]

However, the authors would not want to give the impression that there are *no* variations among companies. For example, the gum content of some gasolines, both majors and independents, was somewhat higher than the suggested limit given above (p. 58). Moreover, the gasoline of at least one of the independents was not quite up to par in several respects—sulphur and gum content were relatively high and the octane number relatively low. It might be noted, however, that the gasoline having the highest octane rating (and evidently rating high in other respects also) is the product of an independent refiner. But while such differences exist, they are of little, if

---

[19] One major company which was selling its premium-grade gasoline as a super-premium product in this market at one cent above other majors, had an octane rating of 91 (research), which was essentially the same as the remainder of the majors.

TABLE 6

AVERAGE RESULTS OF QUALITY TESTS OF VARIOUS BRANDS OF GASOLINE SOLD IN THE LOS ANGELES MARKET, CLASSIFIED BY GRADES AND BY TYPES OF COMPANIES, DECEMBER, 1949

| | Gravity °A.P.I. | Engler Distillation, Per cent Recovered, °F. | | | | | | | | | Resi- dueᵃ | Reid vapor pressure PSI | Gumᵃ ASTM mgs. | TEL mi/gal.ᵃ | Sulfur per cent | Octane no. motorᵃ | Octane no. researchᵃ |
		I.B.P.ᵃ	10	20	30	50	70	90	End point	Recov- ered							
Regular grade																	
Major companies	59.7	78.7	129	161	191	238	281	345	392	97.8	0.97	9.1	1.3	1.01	0.167	76.0	82.6
Subsidiary companies	59.1	81.5	137	173	201	247	283	341	392	97.8	1.00	8.2	2.0	1.40	0.179	76.5	82.0
Independent companies ...	57.5	79.9	137	174	208	256	297	351	390	97.6	1.04	8.3	2.0	1.35	0.182	75.7	81.4
Premium grade																	
Major companies	59.9	78.4	133	157	181	224	268	328	381	97.9	0.89	7.7	2.1	1.76	0.121	81.4	91.3
Subsidiary companies	60.6	80.8	136	158	181	223	259	321	386	98.0	1.00	7.7	2.0	1.75	0.110	80.8	91.0
Independent companies ...	58.1	80.3	135	166	193	239	284	346	387	97.8	1.03	8.1	1.9	2.24	0.182	80.9	89.1

ᵃ Averaged to one decimal place beyond the original data.
Source: Tests made by an independent commercial testing laboratory in this area.

any, importance; it might be added that the quality of the product of each company varies to some degree from time to time, although, again, such differences are not significant.

This analysis of gasoline quality is confirmed by the opinion of one of the laboratory men whose business is making tests and interpreting results. Asked about the quality of the various brands of gasoline tested in this commercial laboratory, he said that there were no appreciable differences in the various brands, given the same quality level; that the motorist could not detect any difference among various brands of regular-grade gasolines or among various brands of premium-grade gasolines. This laboratory man uses any of them, sometimes the product of an independent and sometimes of a major.[20] Moreover, he uses regular grade ordinarily, and puts in premium grade only when his motor starts pinging.

This is not to say that gasoline of poor quality may not be found in the Los Angeles market at times. To begin with, while the 27 companies whose gasoline was tested account for most of the gasoline sold in this market, they do not represent *all* the suppliers in the area; hence some poor-quality motor fuel might slip into the area undetected.[21] Moreover, gasoline which was of good quality when it emerged from the refinery might deteriorate in storage (e.g., become "gummy"). Finally, regular-grade or third-grade motor fuel might be sold as a higher-grade product;[22] such gasoline, while adequate as

[20] The question was asked one laboratory man: "Suppose I were paying you to buy gasoline for me. Where would you buy it and what brand would you buy?" His reply: "I would take you to the nearest place I could buy it cheapest without regard to brand."

[21] From time to time, various major companies have offered for sale to rebranding independents a comparatively small quantity of "degraded" gasoline. Despite this term the quality is only slightly inferior to the product ordinarily offered (possibly one or two octane rating points below average), and the difference would probably not be discernable to the average motorist. According to observers in the trade, these offerings are not of sufficient size or regularity as to constitute a significant part of the total supply in the market.

[22] In a telephone conversation with Frank Berka, of the County Bureau of Weights and Measures, in May, 1950, the following case was cited: A service station operator posting a sign reading "Save 9¢" was brought into court and given four or five days to comply with the court's ruling that the sign was misleading and fraudulent. The operator, upon questioning, stated that the gasoline was Richfield (which later proved to be untrue). Meanwhile the county investigators took samples and found that what was advertised as a premium-grade gasoline tested only 70 octane with no T.E.L. content; it evidently was "white" gasoline, which now is sold primarily for use in stoves, for cleaning, and similar uses, although it can be used as a motor fuel.

lower-grade fuel, would be considered poor quality according to the higher standard established for the high-test product.

One further point: By their choice of advertising schemes the oil companies operating in this market tacitly admit that the product is largely physically homogeneous.[23] Their advertisements generally avoid claims of superiority and simply proclaim the absolute merit of their products or perhaps concentrate on the excellence of the service offered.[24] To the extent that this is true, the oil companies are to be commended; in some industries a high degree of homogeneity is no deterrent to claims of product superiority by brand promoters.

Quality of the Whole Offering

Gasoline is not sold as an isolated item but in conjunction with a number of services. Therefore, the quality of gasoline might be essentially the same among sellers but differences may exist in the amount or quality of the accompanying services offered by various outlets—availability of the product-service at convenient points, keeping the customer's automobile clean, inspection of motor car mechanism, making minor adjustments, and the like.

The quality of the whole offering of major-company outlets and mass-selling independents (especially self-serve outlets) is, of course,

---

[23] The Richfield "rust-proof" gasoline is different, but as one expert commented, in effect, "I cannot think of anything I would worry less about than the possibility of my gasoline tank, fuel line, or carburetor rusting away!" Gasoline containing an upper-cylinder lubricant (e.g., Olympic's thermo-lube) is also different, but again, one questions the significance of the difference.

[24] Most gasoline advertising of the oil companies operating in the Los Angeles area is consistent with this finding. Most companies do not make claims of superiority for their product but rather merely state that their product is of fine quality. For example, Standard Oil advertises its gasoline as "unsurpassed" and having "ping-free power"; and although Tidewater Associated states that its product "gives all cars exceptional road performance," it places major promotional emphasis on "friendly service." Union Oil Company's present advertising emphasizes "the new 76," indicating an improved product but not necessarily one that is superior to that of rivals. Even Shell Oil Company, which advertises "the most powerful gasoline your car can use!" emphasizes high quality but does not claim superiority over the product of its competitors. Somewhat the same thing can be said of Richfield whose new slogan is, "In all the world no finer gasoline" although in this instance the advertising of the company goes a little further. A few companies, however, seem to depart from strict adherence to the truth. As an illustration, there seems to be no basis for the claim of Signal that its product is "The go farther gasoline"—particularly in view of the fact that its gasoline originates from the Standard Oil Company and is presumably no better than the parent company's product. Hancock with its "mileage booster" theme might be placed in the same category.

not the same. The amount of free service is likely to vary considerably. The offering of the major-company outlet is usually dependable; for example, there is little chance that a bad batch of gasoline will slip by or that a slip-shod grease job will be provided. The major-company product-service is available within a few blocks of almost any point in the community, which makes it convenient to patronize such a station. Besides, continuity of high-quality service is available from major companies throughout a wide geographical area, for example, the entire Pacific Coast.

One should not place too much emphasis on differences mentioned but they should be kept in mind. The consumer-buyer may not consider these important, in which case he should acquire his product-service where he can get the "best buy." If the consumer-buyer does value the quality of service (in broad terms) he should pay a little more for his gasoline in order to obtain maximum satisfaction. If he is not satisfied with his purchase, no saving can compensate him adequately.

VI

SUPPLIER-COMPANY POLICIES
AFFECTING RETAIL COMPETITIVE BEHAVIOR

The choice of the method of doing business finds expression in the policies of the companies competing in the market.[1] Competition in gasoline distribution at the retail level is conditioned to some extent by the policies of those supplying the product for resale. Some companies—the major firms particularly—have considerable influence over the activities of their dealers in marketing matters.[2] Other concerns exert little or no control over the retailer's operating policies

---

[1] A policy, according to *Webster's New International Dictionary* (2d ed. unabridged), may be defined as: "A settled or definite course or method adopted and followed by a government, institution, body, or individual."

[2] Company salesmen evidently play an important role in seeing that the policies of supplier companies are carried out. One gathers, however, that educational and persuasive tactics are used to a much greater extent to obtain dealer coöperation than absolute demands for adherence. Of course when the station is leased from the supplier company and a cancellation clause is included in the contract, the company may cancel the lease if the lessee does not adhere to company policies. For example, the cancellation clause in the contract used by one major supplier company in this area reads as follows: " . . . Lessor or Lessee shall have the right at any time during the term or any extension or renewal hereof to terminate this lease on not less than seven (7) days' written notice to the other. . . . If Lessee shall hold over after the expiration of the term [called for in this contract] with Lessor's express or implied consent, it shall be on a month to month tenancy in accordance with the terms hereof and subject to termination as above provided. This lease shall terminate forthwith upon termination of any lease which Lessor may have upon the premises covered hereby." On the other hand, good dealers are hard to acquire, hence supplier companies are reluctant to invoke such a clause.

(although they influence negatively the competitive activities of those acquiring their product by the fact that the retailer is free to act as he pleases). A strategic decision has to be made as to whether the firm will sell the product without strings or will reserve some say in, for example, price making.

Key policies which may influence the nature of retail rivalry are those dealing with the method of wholesale distribution, type of control over outlets, plan used in locating stations, sales promotion, consumer credit systems, maintenance of cleanliness of stations, maintenance of resale prices, and attitude toward promotional price signs, selling split-pump accounts, and rebranding. By means of interviews, supplemented by market observations, the authors were able to obtain information on the marketing policies of the gasoline suppliers in this area. This information is summarized in tables 7 and 8; the former includes information on the major and subsidiary companies[3] and the latter on the independent organizations. In the tables companies are arranged according to the number of retail representatives operating in the Los Angeles market at the time of the study (as determined from market investigation, not from company records).

The policy data contained in the tables apply to 1948–1949. While some of the companies have departed to some extent from strict adherence to these policies during the more dynamic competitive conditions of late 1949 and early 1950—especially those related to pricing matters—this departure, the authors feel, is only a temporary phenomenon and a return to the conditions existing before the price war will result in a return of oil-company operations in accordance with the policies set forth in the tables. Therefore, the material fairly represents the operating policies of gasoline suppliers in the Los Angeles market area in "normal" times.

Major and Subsidiary Companies

Table 7 shows that the policies of the major[4] companies in this

---

[3] These are major companies from the standpoint of their position in this market. However, as was mentioned earlier, two of the seven major firms operating in this area are themselves subsidiaries. Thus, General Petroleum Corporation is controlled by Socony-Vacuum Company, and Richfield Oil Corporation is controlled by Sinclair Oil Corporation and Cities Service Company.

[4] Although there is general agreement as to which companies should be designated "major" concerns in this market area, the term "major concern" is difficult to define. A dozen or so key executives of oil companies operating in the local market were

area—General Petroleum Corporation, Richfield Oil Corporation, Shell Oil Company, Inc., Standard Oil Company of California, The Texas Company, Tide Water Associated Oil Company, and Union Oil Company of California—in many respects follow the same general pattern. More specifically:

1. The wholesale distribution of gasoline[5] in major concerns is largely a company operation in the Los Angeles market, thus providing a closer relationship between the supplier company and the retail distributor; some of the companies, however, employ distributors[6] and a few use "commission agents," [7] so called, particularly in the outlying areas.[8]

---

asked for their definition of a major company but, generally speaking, the replies were not helpful. Perhaps the most useful definition was provided by an executive of one of the subsidiary companies who said that, in his opinion, a major company is one that has to "act like a major" with respect to advertising, service rendered, and the location of service stations. That is, a major company must advertise extensively, offer a high quality of service, and sell its products in a large number of conveniently located outlets.

The authors feel that an oil company should not be considered a major concern unless it possess superiority in a substantial degree. Thus, a major concern should have all of the following characteristics:

1. Well and favorably known brands, generally acceptable to consumer-buyers.

2. Intensive distribution of a wide line of merchandise items over a large geographical area.

3. Large sales volume with a substantial influence on the price of the product in the areas in which it does business.

4. Integration of production, refining, and distribution, including control of crude oil processing, transportation, and marketing facilities.

[5] The distribution of gasoline usually is carried out through what are called "bulk plants" where gasoline is stored pending delivery to retail outlets. According to an executive of one of the subsidiary companies, however, bulk plants are losing out in the Los Angeles area because of the extension of pipe lines and the use of increasingly larger trucking facilities, making it possible for distributors to go directly to the refinery for their products and thus by-pass bulk plants altogether.

[6] These are merchant distributors who accept title to the merchandise which they sell, relying on the margin between the buying and selling price for the revenue from which they pay expenses and make profits, if any; these functionaries may or may not own the physical facilities. They are sometimes referred to as "purchase-and-sale distributors" in this market.

[7] These are not agents in the technical sense, that is, they cannot bind the company whose product they sell. The company consigns stock to them and pays them on a commission basis for what they sell. "Commission agents" (who are also known as "commission distributors" and "wholesale agents") may or may not own the plant and equipment. Sales are billed on company invoices and the company carries the accounts. The "agent" at no point takes title to the goods.

[8] The use of independent distributors is more likely in outlying areas, where organizational problems develop and where profit opportunities are limited, than in cities where the converse situation prevails.

2. By and large, the major companies have a large degree of control over the retail outlets[9] selling their products,[10] although relatively few stations are company-operated.

---

[9] Control is effected through some sort of leasing arrangement, such as (1) ownership of property by the company and lease to the operator, (2) lease of property from the property owner by the company and sublease to the operator, or (3) lease from the operator (who owns or has a master lease on the property) by the company and lease-back to the operator. A leasing arrangement provides for closer coöperation between supplier and dealer because of the possible restrictions incorporated in a leasing contract and the invocation of the cancellation clause in case the dealer is uncoöperative. "Paint contracts," which call for the painting of the service station distributing the company's products, are almost universally used by all types of suppliers. However, they are not considered to be an effective means of control because of the fact that they can be "paid off," on a pro-rata basis by the station operator, or more usually, by the new supplier company, if the operator chooses to change the brand of gasoline sold by the station.

[10] Regardless of the degree of control over facilities, a company may attempt to sell its product on an exclusive contract basis.

The legality of exclusive contracts in the sale of petroleum products and other service-station items to retail distributors was recently tested in a case brought against one of the large oil companies (Standard Oil of California) by the federal government under Section 1 of the Sherman Act and Section 3 of the Clayton Act. (*United States v. Standard Oil of California, et al.,* 78 F. Supp. 850 [1948].) The lower court decided in a lengthly opinion that while exclusive agreements were not illegal *per se*, those under review resulted in a substantial lessening of competition and thus were illegal. The court said (at 872): "Substantiality of restraint or tendency to create monopoly is established by (a) the market foreclosed . . . and (b) the volume of controlled business . . ." The U. S. Supreme Court sustained in a five to four decision the district court decision, finding the exclusive contracts in violation of Section 3 of the Clayton Act and therefore making it unnecessary to consider whether the decree of the lower court might also be sustained by Section 1 of the Sherman Act. In compliance with this decision, Standard Oil sent a letter to its dealers on May 15, 1950, notifying them that they are free to purchase or distribute any petroleum products or automotive accessories they may desire from any supplier they may choose.

However, exclusive contracts would seem to be unnecessary for control in cases where the product is sold through dealers who lease facilities from the suppliers, because refiners may legally require retail distributors to confine the use of leased tanks and pumps to the lessor's own product. Early in the history of the Clayton Act a large number of cases (over forty) developed from contracts covering the leasing of gasoline tanks and pumps by refiners on the condition that the retail distributor use such facilities exclusively in dispensing gasoline sold by such refiners. The Federal Trade Commission held that such contracts were illegal but was reversed by the courts on the grounds that (1) this type of contract did not call for the exclusive purchase of gasoline but only the exclusive use of the equipment in connection with the storage or sale of the particular refiner's gasoline, and (2) no evidence of monopolistic control was shown to exist. (*Sinclair Refining Company* v. *Federal Trade Commission,* 276 Fed. 686 [1921]; *Standard Oil Co.* v. *Federal Trade Commission,* 282 Fed. 81 [1922]; confirmed by U. S. Supreme Court, *Federal Trade Commission* v. *Sinclair Oil Co., et al.,* 261 U. S. 463 [1923].) The Standard Oil notification mentioned above seems to recognize this right. The letter to the dealers stated, in part: "The decree provides, however, that we may restrict the use of any pump, tank, container, or receptacle furnished by us to you and marked as such, to the storage, handling or dispensing of our petroleum products." (See *Automotive Dealer*

3. Generally speaking, retail locations are selected by major companies according to a master plan[11] which calls for (a) blanket coverage of a market area and (b) the establishment of outlets in key spots (in part, for prestige[12] or sales promotional purposes), although the major concerns will, of course, open accounts with dealers who come to them unsolicited, assuming that the applicants give promise of becoming satisfactory sales representatives.[13]

4. Major companies exert considerable sales promotional efforts in behalf of their brands or stations;[14] thus, the products sold by major companies tend to be well and favorably known.

News, May 29, 1950, pp. 1 to 5.) Moreover, if the traditional respect for each other's contracts, which reportedly prevailed among the major, subsidiary, and leading independent companies before the above decision, continues to prevail, a considerable degree of exclusiveness might exist in buyer and seller contractual relations without an exclusive arrangement.

[11] Summaries of two of the schemes which seem to be typical of major-company methods follow:

Company no. 1 has a division of real estate which works closely in conjunction with the sales department on the general selection of service station sites. These selections are made on the basis of studies carried on constantly with regard to population and traffic. Generally, locations where the company plans to or hopes to acquire service-station outlets are spotted at least a year in advance. The actual selection within an area is decided upon by the sales department, and the real estate department carries on the activities with regard to the actual closing of leases, and the like.

Company no. 2 conducts surveys of given areas and an estimate is then made of the potential business. This estimate is based on state tax registrations, auto registrations, and so forth. From this information the company determines the amount of business it may reasonably expect to have with proper representation in this area. In other words, how much business could be obtained with the addition of certain locations. Of course the desirable locations may not be available or they may be prohibitive in price. However, the study is a continuous one, with a separate real estate department carrying on the work.

One of the companies indicated that its plans are made with the end that eventually each area will be covered adequately, in order that people who want to buy the company's products may find them conveniently available; another leading major company reported that it was determined to be "well represented" in any area.

[12] The executive of one major company reported that his concern would not "go too wild" over a location merely for prestige purposes; he said the company would always consider the economics of the location (i.e., whether it would pay its way or not). The executive of another company made a similar statement—that his concern liked to have prime locations but that it always took cost into consideration in selecting them.

[13] An executive of one of the large majors stated that he would find it hard to conceive of an outlet being too small to serve, even to the extent of a few rare instances of having to bucket the gasoline into the pump.

[14] The following were advertising expenditures in magazines, newspapers, and on radio networks, of major oil companies whose markets include the Los Angeles area, in 1947: The Texas Company, $3,066,715; Socony-Vacuum Oil Company, Inc. (of which General Petroleum is a subsidiary), $2,018,303; Shell Oil Company, Inc., $1,234,897; Standard Oil of California, $707,637; Tidewater Associated Oil Company,

5. Major companies provide their dealers with credit facilities so that customers of such stations may purchase their requirements on open account, rather than pay cash.[15]

6. Major companies encourage the maintenance of clean, attractive stations, although with varying degrees of success; these companies evidently feel that stations selling their products should provide the proper setting for a quality product-service.

7. Major companies generally favor (with few exceptions) offering their products at market prices rather than undercutting other major competitors, thus avoiding intensive price competition.

8. Generally speaking, major companies oppose the use of promotional price signs[16] (even more strongly, perhaps, than undercutting the price), which intensify price competition among major outlets.[17]

$599,315; Union Oil Company of California, $466,682; Richfield Oil Corporation, $300,539; (*National Advertising Investments in 1947* [Magazine Advertising Bureau, 271 Madison Avenue, New York 16, New York: 1948]).

[15] All of the major and subsidiary companies have supplier-sponsored credit-card systems; one of the subsidiaries (Rio Grande) does not carry its own credit system but will honor or issue credit cards of its parent company (Richfield).

The supplier companies sponsoring credit systems bear the entire cost of carrying the credit of customers of dealers distributing products of these companies. In order that the dealer may avoid any part of the burden (except the time spent in writing the credit slip), properly executed credit slips are acceptable as cash by the supplier's truck driver for merchandise delivered to the dealer. Technically only credit slips covering the sale of merchandise provided by the supplier company are acceptable by the company, but undoubtedly this rule is not strictly adhered to. Thus, the supplier company finds itself at times carrying accounts covering the sale of merchandise with which it has no connection whatsoever and, indeed, which may have been sold in place of company-supplied merchandise!

[16] One must distinguish between the posted price and the promotional price sign. The posted price is the total price—net price and taxes stated separately—at which the product is offered, and by law is required to be displayed on the dispensing equipment of any retail vendor offering gasoline (*Bus. and Prof. Code of Calif.* Sec. 20820). The promotional price sign, on the other hand, is a large-size advertisement displayed in a conspicuous place on or near the service-station premises, which indicates the price of the product or the savings to be earned by purchasing gasoline from the advertiser.

An executive of one independent company reported that the contracts used by it state the dealer may use and place only advertising material approved by the company. He said, further, that the same clause appears in the subleases of most companies; and that he knows this, because when his company started leasing, the officials copied clauses from major-company contracts to be sure that the company was on sound ground. Assuming his statement is accurate, the supplier company has full control over price signs, although it may not wish to invoke such control.

[17] Despite the opposition of major companies to the use of promotional price signs in stations selling their products in normal times, by May, 1950 their use was almost universal in this market because of the price war.

9. The majority of the major companies indicate that they are not opposed to selling split-pump accounts (the sale of more than one seller's products), but they all attempt to discourage such sales.[18] Thus, major-company dealers are encouraged to concentrate their efforts in behalf of one company's product.

10. Some major companies are opposed to selling their product to rebranders, and some are not.

It should be clear from the foregoing that the policies of the seven major concerns, while similar, are by no means identical.[19] To mention only two points: They differ (1) in their methods of maintaining resale prices, some actually invoking the California Fair Trade Law[20] and others relying on[21] more informal means, such as persuasion,[22]

---

[18] Several reasons for adopting this policy are given by companies which oppose split-pump sales, aside from the obvious one that they want an operator to concentrate his sales effort in behalf of the company's products. It is argued that split-pump operations encourage: (a) the use of company credit cards for the sale of non-company products, (b) mixing non-company (lower priced) gasoline with the company product and (c) passing off the product of another company on which a wider margin is earned for that of the company ("long hosing").

[19] They would be expected to be similar because the companies are similarly situated and are in close competition, but they would be expected to differ enough to indicate independence of judgment on the part of the policy makers of each company in the light of each particular market situation.

[20] The resale-price provision from the contract of one of the major companies reads as follows: "RESALE PROVISIONS. Reseller shall not sell, offer, or advertise for sale any gasoline delivered hereunder at a price lower than . . . [company's] posted retail price, for gasoline of like grade and quality, in effect at time and for the place of resale. Reseller shall not grant any rebates, discounts, or concessions or resort to any device whereby any purchaser may obtain such gasoline at a price lower than . . . [company's] said posted retail price.

"Reseller agrees to resell all gasoline delivered hereunder only under . . . [company's] brands and to maintain . . . [company's] brands, trademarks, and names on the pumps and other facilities through which said gasoline is dispensed and agrees not to mix, substitute, or adulterate said gasoline with any other material."

[21] The legality of resale price-maintenance efforts within limits was well established even before the passage of fair trade laws. While price-maintenance contracts were proscribed, the courts had decided that manufacturers might legally refuse to sell to price cutters and even to threaten to refuse to sell them (*United States* v. *Colgate & Company*, 250 U. S. 300 [1919]) just so long as cooperative means of obtaining information on price cutters' activities were not employed by the seller (*Federal Trade Commission* v. *Beechnut Packing Co.*, 257 U. S. 441 [1922]).

[22] While major oil companies in the Los Angeles area practice price maintenance to a considerable extent, relatively little reliance is placed on the state's Fair Trade Law as a device for preventing price cutting in gasoline. This is not to say that the law is inapplicable to the sale of gasoline in this state. To the contrary, by an amendment to the California act in 1937 the provisions of the law were extended to "any commodity sold through vending equipment, if such vending equipment bears the trade-mark or name or brand of the owner and producer of the commodity,

(2) in the matter of selling gasoline for rebrand purposes[23]—companies may have identical views on the evils of price cutting but may

and if the commodity is in fair and open competition with the commodities of the same general class produced by others." (*Bus. and Prof. Code of Calif.*, 16903). Moreover, much effort was expended in attempting to enforce this act in the early days of its amendment but with very little success. The Retail Petroleum Dealers' Association acted as the prosecuting agency and represented outlets distributing Richfield, Shell, Rio Grande, Gilmore, and Signal products which presumably had an interest in the goodwill allegedly injured by price cutters. While the association received some coöperation from certain supplier companies, the latter did not actively prosecute violators. Reportedly, the effort to enforce contracts under the Fair Trade Law were abandoned in mid-1938. (For a good account of the early attempts to use the Fair Trade Law as a price-maintenance device see *National Petroleum News*, June 16, 23, 30; August 4, 11, 25; September 1; October 6, 13; December 1, 8, 22; 1937. See also January 26; April 20, 27; May 4, 11, 25; June 1, 8, 15, 22; July 20, 27 and August 16, 1938.) The language of the Fair Trade Law is presently used in some of the supplier-retailer contracts but enforcement through court action is seldom if ever resorted to.

It has been argued that price maintenance is impossible to accomplish when, as in gasoline, the product sold by members of the industry carries much the same quality value in the minds of the purchasers. A shift in patronage from those maintaining to those not maintaining prices would probably result, unless all firms move together in their price policy. While this is undoubtedly true, it is not a basic reason for the failure to utilize the Fair Trade Law in maintaining prices. There are, however, several reasons which are valid: (1) Supplier companies are not greatly concerned about the absence of strict adherence to posted prices in every individual sale (e.g., "under the canopy" discounts). They are more interested in maintaining the posted price, and particularly in eliminating promotional price signs which advertise such reductions. (2) There is some question concerning the legality of invoking the Fair Trade Law by companies which distribute a substantial part of their product through their own outlets (e.g., Standard Oil). Such companies are engaged in retailing themselves, hence are retailers; the issuance of contracts to operators of non-company outlets, therefore, might be construed as a horizontal price agreement, which would be a violation of Section 2 of the California Fair Trade Law. (3) The use of the Fair Trade Law by supplier companies, while legal, would require suit and the resulting harassment of dealers would undoubtedly tend to estrange them. (Indeed, there is real doubt whether the actual enforcement of the Fair Trade Law in the type of dealer-supplier relationship that exists in the major-company segment of the industry would be practicable.) (4) The relationship of the supplier and dealer in gasoline distribution is such that price control may be effected by persuasive means without resort to the Fair Trade Law. Just one more point: The maintenance of prices on major-company brands is normally quite effective. Ordinarily most price cutting is in brands of independent suppliers and retail brand promoters, which are not susceptible to control through the use of the Fair Trade Law.

[23] Rebranding gasoline without written authorization from the "true manufacturer" is against the law (*Bus. and Prof. Code of Calif.*, Secs. 20912–20921). According to a top official of one of the small oil companies, the buyer's responsibility in rebranding is to have on hand at all times the letter from the supplier giving the buyer the right to resell the gasoline under a specific rebrand name. This informant surmised that his firm was the only smaller oil company that had an agreement by which the company could resell the gasoline, which it had purchased for rebrand, to another distributor for resale under whatever rebrand the distributor chose to use, assuming

TABLE 7

KEY MARKETING POLICIES OF MAJOR AND SUBSIDIARY GASOLINE SUPPLIER COMPANIES, WHICH HAVE AN INFLUENCE ON COMPETITION AT THE RETAIL LEVEL, LOS ANGELES, 1948–1949

Principal brands of gasoline	Wholesale distribution			Control of retail outlets (Per cent of total)			Selecting locations for retail outlets	Substantial sales promotional effort of company in behalf of	
	Company operation	Distributor	Commission agent	Company-controlled and -operated	Company-controlled, dealer-operated	Uncontrolled		Brand	Dealers
Major companies									
General Petroleum Corp.: Mobilgas, Mobilgas Special	Almost entirely	Small extent	...	...	48	52	Co. plans for blanket market coverage; uses prime locations	X	X
Standard Oil Co. of California: Chevron, Chevron Supreme	Almost entirely	Small extent	Small extent	32	60	8	Co. plans for blanket market coverage; uses prime locations	X	
The Texas Co.: Fire Chief, Sky Chief	Entirely	...	Small extent	...	85	15	Co. plans for blanket market coverage; uses prime locations	X	X
Union Oil Co. of California: Union 76, Union 7600	Almost entirely	...	Small extent	6	74	20	Co. plans for blanket market coverage; uses prime locations	X	
Richfield Oil Corp.: Richfield Hi Octane, Richfield Ethyl	Almost entirely	...	Small extent	...	50	50	Co. plans for blanket market coverage; uses prime locations	X	
Shell Oil Co., Inc.: Shell, Shell Premium	Almost entirely	...	Small extent	...	69	31	Co. plans for blanket market coverage; uses prime locations	X	
Tide Water Associated Oil Co.: Flying A, Flying A Ethyl	Almost entirely	Small extent	...	...	90	10	Co. plans for blanket market coverage; uses prime locations	X	X[f]
Subsidiary companies									
Signal Oil Co.: Signal, Signal Ethyl	Almost entirely	Small extent	Small extent	...	95	5	Some regard for extensive coverage, little for prime locations	X	X
The Petrol Corp.[b]: P.D.Q., P.D.Q. Plus Ethyl	Almost entirely	Small extent	extent	...	95	5	Some regard for extensive coverage, little for prime locations	X	
Rio Grande Oil Co.: Rio Grande Cracked, Rio Grande Ethyl	...	Entirely	...	...	25[e]	75[d]	Some regard for extensive coverage, little for prime locations	Very little	Very little
Seaside Oil Co.: Seaside Silver Gull, Seaside Ethyl	...	Entirely	...	...	95	5	Some regard for extensive coverage, little for prime locations	Very little	Very little

• Originally the company used the brand name *Red Crown* and later changed to the name *Standard*. An official of the company said this was done in order to get away from brand names used by other companies and to place emphasis on the company's name; however, he said, the thinking changed later on and it was decided to emphasize again a brand name as distinct from the company name, hence the adoption of the name *Chevron*.

b The Petrol Corp. became a subsidiary of Standard Oil Co. of California in January, 1948; its stations were later converted to Chevron and Signal Oil Co. outlets.

• All Rio Grande gasoline is marketed through distributors who lease bulk plants and sublease from the company all stations that the company controls by lease or fee in the distributor's territory.

d It is possible that some of these are controlled by distributors through contract or lease.

• Cannot publicize stations because of relatively poor service and appearance.

f Toward creating acceptance of idea of "Friendly Associated Dealer."

TABLE 7 (Continued)

	Supplier company-sponsored retail credit system provided dealers	Maintenance of standards of cleanliness for dealer stations	Extent of price making normally exercised by company at retail level	Attitude toward promotional price signs	Attitude toward sales to split-pump accounts	Attitude toward sales to rebranders
Major companies						
General Petroleum Corp.	Yes	Strong policy, actively implemented with effective adherence	Minimum posted price informally maintained	Opposed with complete success before outbreak of "price war."	Not opposed[k]	Not opposed[l]
Standard Oil Co. of California	Yes	Strong policy, actively implemented with effective adherence	Minimum posted price informally maintained or through company operation.	Declined to state.[h] No signs observed before outbreak of "price war," Jan. 1950.	Opposed	Not opposed[m]
The Texas Co.	Yes	Strong policy, actively implemented with effective adherence	Minimum posted price informally maintained	Opposed with fair success. Scattered signs observed before outbreak of "price war."	Not opposed	Policy opposes
Union Oil Co. of California	Yes	Strong policy, actively implemented with effective adherence	Minimum posted price maintained under Fair Trade Act	Opposed with complete success before outbreak of "price war."	Opposed	Policy opposes
Richfield Oil Corp.	Yes	Strong policy, actively implemented with effective adherence	Minimum posted price maintained under Fair Trade Act[a]	Opposed with complete success before outbreak of "price war."	Not opposed	Not opposed[n]
Shell Oil Co., Inc.	Yes	Strong policy, actively implemented with effective adherence	Minimum posted price informally maintained but not entirely successfully	Neutral. Scattered signs observed before outbreak of "price war."	Not opposed	Policy opposes[o]
Tide Water Associated Oil Co.	Yes	Strong policy, actively implemented with effected adherence	Minimum posted price informally maintained but not entirely successfully.	Opposed with fair success. Scattered signs observed before outbreak of "price war."[i]	Not opposed	Not opposed[p]
Subsidiary companies						
Signal Oil Co.	Yes	Moderate policy, moderate implementation, good results	Minimum posted price informally maintained	Opposed with considerable success. Very few signs observed before outbreak of "price war."	Not opposed	Not opposed
The Petrol Corp.[b]	Yes	Moderate policy, moderate implementation, fair results	Minimum posted price informally maintained	Opposed with complete success before outbreak of "price war."	Not opposed	Opposed
Rio Grande Oil Co.	Richfield credit cards honored	Moderate policy, inadequate implementation, poor results	Minimum posted price maintained under Fair Trade Act	Opposed with complete success before outbreak of "price war."	Not opposed	Not opposed
Seaside Oil Co.	Yes	Moderate policy, effective implementation, good results	Minimum posted price informally maintained	Opposed with considerable success. Very few signs observed before outbreak of "price war."	Not opposed	Opposed

[a] One of the company executives stated that Richfield has used the Fair Trade Act.

[h] One of the company officials stated that he would prefer not to express policy on price signs because of the present (June 9, 1949) "legal position" of the company.

[i] One of the company's local officials stated that the company does everything possible to discourage price signs.

[j] Three day cancellation clause in contract takes care of this.

[k] However, as with all the major companies, this practice is discouraged.

[l] Hancock obtains the gasoline sold under its brand from General Petroleum in exchange for which they supply General Petroleum with crude. Harbor has a deal which is similar to the Hancock arrangement. In addition, Olympic and Pathfinder also buy from General Petroleum.

[m] One of the company officials stated that while they do sell rebranders they are not expanding this operation now. Reportedly, Signal Oil and Gas Co. has a producer-marketer exchange agreement with the Standard Oil Co. of California whereby Signal receives gasoline in exchange for crude oil. It is rumored that some of the finished product so acquired has gone to the Craig Oil Company, in which Signal Oil and Gas Co. is supposed to have a 50 per cent interest. Although the Petrol Corp. operates its own refinery, it buys most of its gasoline from Standard Oil.

[n] Richfield supplies Mohawk, and among others, Parks, a retailer-rebrander. According to the current report in the trade, the arrangement between Richfield and Mohawk is an "exchange deal" whereby Richfield draws its requirements in the Bakersfield area from the Mohawk refinery there, while Mohawk draws its requirements for the Los Angeles area from the Richfield refinery in Los Angeles.

[o] Ben Hur purchases gasoline outright from Shell, and Macmillan trades unfinished gasoline for the finished product from Shell, however.

[p] While one of the company representatives stated "no sales to rebranders" as a company policy, according to an equally authoritative source (April, 1949) the company supplies the major part of the gasoline sold by the Sunset Oil Company.

Source: Interviews with company officials combined with other field investigations.

disagree as to whether individual action on their part would have any restrictive effect on such practices.[24]

In addition to actual differences in policies, differences in implementation of policies exist among major companies also. While policies covering a certain marketing activity may be identical among several firms, differences appear at the tactical level. To take an example: Company A feels that violations should be treated firmly—the dealer posting a sign should be ordered to take it down forthwith. Company B feels that a more effective way is to explain the situation to the dealer and depend upon persuasion to make him recognize the disadvantages of continuing the use of a sign. Company C may go even further and allow the sign to remain in the hope that the dealer will change his mind—which may happen if a nearby competitor threatens to retaliate. Thus, one company may feel that the way to handle the infraction is to "crack down" on the offender, while another one feels that the matter can better be taken care of by watching and waiting.

The subsidiary companies—Petrol Corporation,[25] Rio Grande, Seaside, and Signal Oil—attempt (perhaps unwisely) to operate in much the same manner as the major companies. There are, however, some differences among companies. For example, two subsidiaries (Signal and Petrol) distribute their products at wholesale on a com-

---

he had been granted permission to do so by the company. To make this possible, the company sent a new letter out each month giving such permission.

The following is an interesting slant on the rebrand letter by an independent retail distributor. According to this dealer, the law requiring such a letter was passed at the instigation of the major-supplier companies in order to detect who was selling to the rebranding price cutters. He said that when the law was first put into effect, a representative of the Bureau of Weights and Measures asked to see his rebrand letter. After he showed the letter, the government representative immediately telephoned the office of the major supplier. Shortly thereafter, the major company clamped down on the retailer's supplier, telling him he would receive no more gasoline from this concern if he continued to sell to the rebrander. Subsequently, according to this account, the official from the Bureau of Weights and Measures again asked to see this dealer's rebrand letter. This time he refused to show it until he was brought into court. There the judge read the letter, but the contents were not made available to the investigator from the bureau.

[24] All majors may agree that deep price cutting by those acquiring rebrand gasoline for sale under private label is undesirable; some might feel that they could aid in controlling this "evil" by refusing to sell on such a basis, while others might conclude, probably correctly, that if they did not sell to rebranders some other supplier would.

[25] The Petrol Corporation was in operation at the time this phase of the survey was made but has since been dissolved.

pany-owned and operated basis almost entirely, while the other two (Rio Grande and Seaside) use distributors exclusively. Like the major companies, the subsidiaries (with the possible exception of Rio Grande)[26] have a large degree of influence over the outlets selling their products including the retail prices charged. The subsidiary companies cannot, however, adhere as strictly to stated policies as their parent companies because of (1) their inferior position in the competitive structure (e.g., they cannot afford to be as adamant in insisting on spotless stations or in refusing to sell split-pump accounts) and (2) the limitation of their resources—e.g., they are in no position to consider seriously high-priced locations[27] and large sales-promotional expenditures.

Independent Companies

Table 8 contains policy data for the independent companies supplying gasoline in the Los Angeles market. It shows that the bulk of these companies pursue very different, often diametrically opposed, policies from those followed by the majors and subsidiaries (although this is by no means universally true). We may generalize concerning operating policies of independent companies as follows:

1. Wholesale distribution for the independents is divided between company-operated systems and the employment of merchant distributors. The former alternative is used by a slightly larger number of companies,[28] while a few companies employ both methods. Volume-wise, however, the larger share of the business is done by distributors and commission agents.

---

[26] It is possible, however, that some of the stations listed as uncontrolled by Rio Grande are controlled by its distributors through contract or lease.

[27] However, they do attempt to cover the market fairly extensively, because in part, at least, of their desire to improve the quality of their credit card system by having a large enough number of outlets to provide convenient service to their patrons. One of the small-company executives indicated that it is not essential for his company to have extensive representation because it does not provide credit.

[28] It will be noted that eight companies distribute their product through both company-owned and -operated facilities and wholesale merchants; six firms use only their own distribution facilities; in contrast, five companies distribute all their product through wholesale distributors. Moreover, one company sells its product through wholesale distributors and "commission agents," another uses all three methods to distribute its product. Finally, one company which sells all of its product "at the rack" employs no distribution setup at all; another sells partly "at the rack" and partly through its own facilities.

2. Many, if not most, independent concerns have relatively little control over their retail outlets,[29] except perhaps through the contract covering the purchase and sale of merchandise.

3. The majority of the independent companies either have no policy on the selection of retail locations or operate without a plan.[30] They acquire locations as an opportunity presents itself.[31]

4. Most independent companies do not assume the burden of sales promotion in any substantial amount.

---

[29] Exceptions include Ben Hur, East-West, and Sunland—some of which seem to be special cases. Ben Hur, for example, confines its sales principally to distribution through a small number of large-volume, company-owned self-serve stations.

[30] One small independent (Newhall) reports that it attempts to avoid locating stations too close to one another.

[31] One independent-company executive frankly stated that his company cannot be "fussy" and that it must take the majors' "cats and dogs." Some of these, undoubtedly, are low-gallonage accounts involving small-quantity dumps.

The following figures reported by the Standard Oil Company of California are evidence of a substantial difference in cost depending upon the size of the dump:

AVERAGE DELIVERY COSTS[a]

(Marketing department area trucks—area salesmen salary and truck expense only.)	
Size of Delivery	Delivery Cost
(gallons)	(c per gall.)
50	4.44
75	3.02
100	2.32
300	0.90
500	0.62
800	0.46
1,000	0.41

[a] Source: *National Petroleum News*, November 16, 1949, p. 55.

In southern California two major companies at one time conducted an experiment concerning the control of storage facilities by the supplier and the sale of gasoline to the station operator. The experiment used a meter device in the following way: The company has the keys to the tank so that it can dump gasoline at its own convenience any time of the day or night, thus allowing considerable savings in delivery costs. The gasoline is metered from the tank to the pump. By the use of slugs, purchased from the supplier, the dealer may acquire whatever gallonage he needs at any time. No one else has access to the tank. This scheme has an additional advantage from the standpoint of the company because it provides a means of control of the business by simply controlling the tanks. In other words, the dealer cannot buy from anyone else because the company owns the tanks.

5. While independent companies in some cases provide consumer credit systems, the majority of their dealers do cash business or carry their own accounts.[32]

6. The majority of the independent companies do not emphasize rigorous cleanliness standards for the service stations selling their products.

7. Independents usually do not require the maintenance of resale prices by those selling their products; indeed, some companies expect dealers to use price as a device for inducing patronage.

8. The independent organizations as a group are less strongly opposed to the use of promotional price signs than are the major companies—some may even encourage their use.

9. The independent companies, in general, are not opposed to the sale of their products to split-pump accounts. In fact, they may find a policy favoring such sales advantageous.[33]

10. Independent companies as a group are not opposed to the sale of their products to rebranders. (The significance of this point might easily be overstated in view of the limited capacity of some companies.)

While there are some general differences between the operating policies of major and independent companies, perhaps the most interesting aspect of this part of the study is the great difference in the policies of certain independent companies[34] as compared with others. That is, certain independent companies (particularly the large ones), in contrast with others, have policies which are very similar to those followed by the major and subsidiary concerns. Generally speaking, these independent concerns distribute their products through company-controlled, dealer-operated outlets; and a few[35] are interested in

---

[32] Of the independent companies, sixteen do not have credit systems while eight of the companies indicated to the authors that they do sponsor such a system for their dealers. Four companies formerly had credit card systems but discontinued them. While more of the larger independent companies have credit cards than the smaller ones, two of the largest companies in terms of volume of business (Sunset and Wilshire) are among those which discontinued using them. Two companies which do not use credit cards indicated that in some cases they will help an individual dealer with certain accounts, for example, special commercial accounts or credit to individual customers at a particular station (Golden Eagle and Pathfinder).

[33] As has been indicated by the Socal Company (see footnote (q), table 8.)

[34] Douglas, Hancock, Harbor, Kern, Macmillan, Mohawk, Newhall, Pathfinder, Sunland, and Sunset.

[35] Such as Sunset, Wilshire, Eagle Oil, and Hancock.

covering the market fairly extensively, although they have little interest in high-priced locations. Furthermore, some of these companies have policies which in "normal" times are designed to maintain informally a minimum posted price at the retail level and are opposed to promotional price signs.[36] What is more, a few independents (e.g., Douglas and Hancock) engage in sales-promotional activities. Some also require dealers to maintain clean stations. Finally, some independent companies,[37] like some major companies, are opposed to sales to rebranders. Thus, certain of the independent companies seem to be attempting to behave like major firms—without, one might add, being in a position to operate most effectively in this manner.

By and large, the policies of the smaller and less well-known suppliers are such that their dealers have almost complete freedom of action in their struggle for the custom of the consumers. From a practical point of view, however, they are limited in their choice of methods of operation. They, of course, may have well-located stations and keep them clean and attractive if they choose; in fact, this would undoubtedly be profitable in many circumstances. They may operate on a credit basis but are more likely to sell gasoline for cash, except where the dealer carries his own accounts. They may or may not offer the product of more than one supplier (operate on a split-pump basis) in their stations.[38] As such independent stations are not distributing a well and favorably known brand, however, they are almost forced to cut price and even, possibly, publicize their offerings by use of promotional price signs, if they are to succeed in acquiring sufficient custom to make their operation profitable. Thus, the method of operation of the small company handling a little-known brand of gasoline is determined not by arbitrary act or will, but by market circumstances.

---

[36] Some of the independent vendors normally do not allow price signs on their principal brands, but allow them on secondary brands. For example, in "normal" times Sunset evidently does not allow price signs in connection with the sale of its principal brand, *Sunset,* but does allow signs on its secondary brand, *Air King.* Another example is the Newhall Refining Company, which indicates that while it does not favor price signs, if one of its dealers wants to display a price sign it requires him to use the *Tasco* brand for such purposes. This is supposed to keep the *Newhall* brand "clean."

[37] Harbor, Kern, and Sunland.

[38] One old-timer in the field explained that in the early 'thirties there were many split-pumps in the Los Angeles area; in fact, by far the majority of stations were split-pump accounts, according to him, and there was bitter rivalry among refiners for the pumps in any station.

TABLE 8

KEY MARKETING POLICIES OF INDEPENDENT GASOLINE SUPPLIER COMPANIES, WHICH HAVE AN INFLUENCE ON COMPETITION AT THE RETAIL LEVEL, LOS ANGELES, 1948–1949

Independent companies	Principal brands of gasoline	Wholesale distribution			Control of retail outlets (Per cent of total)			Selecting locations for retail outlets	Substantial sales promotional effort of company in behalf of	
		Company operation	Distributor	Commission agent	Company-controlled and -operated	Company-controlled, dealer-operated	Uncontrolled		Brand	Dealers
Sunset Oil Co.	Sunset Deluxe, Sunset Elkyl	Small extent	Almost entirely	...	...	50	50	Some regard for extensive coverage, little for prime locations	None	None
Wilshire Oil Co.	Wilshire Polly, Wilshire Super Elkyl	Partly	Partly	...	...	10	90	Some regard for extensive coverage, little for prime locations	None	None
Eagle Oil & Refining Co.	Golden Eagle Super Premium, Golden Eagle Radar Elkyl "91"	...	Entirely	...	...	...	100	Some regard for extensive coverage, little for prime locations	Very little	Very little
Hancock Oil Co. of California	Hancock, Hancock Elkyl	Partly	Partly	...	...	80	20	Some regard for extensive coverage, little for prime locations	X	None
Douglas Oil Co. of California	Douglas Aviation Tested, Douglas Aviation Tested Elkyl	Almost entirely	Small extent	...	...	95	5	Some regard for extensive coverage, little for prime locations		X[b]
Fletcher Oil Co.[a]	Veltex, Veltex Super Elkyl	Almost entirely	Small extent	...	...	80	20	No general plan, outlets added on opportunistic basis	None	None
Macmillan Petroleum Corp.	Macmillan Xtra Odane, Macmillan Xtra Odane Elkyl	...	Entirely	...	...	60	40	No general plan, outlets added on opportunistic basis	None	(c)
Harbor Refining Co.	Harbor Tetraethyl, Harbor Elkyl	Partly	Partly	...	...	100	...	No general plan, outlets added on opportunistic basis	None	None
Rothschild Oil Co.	Powerine, Powerine Aviation Elkyl	Entirely	...	...	2	...	98	No general plan, outlets added on opportunistic basis	None	None
Kern Oil Company, Ltd.	St. Helens, St. Helens Elkyl	Entirely	...	...	...	70	30	No general plan, outlets added on opportunistic basis	None	None
Century Oil Co.	Century Crystal, Century Premium Elkyl	Entirely	...	...	...	75	25	No general plan, outlets added on opportunistic basis	None	None
Pathfinder Petroleum Co.	Pathfinder, Pathfinder Elkyl	...	Entirely	...	...	80	20	No general plan, outlets added on opportunistic basis	None	None

a According to observers in the trade there has "always been a close connection between Associated and Fletcher."
b Advertising stresses tie-in with individual dealers; claims to have originated idea of giving away motor cars as premiums.
c While Macmillan does no radio, magazine, outdoor, or newspaper advertising, the company has merchandising deals for its dealers such as "grab bags."

TABLE 8 (Continued)

Principal brands of gasoline	Wholesale distribution			Control of retail outlets (Per cent of total)			Selecting locations for retail outlets	Substantial sales-promotional effort of company in behalf of	
	Company operation	Distributor	Commission agent	Company controlled and -operated	Company controlled, dealer operated	Uncontrolled		Brand	Dealers
Independent companies. (cont.)									
Mohawk Petroleum Corp. *Mohawk* *Mohawk Ethyl*	Almost entirely	Small extent	...	...	3	97	No general plan, outlets added on opportunistic basis	None	None
Newhall Refining Co. *Newhall* *Newhall Ethyl*	Partly	Partly	...	...	50	50	No general plan, outlets added on opportunistic basis	X	None
Olympic Refining Co. *Olympic Quality* *Olympic Ethyl*	...	Entirely	...	...	...	100	No company policy on retail locations	None	None
Socal Oil & Refining Co. *Paragon Long Mileage* *Paragon Ethyl*	...	Partly	Partly	...	25	75	No general plan, outlets added on opportunistic basis	None	None
Sunland Refining Corp. *Sunland HO* *Sunland Ethyl*	All methods used			...	90	10	No general plan, outlets added on opportunistic basis	Little, if any	Little
Ben Hur Refining Corp. *Ben Hur* *Ben Hur Ethyl*	Entirely	...	...	90	10	...	Selects individually on basis of opportunity for mass gallonage	Little, if any[b]	Little
East-West Distributors. *East West* *East West Ethyl*	Entirely	...	...	33	33	34	No general plan, outlets added on opportunistic basis	None	None
Calstate Refining Co. *Calstate Super* *Calstate Ethyl*	Small extent	Balance sold "at the rack"	...	...	...	100	No general plan, outlets added on opportunistic basis	None	None
McCallen Refining Co. ...°	Product sold only "at the rack"			...	...	100	No company policy, almost entire product sold for rebrand	None	None
Time Oil Co. ...°	...	Entirely	...	...	...	100	No general plan, outlets added on opportunistic basis	None	None
Signal Oil & Gas Co.[a] *Padre* *Padre Ethyl*	...	Entirely	...	...	...	100	No company policy on retail locations	None	None
Baker Sales Co. ...°	Entirely	...	...	...	...	100	No general plan, outlets added on opportunistic basis	None	None

[a] This company which was acquired by Standard Oil of California in August, 1947, sells gasoline under the *Padre* brand in Long Beach area, through the Baker Sales Co., and in a small way elsewhere in this market area; the company sells gasoline extensively in the Northwest under the *Padre* brand, however.

[b] While these firms have their own brands, the bulk of their sales are for rebrand purposes.

[c] The company uses a small number of outdoor boards.

TABLE 8 (Continued)

	Supplier-company-sponsored retail credit system provided dealers	Maintenance of standards of cleanliness for dealer stations	Degree of price making normally exercised by company at retail level	Attitude toward promotional price signs	Attitude toward sales to split pump accounts	Attitude toward sales to rebranders
Independent companies (cont.)						
Sunset Oil Co.	No[d]	Weak policy, inadequate implementation, inferior results	Minimum posted price informally maintained	Opposed, except on secondary brand (*Air King*)	Not opposed	Not opposed[j]
Wilshire Oil Co.	No[e]	Moderate policy, inadequate implementation, inferior results	No price-making	Not opposed	Not opposed	Not opposed[k]
Eagle Oil & Refining Co.	No[f]	Weak policy, inadequate implementation, inferior results	No price-making	Favorably disposed[b]	Not opposed	([l])
Hancock Oil Co. of California	Yes	Moderate policy, moderate implementation, fair results	Minimum posted price maintained under Fair Trade Act.	Opposed	Not opposed	Not opposed[m]
Douglas Oil Co. of California.	No	Moderate policy, moderate implementation, fair results	Minimum posted price informally maintained	Opposed	Not opposed	Not opposed
Fletcher Oil Co.	Yes	Weak policy, inadequate implementation, inferior results	No price-making	Not opposed	Not opposed	Not opposed
Macmillan Petroleum Corp.	Yes	Weak policy, inadequate implementation, inferior results	Minimum posted price informally maintained	Opposed except on secondary brand (*Bonded*)	Not opposed	Not opposed
Harbor Refining Co.	Yes	No policy	Minimum posted price informally maintained	Favorably disposed	Not opposed	Opposed
Rothschild Oil Co.	No	Weak policy, no implementation, inferior results	No price-making	Opposed	Not opposed	Not opposed
Kern Oil Company, Ltd.	Yes	Moderate policy, inadequate implementation, inferior results	Minimum posted price maintained under Fair Trade Act	Opposed except on secondary brand (*Mascot*)	Not opposed	Opposed
Century Oil Co.	Yes	No policy	No price-making	Opposed[i]	Not opposed	Not opposed
Pathfinder Petroleum Co.	No[g]	Weak policy, inadequate implementation, inferior results	Minimum posted price informally maintained		Not opposed	Not opposed

[d] Formerly had a credit-card system but discontinued it in late 1949.

[e] Discontinued system during World War II.

[f] Company occasionally helps dealers carry commercial accounts.

[g] Credit card system was discontinued during World War II and has not been reinstated. However, company does help individual dealers carry specific accounts.

[b] Reportedly the contract with Standard provided for no price signs, but Eagle's attorneys advised the company that this provision was not valid, hence the circumscription was disregarded.

[i] Although opposed in principle, company reports "problem hasn't come up."

[j] Some of the gasoline sold through Ben Hur self-serve stations is from Sunset.

[k] In fact, some of the Associated gasoline sold in this area is supplied by Wilshire under the exchange agreement referred to earlier. (See table 2, note c.)

[l] By the terms of the contract with Standard Oil, which was terminated in July, 1949, this company was allowed to place the brand *Golden Eagle* on the product but was prohibited from reselling the product for rebranding purposes.

[m] Company sells to Time, Craig, East-West, among others.

TABLE 8 (Continued)

	Supplier company-sponsored retail credit system provided dealers	Maintenance of standards of cleanliness for dealer stations	Degree of price making normally exercised by company, at retail level	Attitude toward promotional price signs	Attitude toward sales to split pump accounts	Attitude toward sales to rebranders
Independent companies, (cont.)						
Mohawk Petroleum Corp....	No	Weak policy, inadequate implementation, inferior results	Minimum posted price informally maintained	Opposed, except on secondary brand (*Mopeco*)	Not opposed	Not opposed[c]
Newhall Refining Co........	Yes	Weak policy, inadequate implementation, inferior results	Minimum posted price informally maintained	Opposed, except on secondary brand (*Tasco*)	Not opposed	Not opposed
Olympic Refining Co........	No	No policy	No price making	Favorably disposed	Not opposed	Prohibited[a]
Socal Oil & Refining Corp...	No	No policy	No price making	Not opposed	Not opposed[d]	Not opposed[b]
Sunland Refining Corp......	Yes	Weak policy, inadequate implementation, inferior results	Minimum posted price informally maintained	Opposed	Not opposed	Opposed
Ben Hur Refining Corp......	No	Weak policy, inadequate implementation, inferior results	Minimum posted price maintained through ownership of stations	Favorably disposed	Not opposed	Not opposed
East-West Distributors......	No	No policy	No price making	Favorably disposed	Not opposed	Not opposed[a]
Calstate Refining Co.......	No	No policy	No price making	Not opposed	Not opposed	Not opposed
McCallen Refining Co.......	No	No policy	No price making	Not opposed	Not opposed	Not opposed
Time Oil Co..............	No	No policy	No price making	Not opposed	Not opposed	Not opposed
Signal Oil & Gas Co........	No	No policy	No price making	Not opposed	Not opposed	Not opposed
Baker Sales Co............	No	No policy	No price making	Not opposed	Not opposed	Not opposed

[a] In fact the company thinks that split-pump operations are advantageous to Socal dealers.
[b] Mohawk sells to self-serves which in turn sell under private label; brand name *Best* is owned by a Mohawk distributor who uses it from time to time.
[c] Prohibited from so doing under contract with General Petroleum.
[d] According to one of the company's executives, about 30 per cent of its business is on a rebrand basis.
[e] But do not have sufficient supply of gasoline to sell rebranders or self-serve stations.
Source: Interviews with company officials.

VII

NATURE OF RIVALRY
AMONG RETAIL GASOLINE VENDORS
IN THE LOS ANGELES MARKET:
GENERAL CONSIDERATIONS

Gasoline is offered in the Los Angeles consumer market under more than a hundred and fifty brand names (see table 9), through thousands of special outlets.[1] The product is retailed at convenient loca-

[1] These are largely specialty institutions in the sense that only one line of merchandise is sold there (not necessarily in the sense that customers will seek them out at a considerable distance in order to buy the particular product). It is interesting to note that in the early days of the automobile, the local blacksmith often became a garageman. According to one investigator, "He was supplied with gasoline from the bulk plant, but handled it in tins, since that was the way he had previously handled kerosene. The garageman considered gasoline a sideline and did not offer suitable service to the motorist. . . . In 1907, the first filling station was put into operation in St. Louis. It was crude, relative to the standards of our modern service station, but nevertheless it was effective as a business institution. It was so successful, pumping something more than 1,000 gallons a day, that it soon had many competitors. The garageman felt the loss in profits as his gasoline sales declined. To combat the growing competition of the service station, he installed curb pumps in front of his shop. Other retailers, such as grocery stores, car dealers, tire shops, etc., recognized the potential additional profits to be secured from gasoline sales and followed this lead. [Thus] motor fuel developed from a shopping to a convenience good." (Ralph C. Heath, "The Marketing of Consumer Gasoline," [thesis submitted in partial fulfillment of the requirements for the Master's degree in the School of Business Administration, Indiana University] June, 1948, pp. 12 and 13.)

TABLE 9

BRAND NAMES UNDER WHICH GASOLINE WAS RETAILED IN THE LOS ANGELES MARKET,
DURING THE YEAR 1948–1949

Acme	Ethylene Hi Octane	Mohawk	Scout
Admiral	Exeter	Mustang	Seaside Silver Gull
A.E.F.	EZ Hy Test	Naco	Self-Serve
Aeromatic	Father and Son	Newhall	Sequoia
Air King	Federal	Nu Ace	Serv-U High Test
Airport	Fire Chief	Nu Ethyl	Shell
Allstate	Fireball	Nu Gem	Signal
Arc	5 Star	Nu Leader	Silver Green
Arotane	Flying A	Olympic	Silver King
Armor	Gold Premium	Operators	Sky Chief
Atom	Golden Eagle	Orco	Southern
Aviation	Hal's Special	Pacific	Spitfire
Beacon	Hancock	Panther	Sunland H O
Beck	Harbor	Par X	Sunlight
Ben Hur	Herbst	Paragon	Sunset
Best	Hi-fly	Parks	Swift
Bill Whiteheads	Hy-grade	Pathfinder	Tasco
Bonded	Jet	Payless	Thrifti-Tip
Buff's Ethyl	Jetane	P.D.Q.	Tide
Bugle	Joy Juse	Polly	Time
Calstate	Kern	Powerine	Titian
Century	Kimbell	Pursuit	Tom's
Chevron	Kingsbury	Radar	Town & Country
Circo	Larco	Radio	Trojan
Circus	Laughing Gas	R.A.F.	Union
Cloverleaf	Lees	Real Aviation	United States
Convoy	Leggetts	Red Seal	Urich
Community	Lightning	Red Top	U-Save
Craig	Lively	Richfield Hi Octane	Vebee
Delta	Lucky Strike	Rio Grande Cracked	Veltex
Defense	Macmillan Xtra	Royal	Victory
Douglas	Magnum	Russell's Super Ethyl	Vita Plus
East West	Major Aviation	St. Helens	Waggoner's
Ecolene	Mark Bloome	Save 5	Whippet
Economy	Mascot	Sav-More	Wilco
Edwards	Military	Sav $ Mor	Wilshire
El Capitan	Mission	Scotty's	Zip
El Tejon	Mobilgas		

Source: Personal observations by those engaged in the study.

tions, in conjunction with a number of services which vary considerably in quality and quantity among outlets. On a basis of estimated
consumption minus commercial sales the amount of gasoline sold
through service stations in Los Angeles County in 1948 was 1,010,415,-
000 gallons. The number of service stations in operation in the same
year was estimated at 8,000. This is an average of 126,000 gallons per

station per year, or over 10,000 gallons per month.[2] Generally speaking, this is considered good gallonage for a conventional operation. However, while some stations are operating at this volume or even well in excess of it, others are doing much less business. Individual stations, therefore, struggle constantly to obtain or maintain an adequate share of the available volume. This struggle takes various forms and occurs at all levels of production and distribution.[3]

The nature of this competitive struggle will be set forth in broad terms in succeeding sections of this chapter. Thus, a brief analysis of competition in gasoline at the retail level is provided, followed by a classification of the several types of retail competitors found in this market and a short exposition of the dynamic nature of rivalry in this field. Following this summary presentation are separate chapters covering each type of retail competitor: the conservative competitor (chap. viii), the aggressive price competitor (chap. ix), and the defensive price competitor (chap. x).[4]

Nature of Competitive Structure in Gasoline Retailing

Competition in the retail gasoline field [5] is concerned with the rivalry among service station operators for the custom of consumer-

---

[2] This may appear to the reader, as it did to the authors, to be rather high. However, as a check, a computation was made based on estimates of the Standard Oil Company as to the number of stations and gallons of gasoline sold in the Los Angeles basin in 1946 (see p. 104, table 11). This resulted in an even higher average per station, 12,500 gallons.

[3] First, a continual effort at the refinery level to improve the quality of gasoline, each seller evidently being afraid that the other will gain an advantage by obtaining a better product. This is manifested by increases in octane rating, fitting the products to the specific climatic requirements of the area, and so on. Second, a striving by rivals in many ways to improve the amount and quality of service extended patrons at the retail level including making stations more accessible, keeping them clean, checking consumer requirements, making minor motorcar adjustments, and, very important, waiting on customers promptly. Third, the expenditure of effort by sellers—particularly the large firms, and especially at the preretail level—in demand-manipulative activities (such as advertising, house-to-house solicitation, and so on). Fourth, and last, the attempt made by various sellers at the preretail level, as well as at the retail level, to solicit custom by price concessions (either directly by offering cash discounts, or indirectly through coupons, dividend plans, and similar devices).

[4] This classification and the designations for the several types of competitors were devised by the authors to describe the retail market structure as they see it and, as far as they know, are not used in the trade.

[5] Webster defines "competition" in its commercial and economic aspects as: "The effort of two or more parties, acting independently, to secure the custom of a third party by the offer of the most favorable terms. . . ." (*Webster's New International Dictionary*, 2d ed., unabridged.)

buyers of motor fuel.[6] The intensity of rivalry among gasoline vendors depends upon (1) the number of sellers (mentioned earlier), (2) the directness of such competition (discussed immediately below), and (3) the types of competitors found in the market (to be discussed in later sections).

Directness of competition in retailing is a result of two independent factors: spatial proximity or remoteness, and similarity or dissimilarity of offerings.[7] Thus, the relative locations of retail competitors and the degree of product-service homogeneity determine directness of competition. It should be obvious from this that any one retail vendor is faced with varying grades of competition, depending upon the distance of various rivals from the seller's place of business and the similarity of the lines of merchandise and service which are offered by such sellers in comparison to those which he offers in his own establishment.

Because of differing service requirements, the importance of the spatial element, and product preferences, consumers consider only a few stations as completely satisfactory substitutes for one another. That is, only a small number of stations are in *direct* competition with one another: selling the same brands of gasoline and oil, offering the same quality of customer service and located equally conveniently to a group of buyers living in a particular community.[8] The competition of stations which are dissimilar in the quality of the product, the type of service offered, or the spatial separation are only in *semidirect or indirect competition*—selling a different brand of gasoline (a little-known brand instead of a well-known major brand), providing a lower quality of service, and being situated at a more distant or less accessible place. If the differentiating factors are combined, or if there is a great dissimilarity within any one the competition may be *remote*. Because of ease of entering the gasoline field, new rivals may be expected any time when prices become too high

---

[6] Rivalry among buyers for supplies exists also, of course, under some circumstances. This type of rivalry does not develop, however, unless supplies are short (i.e., a sellers' market exists), in which case buyers strive for supplies by offering "most favorable terms" (unless restricted by some sort of price control device).

[7] This analytical scheme is based on that developed by Professor E. T. Grether in his *Price Control Under Fair Trade Legislation* (New York: Oxford University Press, 1939), pp. 225-235.

[8] Even stations selling the same gasoline but located across a busy boulevard are not strictly direct competitors.

or offerings prove to be inadequate; thus, *potential* competition must also be considered as a factor in the retail sale of gasoline.[9]

One must not conclude from the foregoing that indirect or even remote competitors have no effect on one another and that rivals faced only with such competition can act with complete independence, particularly in pricing. Price concessions made by a station selling the same type of product-service, located at some distance from another, has an effect on its indirect rival because of (1) the mobility of consumers of motor fuel, but even more important, (2) the transmitted impact of the price cut through intervening sellers. Moreover, price cutters offering a quite different type of product-service but located close by those with whom they indirectly compete, tend increasingly toward gaining patronage at the expense of such indirect rivals as price differentials widen.[10] However, the effect of indirect rivalry will take place over a considerably longer time and is not as great as in the case of direct rivalry.

Rivals may attempt to attract custom by differentiating their products in the minds of consumer-buyers, by providing a superior product-service, by making concessions from the market price, or by a combination of these. The decision of rivals to compete one way or another will depend upon:

1. The position of the individual firm in relation to the demand for the product, conditioned by the competitive environment of the concern,

2. The astuteness of the management in (a) recognizing opportunities resulting from the company's position and (b) correctly evaluating both immediate and delayed consequences of the firm's actions, and

3. The degree of aggressiveness employed by the entrepreneur in charting the course of action to be taken by the firm.

The following three sections analyze briefly the behavior of the

---

[9] "Potential competition refers to the restraint exercised by the knowledge that an attempt to be too grasping will precipitate competition which is not at present active." (J. Maurice Clark, *Studies in the Economics of Overhead Costs*, [Chicago: University of Chicago Press, 1923], p. 444.)

[10] In any competitive situation some consumers are more price conscious than others. These volatile few would be expected to respond first to the lower-priced offerings. What is more, differences in the responsiveness of consumers to price would be expected to prevail as between depression and prosperous times. See the discussion of diminishing elasticity, above, p. 23–24.

several types of competitors found in the Los Angeles gasoline market
and the reasons why they compete as they do, in theoretical terms.

Conservative Competitors

Conservative competitors, so called,[11] are largely major-company
and subsidiary-company dealers. In normal times an estimated 75 per
cent of the number of outlets in the Los Angeles market fall into the
conservative-competitive category.[12]

This analysis would be simpler if such supplier companies distributed gasoline at retail through company-owned and operated outlets, which is true only to a very limited extent. Actually, there are
two functionaries involved in policy making in the retail sale of
major-company products—the supplier company and the retail dealer
—and the points of view of the two may be, and occasionally are, in
conflict. However, a uniform point of view between supplier and
dealer usually prevails.[13]

Because of the market position and executive astuteness of major
companies, dealers selling the products of such companies need not
and, indeed, may not with impunity compete aggressively in price,[14]
except for limited periods for defensive purposes.[15] Major-company
retail gasoline vendors might find it advisable to operate conserva-
tively for several reasons:

---

[11] The term "conservative" is used here to mean ". . . within safe bounds; moderate . . . believed to involve little risk; not speculative; . . ." (*Webster's New International Dictionary*, 2d ed., unabridged.)

[12] But see the section on defensive price competitors for a discussion of the shift made
by some stations from one category to another when the occasion demands (below
chap. x, pp. 145–148).

[13] The major-company dealer and his supplier are likely to see things in much the
same way, assuming the former understands his own market position. It must be admitted, however, that the dealer tends to see things in somewhat shorter-run terms
than the supplier. But the retail vendor, while nominally free to compete as he
pleases, is greatly influenced by his supplier—thus, major-company policies act as a
crystallizing medium.

[14] In the opinion of a high official of one of the leading major concerns in this area
the seven major companies are so much alike in products and services that they cannot
live in the same market when one of them is cutting the price even a cent under
the others.

[15] Commenting on gasoline prices in mid–1930, a spokesman for the Standard Oil
Company wrote: "Apparently the most destructive 'price war' ever experienced on the
Pacific Coast is ended. The 'war' grew out of price decreases made here and there
throughout the Pacific Coast. This and other companies followed the downward trend
of a series of competitive price reductions until, at some points, suppliers and dealers
were selling gasoline at or below cost." *Standard Oil Bulletin*, XVIII (July, 1930), p. 1.

1. The product sold by such companies is well and favorably known,[16] hence by a substantial section of the consuming public considered superior to that sold by independent concerns (which, however, is not necessarily true). Therefore the major-company dealers *can* exact a somewhat higher price for their product. Incidentally, the fact that the major-company brands are well and favorably known makes price reductions more effective, since they do not create doubts in the minds of consumers about product quality.

2. Although one group of consumer-buyers considers the major-company product superior to that of independent firms, another substantial group believes the gasoline[17] to be essentially the same as that sold by other major concerns. Thus, any open price reductions by one major company must in time be met by others, if they are to avoid serious loss of business. That is, the product of the individual major company has a high degree of cross elasticity—especially if such price reductions are publicized. Assuming prices are met, no advantage would accrue to a price cutter unless the generic demand for the product were elastic, which, as has been pointed out, is contrary to fact.[18] Therefore, the wise vendor in this position will practice restraint in reducing prices.

3. As was mentioned previously, gasoline is purchased largely on a convenience basis. Therefore, if the vendor is to cultivate the entire market (as a major seller must) rather than just ladle off the cream, he has no choice but to place outlets at a large number of points in each market so as to maximize convenience to all consumers located in it. Numerous conveniently located service stations make possible the easy shift of patronage from one vendor to another selling the same brand of product. If such shifts are induced by open price concession, they are bound to create ill-will among other company dealers and might even produce a "civil war." [19]

[16] But each company's product is not necessarily equally well and favorably known.

[17] Obviously, however, the product services of major-company gasoline dealers are not considered absolutely homogeneous by all buyers. If such homogeneity did prevail, no open price differentials could exist among such sellers (except where a price cutter was very small), because any vendor offering his product at a lower price would get all the business.

[18] However, the degree of elasticity of demand for the product-service of major-company sellers as a group might be quite high. Hence price cutting might make sense if major-company dealers as a class—but not necessarily acting in concert—are attempting to gain or recover volume from independent-company sellers, as a class.

[19] That is, a war among dealers distributing the same brand of product.

4. Major companies are at a disadvantage in dealing effectively, by direct means, with a price competitive situation involving one or only a few sellers in a particular locality, that is, by adjusting prices to those of certain rivals. In contrast to an operator whose price-making decisions concern only the particular outlet under consideration and a brand of product that is acceptable to only a small part of the consumer market, a major company selling through a large number of outlets would endanger the price stability of all its stations in the area[20] by openly meeting a price cutter's prices in a narrow segment of the market.

Consequently, major-company stations must stress the quality of the product-service as well as semi-price and non-price competitive methods in their rivalry[21] (superior locations, attractiveness of stations, completeness and promptness of service, sales promotional efforts, and so forth). Such a course does not mean that the major-company stations are not engaged in price competition at all; it does mean, however, that their position in the market forces them to emphasize other than price-competitive schemes in seeking custom. The criticism often leveled at major companies for competing on a non-price rather than a price basis (which, incidentally, is technically inaccurate[22]) and offering their product through what appear to be an excessive number of outlets, largely results from the market position in which the companies find themselves.

One might infer from the foregoing exposition, then, (1) that because of the inelastic nature of the demand for the generic prod-

---

[20] This again is a result of the high degree of demand elasticity prevailing for the product of an individual major seller; and the fact that submarkets overlap and that such a move would spread to other market segments.

[21] Actually, competitive behavior may be classified in five ways based on the methods used to stimulate the amount taken: (1) Non-price competitive activities—in which reliance is placed on persuasive effort in attempting to manipulate demand; (2) product rivalry—in which increases in the amount or quality of the product-service are used to attract patrons; (3) indirect (or, perhaps semidirect) price appeals—in which concessions are made but on some related product or service rather than on the principal item sold; (4) selective price concessions—in which discriminatory discounts are made where necessary to hold or gain patronage; and (5) direct price concessions—in which open reductions are made in the price of the principal product. Vendors may, and often do, use all these devices in their competitive activities but typically stress one, or perhaps two, more heavily than the others. Thus, two rivals typically use the same competitive devices but with different emphasis, hence may be competing quite differently.

[22] The point is that they *stress* other competitive devices than price.

uct, a high price level would be advantageous to all major-company sellers (assuming it did not attract new competitors and seriously reduce volume) and (2) that without the aggressive price competitors an effective oligopolistic situation might exist, which possibly would result in higher prices than actually prevail. This suggests the important role which is played by the aggressive price competitors in this market in keeping prices within bounds.

Aggressive Price Competitors

Aggressive competitors recognize (1) that a substantial segment of the market is very price conscious and therefore is willing at any time to take advantage of low-priced offerings and (2) that they are in a peculiarly advantageous position to serve this demand. Unlike major-company sellers, who are not in a position to take the price offensive (and who very possibly would not care to anyway), some independent sellers not only are in a position to engage in price competition, but seem to welcome the opportunity to do so. Probably 10 to 15 per cent of the outlets retailing gasoline in the Los Angeles market (representing a possibly greater percentage of the volume) normally operate in an aggressive manner concerning prices.[23]

A number of factors place such sellers in a position, indeed even force them, to compete aggressively. First, the brand of the product the independents sell is less well known than that of majors, with the result that (1) some concession must be made in order to sell it and (2) the price concession does not inevitably result in retaliatory reductions by competitors.[24] Second, this opportunity to gain an advantage through aggressive price tactics has drawn some aggressive-minded, imaginative individuals into the field who have begun to think in terms of volume operations. Third, once established, large scale outlets *require* substantial price concessions, since they must reach beyond the contiguous area for custom in order to induce sufficient patronage to insure a profitable operation. Hence, such sellers often not only can, but must undercut.

---

[23] In the sense of (a) seeking custom in an extremely energetic manner and (b) making use of price concessions to accomplish the purpose. Aggressiveness may take other forms, of course, such as establishing new outlets or soliciting custom through personal calls.

[24] The low prices for a non-major brand will affect only a small proportion of the market, so that the result is likely to be a low rate of cross elasticity of demand for most competing sellers.

Aggressive price-competitive operations in gasoline distribution are based on three related principles:

1. While the demand for gasoline in general is inelastic,[25] the demand for the product of any one seller may be highly elastic, assuming price reductions by the one seller are not met by competitors. Thus, a price cut by one seller which is not generally met by competitors will result in a substantial increase in the amount taken of that seller's product. This, in short, means gaining volume not from former nonusers but from those formerly purchasing from others. This assumption of the existence of a high rate of response accompanying a substantial price cut by one seller is certainly borne out by the evidence derived from the market place.

2. Cutting price will result in a narrower margin per unit of product sold, but this narrower margin often will be more than offset by the increase in units sold, and as a result total dollar margin[26] may be substantially enhanced. The aggressive price competitor is often completely independent (having no operational tie-ups with suppliers), and since many refiners compete for his business, and the trucking costs involved in one-stop deliveries are less, he is in a position to acquire supplies at a somewhat lower figure than that paid by orthodox distributors. His theoretical potential margin, therefore, is much wider. But in order to do a large-volume business, the aggressive competitor passes on to the consumer all this increase in unit margin, plus a part of the remainder, in the form of a price reduction. Thus the increase in the number of sold units more than makes up

---

[25] Elasticity is not considered here in its narrow sense as the rate of response to a *minute* change in price, but in its broader aspect as the rate of response to any change in price. It is very possible that the demand is quite inelastic in the former sense around the price point at which most sellers are offering their products, but that a substantial price cut would result in a significant increase in sales. As a matter of fact, this phenomenon undoubtedly prevails in the gasoline field—a small cut (of half a cent, for example) would have little effect on the amount taken, while a large cut (5 cents) would result in a heavy response by consumer-buyers, assuming of course that competitors did not meet the cut. Thus, we have the interesting phenomenon, which the authors feel is fairly typical of many demand situations, of a very different rate of elasticity of demand in a segment of the demand curve from the same price point, depending upon the extent of the reduction.

[26] Roughly speaking, margins may be considered from two points of view: (1) The per-unit margin—the difference between the purchase price and the sale price of a single unit of the product (which may be expressed in dollar terms or as a percentage of sales). (2) The dollar margin—the differential per unit times the number of units sold. For a fuller consideration of the subject of margins, see chap. xi, pp. 156–168, below.

for the reduction per unit (e.g., ten thousand times four cents equals four hundred dollars, versus one hundred thousand times two cents equals two thousand dollars).

3. Operations on a much larger scale than were previously thought possible are practicable in the service-station business. The costs accompanying such operations do not increase at the same rate as sales volume. Not only may unit volume and dollar margin be enhanced by a low-price policy, but unit costs may be reduced by it. The principle of low unit cost accompanying narrow-margin operations is a well-known phenomenon. The gasoline field offers a particularly interesting application of the principle. Lower unit costs result from (a) a much less than proportional increase in the fixed plant relative to the volume, (b) a more effective utilization of manpower, and (c) (in self-serve operations only) the reduction in the number of attendants[27] and the amount of skill required by them.

Just one concluding point: While only an estimated 15 to 20 per cent of the gasoline sold at retail in the Los Angeles area is normally distributed by aggressive price competitors, this percentage does not fully reflect the competitive importance of this type of vendor. He is a major factor in keeping retail gasoline prices under control.[28]

Defensive Price Competitors

Some gasoline vendors are neither in a position to offer their products at market prices nor to seek volume sales through drastic

---

[27] In an interview (July, 1949) a spokesman for the Teamsters' Union indicated that his union was definitely opposed to self-serve stations because they tended to create unemployment. However, because of its weakness—this group is only 10–15 per cent organized—nothing can be done by the union. Legislation is its only hope. The union was a factor in enacting the City of Los Angeles ordinance which proscribes self-serve operations within the city limits (see below, p. 124, table 15). This opposition to self-serve operations has been ostensibly based on the fire-hazard factor, *not* on the unemployment aspect. Reportedly, in Seattle (but not in Los Angeles) the majors and the union coöperated in outlawing self-serve operations. In Seattle, the ordinance passed was vetoed by the mayor, but subsequently passed over the veto; a petition was being circulated to present it to the people in a general election.

[28] Those gasoline vendors who seek custom by aggressively competing in price are quite a different type of retailer than those who typically pursue such tactics in some other field, such as groceries. In the former, the aggressive price competitor is the non-affiliated (independent) concern, while in the latter, the aggressive competitor typically is the integrated (chain) distributor. There are several possible reasons for this, including differences in elasticity of demand for the firm's products, the contrasting buying habits of purchasers of the two products, and the type of thinking done by business executives in the two fields.

price cutting. Typical of vendors falling into this category are those operating small, poorly located, and possibly untidy stations, and selling a little-known brand of gasoline. Such vendors are by their competitive situation in the odd position of being forced to cut, but not being able to go all out. An estimated 10 to 15 per cent of the outlets in the Los Angeles market operate on this basis in ordinary times.

On the one hand, defensive price competitors are like conservative competitors: they are small, full-service operators; on the other hand, they are unlike conservative competitors: they are unable to sell their product at the market price and must therefore induce patronage by offering a discount. Defensive as well as aggressive price competitors must operate on a cut-rate basis, but the price reductions of the defensive type are modest rather than drastic. Normally, defensive competition is confined to independent-company dealers, because they must have considerable freedom in pricing.

Such competitors, therefore, must cut price enough to offset some disadvantage (hence cuts may vary among sellers, depending upon the extent of the disadvantage faced). They must, however, avoid deep cuts as they are not in a position to handle the volume necessary to offset the narrower unit margin created by the cut. In addition, because the product is not well known, a drastic cut might create a suspicion of low quality, hence result in little, if any, increase in volume.

As was mentioned earlier, vendors of major-company products as a group are normally in a competitive position that makes for a considerable amount of independence in pricing.[29] At times, however, they are forced into a defensive position by loss of volume to their more aggressive rivals. Thus, some major-company dealers at times may find themselves in the anomalous situation of having to shift their position from that of conservative competitors to that of defensive price competitors. The basic reason, then, for a major-company dealer going on the defensive at times is that he finds himself at a disadvantage as a result of the price-cutting activities of some independent rivals; but a contributory reason might be that the major-company dealer is not well located, or that his station is not

---

[29] *Independence in pricing matters,* which is concerned with the retail vendor's relationship with rivals, is not to be confused with *freedom in pricing matters,* which refers to the retail seller's relations with his supplier.

attractive. Indeed, such outlets are likely to be in the vanguard of those taking defensive price action when serious loss of volume is felt by major-company dealers, assuming the operators of such stations are aggressive-minded.

Usually when such stations are faced with the described price disadvantage they attempt to overcome it by semi-price or non-price means. However, occasionally major-company dealers will choose to make price concessions to customers, although the discounts may possibly be only "secret" ones at first. Open price cutting by a major-company dealer will (at least) be frowned on by the supplier company if the action is taken for aggressive purposes.[30] A major-company dealer faced with seriously declining patronage may either (1) take matters into his own hands, despite the fact that he ordinarily has little freedom in pricing, or (2) be given permission by his supplier to meet the lower prices of his competitors.

When major-company stations cut their prices they not only take business from aggressive price cutters but from conservative dealers —including those selling the same brand, as well as those selling other major-company brands. Therefore, concessions made for defensive purposes almost inevitably lead toward similar action by other major-company sellers. Thus, when one major-company dealer becomes a defensive price competitor, another will find it necessary, in turn, to act defensively to protect himself. It is by such means that a large segment of the conservative competitive group may temporarily shift to a defensive position. Such a shift actually occurred in the Los Angeles market in early 1950. This will be discussed in detail below.[31]

Competition a Dynamic Phenomenon

An attempt to describe competition in any field is likely to result in a static, rather than dynamic picture. Actually, one would require a motion picture of the competitive struggle to depict the scene with any degree of realism, since rivals are constantly contending with each other to retain or increase their share of the market. Moreover,

---

[30] The spokesman for one large company stated: "Among the causes destructive of stabilized marketing conditions is the dealer whose only aim, regardless of the reasonableness of prevailing prices, is to take the business of his neighbor by selling below the latter's price." *Standard Oil Bulletin*, XVIII (July, 1930), 2.

[31] See below, chap. x, pp. 146–148.

new sellers are invariably appearing, different appeals are being used, and changed demand conditions are presenting themselves. Competition is especially intensive in gasoline since the demand for the generic product is inelastic as has been pointed out, hence, generally speaking, any custom gained by one seller is at the expense of others —a competitive pattern which does not exist in the sale of candy or taxicab service, for example.[32] That is, gasoline competitors concentrate their efforts on taking business away from one another.

Gasoline retailing, therefore, is a kind of economic free-for-all, in which each contender fights the pack[33] within his own sphere of influence.[34] Thus, (1) major-company dealers are competing with dealers selling the same major-supplier's product; (2) major-company dealers are competing with dealers selling different major-suppliers' products; (3) major-company dealers are competing with dealers selling independent-suppliers' products; (4) independent-company dealers are competing with dealers selling the same independent-supplier's product; (5) independent-company dealers are competing with dealers selling different independent-suppliers' products; and (6) independent-company dealers are competing with dealers selling major-suppliers' products. Superimposed upon this is the struggle among suppliers at the policy-making level, each attempting to outdo the other in devising more effective ways of obtaining his share of the market.

Vendors use various devices in their attempt to attract the custom of the motorist. These include, among others, offering price concessions; providing credit to customers; increasing the number or size, or changing the layout of stations;[35] improving or at least differentiating the product[36] or the service;[37] and increasing or improving

---

[32] For an exception to this general proposition developing out of expanding market conditions, see below, pp. 104–105.

[33] Although obviously the impact of each rival's efforts varies considerably from that of others depending upon the location, the product line, and the type of competitive weapons used.

[34] It is incorrect to say that the competitive struggle pits each seller against all others in the whole market area; rather, the struggle is mainly among small numbers of sellers in a large number of submarkets, indirect competition prevailing only among sellers located in different submarkets.

[35] Substantial improvement is constantly being made in the Los Angeles area in the attractiveness of stations, including ease of entrance.

[36] "Rust-proof" gasoline, developed by Sinclair Oil Corporation and offered on the coast by Richfield Oil Corporation, is an example of this, although one cannot help

methods of publicizing offerings. Rivals are constantly jockeying for position by adjusting their offerings in order to retain or attract the patronage of consumers with varying service requirements, brand preferences, degrees of price consciousness, and market knowledge. These adjustments vary with the type of seller and take the form of narrowing or widening price differentials (open or secret); providing or withdrawing special values on related items, when bought in connection with the purchase of gasoline; offering or ceasing to offer gifts, premiums, or prizes to patrons; varying the amount and quality of free service.[38] The form of the adjustment will ordinarily vary with the position and attitude of the seller.[39] He must always keep in mind that in the sale of gasoline, sellers in direct competition are relatively few (i.e., oligopoly prevails), hence reactions of competitors to the sellers' actions must be considered (i.e., sellers must show foresight).

While rivalry among service stations is largely confined to dealers operating within relatively small trading areas, the effect of the intensive struggle (particularly concerning the price) is transmitted from one area to another through the action of rivals located on the periphery of each submarket area. Latterly, the influence of sellers' actions on distant rivals has increased substantially, because of the establishment of large-scale, mass-selling retail institutions whose deep-cut prices attract custom from afar.

---

but wonder about the seriousness of the hazard from which the product is supposed to protect the motorist, even assuming it possesses the qualities claimed for it.

[37] Most, if not all, major companies provide maps for tourists. One subsidiary company in this market recently offered booklets which contain information on eating places, motels, and the like for those planning trips. Other companies concentrate on other types of services. One major concern provides "certified rest rooms" as an important part of its promotional campaign.

[38] Reportedly, one large West Coast company, when faced with intensive competition, increased the number of attendants in a station so as to assure prompt and effective service, and thus increased the attractiveness of that particular outlet.

[39] Competitive activities might even be in the form of harassing tactics. The following excerpt from a letter from one of the pioneers in "gasateria" operations in the Midwest is illustrative: "In the beginning these stations sold anywhere from 350,000 to an average of 225,000 gallons per month. Competitors were baffled as to how to meet this type of competition. Every kind of a hindrance or obstacle known to the industry was used against them to retard their progress, such as injunction suits, using political pressure to get Fire Marshal disapproval. Competitors even instructed their employees to tell the public that this low price marketer was selling inferior merchandise. . . . The failure of the major oil company to accept this type of competition as a part of the industry eventually led to a very long and destructive price war."

TABLE 10

BRANDS OF GASOLINE USUALLY PURCHASED BY CONSUMERS IN THE LOS ANGELES MARKET, JANUARY AND JUNE, 1948–1950

(Per cent of respondents indicating use of each brand)

Brand	Producer-brand promoter	Jan. 1947	June 1947	Jan. 1948	June 1948	Jan. 1949	June 1949	Jan. 1950
Standard	Standard Oil Company of California	20.2	18.1	20.8	20.0	18.3	16.1	16.7
Union	Union Oil Company of California	9.3	13.8	14.2	12.5	10.9	13.3	10.5
Mobilgas	General Petroleum Corporation	8.9	8.5	9.8	7.2	9.3	9.1	8.5
Texaco	The Texas Company	9.9	8.5	10.2	8.6	7.2	7.6	8.3
Richfield	Richfield Oil Corporation	6.1	6.7	4.2	8.0	5.8	7.5	7.7
Shell	Shell Oil Company Inc.	11.8	9.8	7.4	7.4	6.9	8.6	7.1
Golden Eagle	Eagle Oil & Refining Company, Inc.	1.9	1.2	1.0	2.5	3.4	2.8	3.8
Signal	Signal Oil Company	2.5	2.2	1.6	1.9	3.2	2.0	3.0
Associated	Tide Water Associated Oil Company	3.2	3.5	1.6	2.2	2.0	2.2	1.9
Hancock	Hancock Oil Company of Calif.	—	—	1.8	1.8	1.6	1.2	1.5
Douglas	Douglas Oil Company of Calif.	—	—	1.2	1.2	1.8	1.0	1.5
Polly	Wilshire Oil Company, Inc.	1.1	1.4	0.6	0.4	0.2	0.4	0.9
P.D.Q.	The Petrol Corporation	2.3	2.0	0.8	1.0	1.0	1.0	0.4
Sunset	Sunset Oil Company							0.4
All others[a]		14.2	15.3	12.6	16.3	15.9	16.3	16.5
No preference		8.6	9.0	12.2	9.0	12.5	10.9	11.3

[a] Including the following: Atom, Beck, Ben Hur, Century, Craig, Harbor, Kingsbury, Macmillan, Magnum, Nu Ace, Mark Bloome, Pacific, Paragon, Parks, Phillips, Powerine, Rio Grande, St. Helens, Sears, Seaside, Urich, Vebex, etc.

Source: The Los Angeles Times, "Continuing Home Audit Los Angeles County."

Table 10 presents Los Angeles market brand-preference data semi-annually for 1947–1950; these indicate the results of the competitive struggle. The heavy concentration of preference for the brands of major companies will be noted. (This phenomenon is discussed in a later chapter.)[40] It should be noted, also, that the share of the market enjoyed by major companies changed materially from January, 1947, to January, 1950. (This, too, is discussed in a later chapter.)[41]

Four additional points concerning the dynamic nature of competition in the gasoline field may be of interest:

1. There is evidence of a high degree of correlation between a company's share of the retail gasoline market and the number of outlets through which its product is sold. Table 11,[42] which shows estimates of the number of stations and the gallonage of the seven major companies in the Los Angeles market, and the minor and secondary companies as a group, indicates that in every instance save one, the per cent of stations in the Los Angeles market and the per cent of gallonage are close to identical. The one important exception is Standard Oil Company of California whose company-owned stations (operated by Standard Stations, Inc.) do almost twice as much volume as would be indicated by the number of stations which it operates. One further exception, though rather unimportant, is the non-major sellers as a group, whose percentage of gasoline gallonage is slightly less than the percentage of outlets selling their brands.

While it can hardly be denied that the more stations a company has, the greater will be the gasoline sales, one should not conclude that consumer preference for certain brands of gasoline is merely a matter of the number of outlets. Actually, the opposite is probably true: a firm has a large number of outlets because the preference for its brands exists. Moreover, the preference for the product of major companies undoubtedly exists, but is offset by price concessions made by non-major sellers; so that while the opportunity for purchase is enhanced by the increase in the number of outlets, the existence of a large number of service stations is by no means a guarantee that

---

[40] See below, chap. viii, p. 110.

[41] See below, chap. x, pp. 146–148.

[42] At first glance, tables 3 and 11 seem to be in conflict as regards the relative amount of business done by major and minor companies in this area. However, each shows approximately 60 per cent of the service station business going to major companies and 40 per cent of the business going to the subsidiary and independent firms.

such stations will be patronized. Hence, the successful exploitation of a market cannot be effected simply by multiplying the number of retail outlets.

2. The California gasoline market as a whole (including the Los Angeles area) has been expanding at a tremendous rate, especially

TABLE 11

Estimated Number of Service Stations and Volume of Gasoline Sales, and the Per Cent of Total Stations and Sales for Each of the Seven Majors and for Minor and Secondary Companies Combined, Los Angeles Basin, 1946

Companies	Number of stations supplied	Gallons sold annually	Per cent of available gallonage	Per cent of total stations
Standard Oil Co. of Calif......	519	104,005,176	11.14	8.38
Standard Stations, Inc.......	(291)	(81,325,716)	(8.71)	(4.70)
Chevron dealers...........	(228)	(22,679,460)	(2.43)	(3.68)
General Petroleum Corporation	689	103,225,360	11.06	11.13
Union Oil Company.........	508	81,473,700	8.73	8.24
Shell Oil Company..........	425	69,755,000	7.47	6.86
Texas Company.............	446	65,570,800	7.02	7.20
Richfield Oil Company.......	420	63,455,000	6.80	6.78
Tide Water Associated Oil Company.................	264	38,830,400	4.18	4.26
Minor and secondary concerns	2,919	406,961,820	43.60	47.15
Total....................	6,190	933,277,256	100.00	100.00

Source: Summary of Testimony on the Trial of Civil Action No. 6159-Y, *United States* v. *Standard Oil Company of California, et al.* (Wayne Goble Publications, 1948) Tenth Day, p. 1.

during the past decade or so. The data in table 12 indicate that the bulk of this growth is the result of the increased number of motor vehicles; some, however, is due to more intensive use of the vehicles. Such a market expansion (in the absence of an equivalent increase in the number of outlets) tends to have a mitigating effect on the intensity of competition among outlets. That is, competition is likely to be "softer," because sales may be gained from new customers in the market rather than from rivals.[43] This does not mean that competition under such conditions is not intensive, but only that it very

---

[43] That is, competition is likely to be softer under such conditions because vendors are not as "hungry" for business. It is easier to obtain a satisfactory volume, hence vendors do not find it necessary to strive so vigorously. This tendency reaches its ultimate stage when—as in some cases of wartime community growth—all sellers are bound to get adequate volume because of the fact that demand taxes all the available facilities and consumers are forced to patronize any vendor that can serve them.

likely would be more intensive in the absence of such market expansion, other things being equal.

It is noteworthy, however, that because of this growth element some vendors may be losing position in their share of the market. It goes without saying that with the cessation of expansion, com-

TABLE 12

Indexes of Taxable Distributions of Gasoline in California and of Motor-Vehicle Registrations in California and Los Angeles County, 1939-1949

(1939 = 100)

Taxable distributions of gasoline		Motor vehicle registrations		
Year	California	Year	California	Los Angeles
1938-1939	100.0	1939	100.0	100.0
1939-1940	104.4	1940	106.4	107.4
1940-1941	117.2	1941	113.7	115.6
1941-1942	104.4	1942	109.1	111.2
1942-1943	90.0	1943	106.0	106.9
1943-1944	92.1	1944	107.3	107.9
1944-1945	110.2	1945	110.3	110.0
1945-1946	145.8	1946	120.0	120.5
1946-1947	166.4	1947	135.0	135.8
1947-1948	176.2	1948	144.6	145.9

Source: Reports of the California State Board of Equalization and the California State Department of Motor Vehicles.

petitors who have been sustained by the new business coming into the market, rather than by maintaining or expanding their share of the market, may be faced with disaster.

3. Considering the necessity of intensive cultivation of markets by major companies, it would seem that they not only would have to stress non-price and semi-price competitive schemes, but might attempt to divide territories for the purposes of enhancing their sales volume per outlet and cutting costs. Table 13, which shows the number of stations representing each major and subsidiary company in each of the forty-eight subareas in the Los Angeles market, has been provided for the purpose of determining whether such a plan is being followed.

These data indicate that major companies are not only represented in most submarkets but are represented in considerable numbers, in most instances. Hence, there is no evidence of sharing mar-

TABLE 13

NUMBER OF SERVICE STATIONS CARRYING MAJOR- AND SUBSIDIARY-COMPANY PRODUCTS
IN EACH SUBMARKET OF THE LOS ANGELES AREA, BY MAJOR AND
SUBSIDIARY COMPANIES REPRESENTED, 1947

	Submarkets	Majors							Subsidiaries			
No.	Location	Gen. Petr. Corp.	Rich. Oil	Shell Oil	Stand. Oil	Texas Co.	T.W. Assoc.	Union Oil	Petrol Corp.	Rio Grande	Sea-side	Signal Oil
	Downtown	25	13	14	34	16	12	18	1	2	5	13
1	Westlake	13	11	12	23	11	4	11	—	1	3	6
2	Elysian Park	15	5	5	10	7	3	8	1	2	1	5
3	Glendale	39	29	21	35	24	18	24	5	5	4	13
4	Burbank	14	7	12	8	7	8	9	4	5	5	12
5	San Fernando	3	7	3	4	5	5	10	—	—	1	3
6	Valley	12	15	13	9	10	10	11	11	4	3	6
7	North Hollywood	11	8	7	9	6	8	12	6	4	4	3
8	Hollywood	24	22	26	35	23	15	19	4	2	1	8
9	Wilshire Center	23	20	16	27	14	6	20	1	—	—	7
10	Miracle Mile	22	14	14	18	15	5	13	2	1	4	9
11	West Hollywood	9	7	9	10	12	6	8	2	5	3	4
12	Beverly Hills	18	10	7	12	8	8	12	2	—	5	5
13	Westwood	3	6	4	10	5	4	12	—	2	—	3
14	Santa Monica	22	15	17	38	23	24	16	7	11	5	18
15	Culver City	4	5	5	7	6	3	12	1	3	2	5
16	Wash.-Jefferson	18	11	11	18	12	6	13	3	6	4	7
17	Crenshaw	22	18	15	14	12	7	15	4	6	1	6
18	Inglewood	19	7	8	9	18	7	8	3	3	2	2
19	Westchester	—	1	1	2	—	—	4	—	—	—	—
20	Manhattan-Redondo	9	4	4	11	10	6	4	4	3	1	3
21	Torrance	6	2	3	2	11	3	4	—	—	2	5
22	Morningside-Gard	27	12	12	7	12	5	7	11	8	2	4
23	South Downtown	14	10	15	12	5	1	5	3	1	—	5
24	South Central	40	18	21	15	8	9	12	12	13	4	12
25	Compton	25	4	8	7	9	5	8	7	2	3	5
26	Dominguez	1	1	1	—	3	—	—	3	1	—	3
27	Wilmington-San Pedro	13	11	5	11	12	8	10	2	—	3	9
28	Long Beach	47	28	24	39	40	9	22	14	3	4	34
29	Downey	9	5	5	5	8	5	6	2	—	—	10
30	Huntington Park-South Gate	30	12	11	11	11	4	10	7	10	—	12
31	Vernon-Maywood	23	5	7	7	3	2	7	4	3	2	9
32	Lincoln Heights	8	6	6	6	4	—	3	1	1	1	7
33	South Gate	6	10	5	7	9	4	7	1	3	3	6
34	Pasadena	32	25	11	29	24	17	44	11	5	2	7
35	Foothills	11	8	7	9	11	5	10	4	1	5	3
36	Pomona	21	13	11	11	18	7	13	17	2	4	7
37	Baldwin-Covina	8	1	4	4	2	1	2	2	1	1	2
38	El Monte	13	5	6	4	2	5	6	4	1	1	4
39	Alhambra	24	11	12	15	13	10	14	9	4	3	11
40	Boyle Heights	20	9	8	12	8	2	9	5	—	2	12
41	Belvedere	20	5	5	5	5	2	4	3	2	3	2
42	Montebello	4	1	2	2	3	2	3	1	3	—	1
43	Whittier	12	1	6	7	8	5	11	1	—	—	1
44	Fullerton	6	5	4	8	8	4	11	1	—	1	1
45	Anaheim	10	8	2	5	9	7	5	1	—	2	6
46	Santa Ana	15	8	8	8	14	7	9	3	2	2	10
47	Orange Coast	13	10	9	17	20	7	12	7	2	1	5
	Totals	783	469	442	609	531	301	513	197	133	105	331

Source: *Service Station Route List*, Hearst Publications, Inc. (*The Los Angeles Examiner* Dept.), 1947, supplemented by field investigation (June, 1949).

kets among major firms in the Los Angeles area. The subsidiary firms are not represented in all subareas in the Los Angeles market, but this does not suggest division of territory. Rather, it is a reflection of the fact that the subsidiary concerns (particularly Rio Grande and Seaside) do not have a policy of blanket coverage of the market.

4. A relatively large part of the gasoline gallonage sold in the Los Angeles area is marketed through independent (or at least non-major) outlets. This is indicated in the figures for California as a whole compared with Los Angeles,[44] and in those for San Francisco compared with Los Angeles.[45] While dealers of non-major companies (sometimes also called minor or secondary companies) did 43.6 per cent of the business in the Los Angeles market area, such dealers in the state as a whole did only 18.2 per cent and in San Francisco 23.94 per cent. This would indicate vigorous competition in the Los Angeles area because of the larger-than-average percentage of competitors which normally use price as a major competitive weapon.

[44] The figures for California as a whole compared with those for Los Angeles are as follows:

	California[a]	Los Angeles[b]
	(per cent)	(per cent)
Major-company dealers..................	81.8	56.4
Minor- and secondary-company dealers......	18.2	43.6
	100.0	100.0

[a] Based on data obtained from California State Board of Equalization on taxable distributions of gasoline for 1946.
[b] Summary of Testimony on the Trial of Civil Action No. 6159-Y, *United States* v. *Standard Oil Company of California, et al* (Wayne Goble Publications, 1948) Tenth Day, p. 1.

[45] The figures for the San Francisco Bay area compared with the Los Angeles area are as follows:

	San Francisco[a]	Los Angeles[b]
	(per cent)	(per cent)
Major-company dealers.................	76.06	56.40
Minor- and secondary-company dealers....	23.94	43.60
	100.00	100.00

[a] Summary of Testimony on the Trial of Civil Action No. 6159-Y, *United States* v. *Standard Oil Company of California, et al* (Wayne Globe Publications, 1948) Tenth Day, p. 1.
[b] *Ibid.*, p. 1.

VIII

NATURE OF RIVALRY:
CONSERVATIVE COMPETITORS

Perhaps the two distinguishing characteristics of conservative competitors in retail gasoline distribution are (1) the stress on other than price-competitive devices in their attempt to attract patronage and (2) the substantial interest taken by supplier companies in the marketing activities of their dealers. In short the supplier companies recognize their position in the market and operate in such a way as to maximize results.

Such suppliers exert a considerable influence over the operating methods of the retail vendors who distribute their product. They have a substantial—if not complete—control over the quality of the product, the brand, the form and extent of sales promotional effort; in addition they have an influence over the prices, the type of equipment, the layout of the facilities, and even (often) the location of the outlet.

Thus, the supplier decides in large part what method of competition is to be followed and what competitive tools are to be employed. This places the dealer in a position of specializing in the operation of his business in accordance with policies determined to a large extent by supplier companies, and is an application of the

Taylor principle of separating the responsibilities of planning and doing.[1]

Method of Operation of Conservative Competitors

As mentioned earlier, a seller is not free to choose any form of competition. Because of his market situation, as well as the attitude and astuteness of those responsible for business policy, any seller is considerably limited in his choice of competitive methods.

The conservative-competitive stations are (1) advantageously situated so as to be able to sell their product on a quality basis and (2) vulnerable pricewise, with the result that they strongly tend to stress superior locations, attractiveness of stations, completeness and promptness of service, and the like, rather than low price. This, of course, does not mean that such stations do not engage in price competition at all. On the contrary, they must stand ready to adjust their prices to changes of rivals as the occasion demands. It does mean, however, that their position in the market (combined with the foresight of their supplier in market matters) causes them to emphasize the quality of the product-service rather than price, in attempting to attract custom.

Stations distributing the products of the seven major companies—General Petroleum, Shell Oil, Standard Oil, Richfield Oil, the Texas Company, Tide Water Associated, and Union Oil—may generally be classified as conservative competitors. Outlets of subsidiaries—Rio Grande, Seaside, Signal Oil, and the Petrol Corporation[2]—operate in much the same manner. Even the stations of a few of the independent companies—until recently at least—have attempted oddly enough to conduct their business on a similar basis.[3]

---

[1] According to Taylor's principles of scientific management (Frederick Winslow Taylor, *The Principles of Scientific Management* [New York and London: Harper & Bros., 1929]) management should plan the work (i.e., decide on the best methods to be followed, such as select proper tools) while labor performs the task according to the plan. Thus, each specializes in one phase of the operation and in the phase that he is best able to perform.

[2] Petrol Corporation became a wholly-owned subsidiary of Standard Oil Company of California in January, 1948. Subsequently, its operations were terminated by the parent company.

[3] Neither their locations nor the extent of consumer preference for their products would seem to justify conservative marketing of their products. Because of the importance of these elements in operating in the manner indicated, one successful independent-station operator is of the opinion that it is useless for an independent dealer to try to compete with majors unless he cuts price.

A large number of the stations in the Los Angeles market—an estimated 75 per cent in normal times—attempt to attract custom by the brand [4] of product and quality of service rather than by concession from the market price.

Operational Techniques. The operation of a service station under major-company sponsorship would appear to be simple. However:

1. Such operation involves a considerable amount of behind-the-scenes (foundational) work—finding locations, planning layouts, promoting sales, providing delivery, devising record systems, determining prices, and so forth.

2. The simplicity of service-station operation is more apparent than real. Actually, the successful operation of a station is the product of considerable practical knowledge and assiduous attention to detail in attracting patronage, providing for customer requirements[5] and conducting the business affairs profitably.

While the suppliers' part in marketing is extremely important, it is of no avail without intelligent, energetic, and honest management at the service-station level. A good operator may mean the difference between the success and failure of a station.

Typically, the stations of conservative competitors are operated in the following manner:

1. Stations are clean, well equipped, and conveniently accessible[6] to consumers.[7]

---

[4] This same strong tendency toward the purchase of major brands of gasoline prevails in other markets also, as evidenced by the data found in available consumer-preference studies. For example, in Columbus, Ohio, over 85 per cent of the consumers reporting indicated that they bought one of the major brands of that area, including *Sohio X-70, Sunoco, Shell, Pure Oil, Gulf, Sinclair, Texaco,* and *Mobilgas* (*Consumer Analysis of the Greater Columbus Market* [*Columbus Dispatch,* 1948]). Likewise, in Philadelphia, of those questioned as to the brand of gasoline they usually bought, 90 per cent mentioned the name of a major brand, including *Atlantic, Esso, Sunoco, Gulf, Texaco,* and *Mobilgas* (*Consumer Analysis of the Philadelphia Market,* [*Philadelphia Bulletin,* 1948]). Finally, in St. Paul, well over 80 per cent of those reporting indicated their use of some one or more of the major brands—*Phillips 66, Standard, Texaco, Pure Oil, Mobilgas, Shell, Cities Service, Skelly, Sinclair,* and *Tydol* (*Consumer Analysis of the St. Paul Market* [*St. Paul Dispatch-Pioneer Press,* 1948]).

[5] For an interesting article concerning the effective operation of a major-company dealer station see F. A. Bean, "Mr. Bean Approves" (*National Petroleum News,* November 23, 1949, p. 34).

[6] Often on high-traffic intersections. The location of service stations is restricted by zoning ordinances, however. In the city of Los Angeles, for example, filling stations are prohibited in all zones classified A (agriculture), RA (residential agriculture), and R

2. Outlets are relatively small[8] (three to six pumps) and designed to distribute only a moderate volume (10,000 to 20,000 gallons per month).[9]

3. The custom of each station is largely drawn from the immediate area contiguous to the station (except those located on highways and designed to serve tourists).[10]

4. The brand of gasoline offered is well publicized[11] and favorably known.[12]

(residential); they are also prohibited in areas designated as CL (limited commercial) except in cases of special variances. Automobile service stations are permitted in the remaining C zones (various gradations of the commercial classification), CM zones (business), and all M zones (industrial). There is a provision that ". . . any tube and tire repairing, battery charging, and storage of merchandise and supplies must be conducted wholly within a building. Provided, further, that any lubrication or washing, not conducted wholly within a building shall be permitted only if a masonry wall six (6) feet in height is erected and maintained between such uses and any adjoining 'RA' or 'R' zone."

[7] The distribution of gasoline through numerous attractive outlets has several sales promotional aspects: (a) a large number of attractive stations is a form of advertising *per se;* (b) a large number of stations makes the use of other types of advertising practicable since there is no waste circulation; and (c) the large number of stations provides a purchasing opportunity for the whole market, hence sales are likely to be enhanced.

[8] The clientele of each conservative-competitive outlet is small enough so that personal attention can be given customers.

[9] While no detailed service station operating data are available for this area, the Standard Oil Company (Ohio) figures published in 1948 by Professor Learned (Edmund P. Learned, "Pricing of Gasoline: A Case Study," *Harvard Business Review,* November 1948, p. 749) may be considered generally indicative of the relationship between volume and operating results. Thus, one may infer from these figures: (1) Increased gallonage is sometimes, but not always, enough to more than offset any reductions in per-unit margin, and thus enhance *dollar margin* resulting from gasoline sales, although such increases are not likely to be great. (2) Increased gallonage is invariably accompanied by substantial increases in dollar margin resulting from enhanced sales of other merchandise and service. (3) While operating expenses (such as rent or labor,) increase with additional gallonage, such increases are not at the same rate as the increase in dollar margin; hence, the large volume of sales at a lower per-unit margin results in an increased net profit for the operator. (4) Assuming an allowance of $250–$300 for the operator, the break-even point for Sohio stations in 1941 appears to have averaged around 10,000 gallons on a 3½-cent-margin operation, and around 12,000 gallons on a 2½-cent-margin operation (somewhat less, if the salary allowed the operator is reduced).

[10] As mentioned, the demand for the product-service of an outlet located on a highway is likely to be quite different from that within a community. This is not to suggest that customers are made up of different classes of people in each instance, merely that consumers are likely to react differently to offerings when they are on a trip than when they are going about their everyday affairs in their home communities (see above, p. 12).

[11] It should be emphasized that sales promotion for such stations is largely, if not wholly, undertaken by the supplier company.

[12] The authors feel that the effect on consumers of seeing numerous, easily identifiable, attractive-looking major-company dealer stations may be one of their most important advertising mediums, and that prestige locations are extremely important from a sales promotional standpoint.

5. Appeal for patronage is made by friendly service, courtesy, and quality of product-service rather than low price.[13]

6. Supplier-sponsored credit[14] is offered to service-station patrons.[15]

7. Dealers depend for a substantial amount of their revenue on the sale of services and products other than gasoline.[16]

Service the Key Factor. As mentioned above, generally speaking, the stress is on the offering of service in major-company dealer stations. While this is usually not as sharp a competitive device as

---

[13] It follows, then, that major-company outlets normally avoid the use of promotional price signs. Interesting in this connection are the point-of-sale signs which were displayed by Standard Oil and Richfield Oil before January, 1950. The Standard Oil signs read: "Don't be confused by discounts—Compare our quality prices and service"; while Richfield's signs read: "Don't be tricked by cut-price gasoline signs—We give quality and service."

[14] The experience of one large major company with credit operations is interesting: "Comparing our analysis of 180,000 credit purchases with detailed personal observations in stations, we were interested to find that the average credit card user buys 47% more gasoline per trip to the station, than does the average cash customer; and that the credit card customer's purchases of lubrication and products other than gasoline were two-and-a-half times greater per trip to the station than the cash customer's purchases.

"It was amusing to chart the consolidated history of credit card accounts over a period of time. The first month that the credit card customer receives his credit card, he really splurges and buys a lot. Apparently, he quickly finds out, however, that he has to pay for it just the same, because the next month his purchases level off and thereafter create an almost steady line at the figure I just mentioned." (H. C. Grimsley, "The Application of Market Research to the Oil Business," p. 14 [an address before the American Marketing Association, October 19, 1949, Los Angeles, California].)

[15] Less than 22 per cent of the homes composing the sample of the *Los Angeles Times* "Continuing Home Audit" had credit cards in the spring of 1949. Of these, close to 64 per cent used them in "nearly every purchase," approximately 13 per cent used them in the "majority of purchases." The rest were accounted for as follows: "seldom used in town"—about 9 per cent, "trips only"—about 8 per cent, and "never used"—about 6 per cent.

It has been suggested, incidentally, by some credit men in the petroleum marketing field that requests for credit cards can be satisfied, in part, at least, by the issuance of one or more $10.00 coupon books. The use of the coupon books has the advantage of setting a maximum on the amount which may be bought, as compared to the unlimited purchases which can be made with credit cards. It appears that for some purposes customers really prefer coupon books.

[16] According to the Learned study (Edmund P. Learned, *op. cit.*, p. 749) the percentage of dealer dollar margin derived from merchandise (other than gasoline) and service sales in 1937 varied from 20.7 (for stations selling an average of 8000 gallons per month and with exposed lubricating facilities) to 28.0 (for stations with 8800 and 9800 gallonage and with exposed and enclosed lubricating facilities); in 1941, these same percentages varied from 33.5 (stations with 8800 gallonage sales and exposed lubricating facilities) to 48.0 (stations with 15,000 gallonage sales and enclosed lubricating facilities).

Evidently (1) the amount of margin revenue derived from such sales has increased materially from 1937 to 1941, and (2) non-gasoline revenue increases with increased gasoline sales.

price, it can be effective in acquiring custom, assuming the term "service" is not a mere shibboleth. Special mention should be made of at least three aspects of service as a competitive tool:

1. The service performed by some station operators goes far beyond the type of activity usually thought of as falling into this category. Such ultraservice may include periodic reporting on the condition of the motorcar, adjustments and even minor repairs on the customer's automobile, advice concerning the need for renewal of parts, and calling for and delivery of the patron's automobile. It should be kept in mind, however, that some patrons do not desire much service; the intelligent operator will attempt to provide service in accordance with the wishes of the customer.[17]

2. Service not only involves work well done (clean windshields, neatness in handling gasoline and oil, and the like) but promptness in responding when customers enter the station. One of the important cost elements in a full-service operation is the provision for prompt service. This, note, is different from the amount of service extended—a patron might be given complete service at a little extra cost if the seller were allowed to perform such service at his own convenience. The offering of prompt service requires that an adequate staff be maintained. This calls for the maintaining of a larger staff than would be needed otherwise, to take care of peak requirements. Some companies seem to offer this type of service in their own outlets in markets where the struggle for business is particularly intensive.

3. An important element making for success of a filling station stressing service is the personality of the operator and of his attendants so that the visit to the station is a pleasant experience. The

---

[17] The Union Oil Company in early 1950 introduced an ingenious promotional-service device in this market based on the idea, fairly well confirmed, that different customers desire different amounts of service—and even the same customer differing amounts depending upon the circumstances surrounding the purchase. This new scheme was designated the "Minute Man 1-2-3 Service System" and permitted the customer to select the amount of service desired, simply by means of a one-, two-, or three-finger signal given upon driving into the service station. The classes of service indicated by the signals were as follows: 1, the full treatment (10 different services, including filling the tank with gasoline, checking the oil, water, and battery, cleaning all windows and headlight glass, emptying the ash trays and cleaning the interior with a whisk broom; 2, the regular service (pumping of gasoline into the tank, checking the oil, water and battery, and cleaning the windshield); 3, the "quickie" (supplying gasoline, checking oil, cleaning the windshield).

dealer blessed with a pleasing personality has a distinct advantage
not only in terms of the number of patrons, but also in terms of the
amount of the customer's business he obtains (tires, oil changes,
wash jobs, batteries, accessories). The personable retail dealer who
represents a good company and has the proper amount of knowledge
and intelligently applied energy[18] cannot help but be successful in
acquiring or retaining customers.

Indirect Price Competitive Schemes. One should not interpret
the foregoing as indicating that there is no aggressiveness among
major-company distributors. Indeed, majors establish stations with
the idea of obtaining a share of the market; this alone is an aggressive activity. They strive vigorously for volume; sometimes actual
house-to-house solicitation of customers is practiced. However, the
aggressiveness that does prevail usually takes some non-price or
semi— or indirect-price competitive form. The indirect form has
several variants:

1. Special rates on some service or non-gasoline merchandise. A
common competitive device used by some vendors who don't cut
the price (as well as price cutters) in this market has been the low-
price car wash (89 cents seems to be the prevailing price). Moreover,
discounts from the regular price are offered on various pretexts: (a)
One major-company dealer charges 89 cents regularly for a car wash
but only 69 cents when the service is bought in connection with the
purchase of 10 gallons of gasoline[19] and (b) one Tide Water Associated station (perhaps others) features a "Get acquainted offer" of
a purported $5.50 value, including two chassis lubrications, one
crankcase flush, one sparkplug cleaning, etc., for $1.50.

---

[18] According to the *National Petroleum News* (November 9, 1949, p. 11), a unique,
but not new, service is being offered in Walla Walla, Washington. A dealer has two
men check the downtown parking meters to see whether there are any violations. If the
car is overparked, the checkers insert a nickel and leave a card which reads: "Please
accept this through the courtesy of John Doe's service station as we hate to get a ticket
ourselves. If we have saved you a traffic violation, we are being of service to you which
is our aim at our service station. If you are by our way, we would enjoy seeing you and
giving you a sample of the kind of service we have to offer there." Signal Oil Company
recommended this type of service to its dealers, saying that the Walla Walla dealer had
won many new customers.

[19] One large independent super station offered a wash job for 59 cents to students and
faculty of the University of California, Los Angeles, on Monday, Tuesday, Wednesday,
and Thursday only, for a limited time. The appeal of such offers is not always confined
to price; often the service offered is distinguished also by the rapidity with which it is
performed (e.g., a five-minute car wash).

2. Contests of various types with prizes to those holding winning tickets. One small major-company station in the Palms district used a premium scheme with considerable success, increasing business substantially. Each patron was given a ticket; around its outer edges were numbers to be punched when the corresponding number of gallons of gasoline was purchased. When the ticket was completely punched, a center panel was lifted out and inside was found a number which indicated the nature of the premium to which the holder was entitled—such as a quart of oil, five gallons of gasoline, lubrication.[20]

3. Other indirect competitive schemes used at one time or another: (a) Kelly-Springfield tires were offered at dealer's cost plus $1.00 by one major-company dealer in this area. (b) A special of 89 cents for a lubrication job for Tuesdays and Wednesdays (presumably off-peak days) was offered by a major-company dealer station in the Los Angeles market recently.

We may conclude that the type of competition stressed by major-company dealers normally may be expected to take one of the following forms:

1. Non-price competitive activity (attempts at differentiation and persuasion).[21]

2. Product appeals (faster[22] and better-quality product-service).

3. Indirect-price competitive schemes (specials on washes, lubricating, and the like).

4. Selective price concessions (discounts from the regular price to certain customers).

The occasional open price cutting by normally conservative competitors in the Los Angeles market requires some explanation. One aspect of the practice is presented in the next subsection.

---

[20] Despite substantial success, the supplier company frowned on the scheme and the operator acceded to its request to discontinue its use.

[21] An excellent example of this type of appeal is offered by Shell Oil Company whose stations in May, 1950, were conspicuously featuring giant (10 foot) humorously illustrated signs carrying the statement: "The Most Powerful Gasoline Your Car Can Use!"

[22] According to a trained observer in the field (*National Petroleum News*, December 28, 1949, p. 9) during the year 1949 an increasing number of stations advertised *quick* oil changes. These stations claimed oil changes in periods of time ranging from five to seven minutes; a sign has recently appeared in Los Angeles advertising a three-minute oil change.

Conflict Between the Interests of the Major Company and Its Dealers

Normally, control of the product is not retained by the supplier throughout the distribution process but, rather, title to the product passes from the company to the retail dealer, who in turn conveys it to the consumer. In view of this, the major-company supplier has the choice of two alternatives regarding price making: (1) he may divest himself of all price-making responsibility (by selling the product to the dealer without any strings attached), or (2) he may assume some, perhaps a major part, of the price-making function (by employment of some sort of price-maintenance scheme).

Generally speaking, major oil companies in the Los Angeles area retain considerable interest in determining the price at the retail level. Thus, price making is shared by the gasoline supplier and the retail dealer in the typical major-company distribution setup. It should be apparent that the two parties may not see eye to eye in pricing matters. Differences in point of view might be due to the fact that (1) the dealer is looking at the problem from the single-station viewpoint, while the supplier sees it from the point of view of all the sellers in the market area; (2) the dealer is apt to see the problem only in short-run terms, while the supplier is considering it in terms of a longer period of time; and (3) the dealer may be viewing the problem with inexperienced eyes, while the supplier may be looking at it with the perspective of long and broad experience.[23] Thus, an individual retail seller might consider it to his advantage to cut prices under certain circumstances[24] when a supplier would judge such a move disadvantageous.

When this study was first started, in the spring of 1948, there were few, if any, instances of major-company dealers advertising a price cut in the Los Angeles market area. Even as late as July,

---

[23] This is not even to mention the fact that there are individual differences among service station operators, both in terms of the degree of aggressiveness which they possess and their particular business situation, such as location or size of establishment.

[24] While an individual seller of major-company products may not *raise* prices with impunity, he may in combination with his competitors succeed in enhancing prices above the level contemplated by the supplier. Such an increase was effected in Oakland, California, in December, 1948, when the retail dealers raised the price a cent in order to widen the dealer margin. Even this type of price manipulation may be costly because it may make more effective the competition of those cutting under the market price.

1949, the authors had observed, or had reported to them, less than a dozen instances of promotional price signs used by stations selling major brands of gasoline. All except one[25] of these several price cutters represented two major companies—Shell and Tide Water Associated. There was no evidence of price cutting by dealers selling Standard Oil, Union Oil, General Petroleum, or Richfield Oil Company products.

It might be enlightening to examine the competitive behavior of the first few nonconformists in the post-World War II period to discover, if possible, something about their motivation. As one might expect, considerable differences were found in the reasons for price cutting by major-company dealers. To begin with, two dealers who departed from the normal competitive pattern in those early days of major-company dealer price cutting used this device only to test results.[26] In at least one instance, the price cutter had an unusually large establishment which required more volume than could normally be expected to be obtained from the immediate area.[27] On the other hand, some of those who departed from the

---

[25] For a short period of time in February, 1949, a large Texaco dealer on Beverly Boulevard was offering Ethyl at a saving of 3.4 cents and regular-grade gasoline at a saving of 2.7 cents, compared with Standard Oil Company prices at that time in this area. The owners of the station reported a 31 per cent increase in business in twelve days, the volume running at the rate of 65,000 gallons a month at the end of that time and with a good prospect of doing 100,000 gallons within a few months. Three weeks after the interview with this dealer, the station was no longer selling Texaco products but had switched to those of an aggressive independent, the Eagle Oil & Refining Company (*Golden Eagle* brand); but see below, chap. ix, p. 140, n. 67.

[26] One Shell station displayed a sign, "Save 3¢ on Ethyl" on a Saturday and Sunday as an experiment with very favorable results. It did not continue the use of the sign as it felt that the company would not like it and knew that it was wise to go along with the company.

Another Shell station featured a week-end "3 cents off" special over the Fourth of July holiday. This operator reported that he and his employees estimated the amount of business that they felt they should do over the three-day period, and that the amount of business actually done with the help of the sign was only 86 gallons more than this estimate. On a basis of this experience, together with the fact that his competitors did not like the sign, and his feeling that the company would prefer that he did not use price signs, he decided to stick to his quality appeal.

[27] For many years Muller Bros. has operated a large nine-pump station in the Hollywood district, selling Associated products, moderately cutting price. The size of the Muller investment, and the resulting overhead, is such that the station must have traffic; the only question then becomes whether they handle Associated products or those of some other company. The operators have very likely been able to continue on this basis largely because the promotional stress is not on the price of the gasoline but on service specials.

Another example of this is a large Shell station on heavily traveled Olympic Boule-

normal major-station pattern seemed to feel that they were forced
to compete in this way by their price-cutting rivals.[28] Finally, one
station which was disadvantageously located cut prices, evidently
in an attempt to offset its competitive disadvantage.[29]

It should be especially noted that most of the early cut-price outlets
were those in which the dealer, rather than the supplier of the
gasoline, controlled the property; hence, the operator had at once a
wider margin from which discounts could be made[30] (see below, pp.
162 to 164) and a relatively large degree of freedom in his compet-

---

vard which displayed a sign offering gasoline at 2 cents less than competing major-
company stations. This station has only six pumps but it is located on a large, high-
value lot, with first-class supplementary service facilities (wash rack, paint shop). Again,
this operation requires more than the normal amount of traffic in order to make it pay.

[28] (1) The price sign on one small Shell station—not too well located—read "2¢ off,"
and in very small letters at the bottom, practically unreadable, "with purchase of ten
gallons or more." The operator put it up in desperation, even though this is company-
leased property, because, he reported, business was being drained away by the Shell
station approximately two miles farther down on Olympic. Sales of the station, which
had fallen below 100 gallons per day, jumped to 200 gallons per day after the cut.
Although the gallonage was doubled, his margin was cut almost in half (formerly 4.3
cents, minus 2 cents discount equals 2.3 cents). Hence, even assuming that costs remained
the same and that no additional revenue was forthcoming as a result of the enhanced
gallonage, he would be in about the same position as he was before, except, of course,
that he would be inviting retaliation from a near-by major-company station; if this
happened, it would place him in the position of having a small volume at a narrow
margin. However, the operator expected that his volume would reach as high as 300–400
gallons a day in time.

(2) An Associated station displayed a sign, "Save 3¢ in coupons." This station is right
across the street from a Veltex station which posted a "Save 5¢" sign; the latter gave a
discount on gasoline dispensed from a pump designated *Bob's Ethyl*—a rebrand. Next
door is a Harbor station which the Associated dealer stated sold at a discount but which
posted no sign. The Associated outlet boosted its gallonage substantially after the
price sign appeared. The manager of the station was sure that the supplier company
did not like the sign but felt that it was not in a position to do very much about it
because he had the master lease on the property.

[29] This Associated station is on busy Vermont Avenue but at the intersection of a
narrow side street; it also occupies a very small and hard-to-enter lot. While it is
difficult to isolate the effect of poor location, this station was among the first of the
major-company representatives to display a sign advertising a discount from the regular
price.

[30] In one Associated station the sign read "Save 3¢. . . ." When the operator was
asked why he put up the sign, he said: "Because of the self-serve stations with the 5¢
signs." The Associated dealer owned the master lease so the company could not do
anything except cease selling him gasoline. The operator reported that he still retained
a fair margin because he made 1½ cents more per gallon than someone who leased
from the company. In other words, the ordinary dealer earned a margin of 4 cents on
regular and 4½ cents on Ethyl, at that time, whereas this particular dealer was earning
margins of 5½ cents and 6 cents. The sign helped his business a great deal; he did not
report exactly how much.

itive activities.[31] It should be noted, also, that while counteractivities may not be immediately forthcoming,[32] price cutting by major-company dealers tends to cause further price cutting by stations of the same type.[33]

Thus, several factors seem to underlie the price cutting among those retailer-vendors who normally could be classified as conservative competitors. The fact that the outlet is a large-capacity establishment, disadvantageously located, or affected in volume by low-price competitors, may tend to cause an operator to undercut the market, especially if he holds the master lease on the station, and thus has more than the average amount of freedom in price policy. These, note, are largely defensive reasons. A dealer therefore who has one of these reasons and the freedom to act will almost inevitably cut prices, especially if he is an aggressive person. However, an operator who has such an attitude would be apt to seek complete freedom in pricing by acquiring the product from a concern which condones or even encourages price cutting of its brand, or by buying gasoline for rebranding and assuming the role of a brand promoter and aggressive price cutter. This type of person, in short, is likely to operate as an aggressive price competitor. He is the subject of the following chapter.

---

[31] Under such conditions the retail distributor has control of the lease, so that at worst he is forced to find another supplier. See footnote 25, above.

[32] The effect of price cutting on competitors is interesting:

(1) An interviewer asked the operator of a Texaco station if the promotional price sign displayed by the station next door was helping that station. The reply was exceedingly profane. When asked why he did not do the same thing, he said that (a) his margin was not adequate (reportedly only 3½ cents), (b) the company, he felt, did not want him to put up a sign and, therefore, the displaying of such a sign would be impracticable. It should be noted that if the dealer *feels* that the use of the sign is impracticable because he *thinks* the company would be displeased, it has much the same effect as though the company actually does have such a policy.

(2) Another competitor of this price-cutting station (a Chevron dealer), when asked why he did not cut the price to meet the other station's price, said he did not have enough margin. He added, that assuming he did cut the price and gained increased volume, he would not want to try to handle such a big volume. He would prefer to handle the smaller amount of business himself and work on enhancing his gross revenue through the sale of lubricating service, and other services. He commented on the fact that while his supplier had indicated that he was free to do whatever he pleased concerning the price, he knew that the company did not like price signs.

[33] At the time of this writing (May, 1950) most major-company dealer stations have entered into the price-cutting competition. However, this development will be discussed later in the chapter on defensive competition (see chapter x, below).

IX

NATURE OF RIVALRY:
AGGRESSIVE PRICE COMPETITORS

Unlike the conservative competitor, the aggressive price competitor in retail gasoline distribution assumes almost complete (if not complete) responsibility for the formulation of the policies under which he plans to operate. This competitor typically chooses his own location, plans his layout, selects the product to be offered to the public, promotes his own brand, decides on the price he will charge, determines the amount of service to be offered, and so on. In short, the aggressive competitor assumes the role of policy maker as well as the executor of policies.

The aggressive price competitor offers his product at a considerable discount from the market price because he (1) thinks aggressively, (2) is in a market position which favors such action, and (3) is free to act as he pleases. The aggressive price competitor, therefore, has an extremely important function in any market, because of the depressive influence he has on the price level. However, the aggressive price-competitive retailers are not the only factors of importance in this connection; gasoline suppliers are also key factors in this type of rivalry, since they provide the product.[1] Table 14 is de-

---

[1] Actually, there are (1) those suppliers who promote a brand and sell their product to price-cutting retailers, who in turn sell to the public under that brand name (e.g., Eagle Oil & Refining Company); (2) those suppliers who sell to price-cutting retailers,

TABLE 14

CHARACTERISTICS OF REPRESENTATIVE AGGRESSIVE PRICE-COMPETITIVE FACTORS
IN THE LOS ANGELES RETAIL GASOLINE MARKET, LATE FALL, 1949

Reported source of gasoline	Size of stations: number of pumps			Number of stations	Type of service			Degree of price cut			Display promotional price signs		Other sales promotional activities
	Small	Medium	Large		Full service	Semi-self-serve	Self-serve	Large	Moderate	Small	Advertise discounts	Advertise actual price	
Aggressive retailers[a]													
Consumer's Cooperative[b] — General Petroleum Corp.	6			1	1			X				X	Patronage dividends to members
Craig Oil Company — Hancock, Signal Oil and Gas			18-24	5	5				X			X	Merchandise coupons
Foster Oil Company — Douglas Oil Co.			15	1	5	1		X			X	X	Full service to women, older men
Gilmore Service Station — Olympic Refining Co.			21-24	2	10			X			X	X	
Hane Bros. — Various majors and independents			12-22	10		1	1	X			X		
Hutton's Shell Service — Shell Oil Co.			12	10			1						Prizes to patrons
Mark Bloome — Eagle Oil & Refining Macmillan			6-18 9	6 1	5		1		X X				
Muller Bros. — Tide Water Associated				1			1			X		X	Free gasoline to those waiting over 5 minutes
Parks Service Stations — Richfield Oil Co.		6	18	13	13			X		X	X		Merchandise coupons, drawing for free automobile
Rothschild Service Stations — Own refinery			18	4			4	X					Drawing for free automobile
Sears, Roebuck & Company — Standard Oil Co. of California		6	20	8	8			X	X		X	X	
Tide Oil Company — Various majors and independents				1			1	X			X	X	
Urich's Self-Serve — Own refinery and various majors			18	15			15	X			X	X	
Victory Petroleum Co. — Various majors and independents	5-6			5	5			X			X	X	
Supplier-brand promoters													
Eagle Oil & Refining Co. — Union Oil Co. and others		3-18			X		X	X			Usually		
Olympic Refining Co. — General Petroleum Corp.		3-18			X		X	X			Usually		
Rothschild Oil Co. — Own refinery	3-6				X		X	X			Usually		

[a] Other aggressive influences are (1) direct supply factors and (2) indirect supply factors, as listed below.

Direct supply factors (sales made directly to aggressive price competitors):
Calstate Refining Co.   Douglas Oil Co.   Macmillan Oil Co.   Mohawk Petroleum Co.   Richfield Oil Co.   Standard Oil Co. of California   Time Oil Co.
Century Oil Co.   Fletcher Oil Co.   Harbor Oil Co.   McCallen Refining Co.   Newhall Refining Co.   Socal Refining Co.   Sunset Oil Co.   Wilshire Oil Co.
Hancock Oil Co.

Indirect supply factors (sales made to direct suppliers who, in turn, may sell to aggressive price competitors):
General Petroleum Corp.   Shell Oil Co.   Tide Water Associated Oil Co.   Union Oil Co. of California

[b] No longer in business.

Source: Field survey.

signed to present the various phases of the aggressive price-competitive situation in the Los Angeles market area.

Self-Serve Stations. One of the most interesting types of aggressive operation in the retail gasoline field is the self-serve outlet.[2] While self-serve stations are far from new,[3] the first serviceless outlet in the Los Angeles market area[4] was installed as recently as 1947 by Frank Urich. Although self-serve stations are restricted by legislation (they are actually outlawed in certain communities, including the city of Los Angeles[5]—see table 15), by July, 1950, there were some 160–175 of them in this market area, including conversions which are not too successful.[6] Among the leading operations in this area

who in turn sell to the public under their own brand name (e.g., Hancock); and (3) those suppliers who act only as ultimate suppliers since they sell only to supplier brand-promoters, who in turn sell to retailers (e.g., General Petroleum).

[2] For survey of self-serve operations in southern California see *National Petroleum News*, November 3, 1948, pp. 26–41.

[3] The following is an excerpt from a letter to the authors by one of the pioneers in the self-serve field: "The self-serve stations in Los Angeles are a duplicate of the type of stations we have built for the last twenty years in this country. . . . Their spacing, their appearance, their lighting and the location of the buildings are almost identical to our original plan. Apparently the designer of the stations in California must have come to Indiana and did some measuring and studying of our system because they are identical. The dispensing equipment and arrangements are the same. In the early days we had no safety features and today we use the automatic safety nozzle. We have found that we can handle greater volume by rendering whole or partial service. . . . We did not operate the first self-serve filling station. However, we had the first design to handle volume and we were the first ones to apply for a patent."

According to the board chairman of Hoosier Petroleum Company, Inc., of Indianapolis, Indiana, that company opened the first self-serve station (about 1930) in Cambridge City, Indiana. This particular venture was unsuccessful due to insufficient traffic. The company then opened a highly successful self-serve station at North Capitol and Twenty-second streets in Indianapolis, and in quick succession opened similar stations in Chicago, St. Louis, Memphis, and Louisville, all of which operated profitably. When depression conditions became serious, the company was prevailed upon to revert to the offering of service, in order to spread employment; this reportedly was a costly error.

[4] Other large cities that have self-serve stations include Charlotte, North Carolina; Chattanooga, Tennessee; Houston, Texas; New Orleans, Louisiana; Norfolk, Virginia; Oklahoma City, Oklahoma; Richmond, Virginia; Sacramento, California; San Antonio, Texas; San Diego, California; Tacoma, Washington.

[5] As will be noted in table 15, the anti-self-serve ordinance in effect in the city of Los Angeles forbids anyone but the owner or regular employee of a gasoline station to pump gasoline; therefore the motorist is liable to prosecution under the law in case he dispenses the motor fuel—the owner or operator is merely the accessory. It has been reported (*National Petroleum News*, February 1, 1950, p. 13) that the Board of Fire Commissioners of the City of Los Angeles has proposed that the anti-self-serve ordinance be amended so as to shift the liability in case of violation from the motorist to the station operator.

[6] This may be due to the fact that they are poorly located for mass selling, improperly laid out to handle large volume, or not spacious enough to be attractive to patrons.

are those owned by Gilmore,[7] Hane,[8] Rothschild,[9] and Urich.[10] Most of the specially designed self-serve stations have been successful (pumping at least 10 times the volume of an average conventional-type station before the price war); many of them have had phenomenal success (doing from 40 to 60 times as much gallonage as the average service station previous to the break in prices).[11]

Self-serve stations rely on large volume for success. Generally speaking, they are characterized by the following principles and techniques:

1. Self-serve stations specialize in the sale of gasoline,[12] and offer it for cash at substantial discounts from the price charged by conventional dealers.[13]

---

[7] The twenty-four-pump Gilmore self-serve station is in the unique position of being well located on a highly traveled boulevard (Beverly) but on a small Gilmore-owned county "island" (where self-serve operation is permissible) and surrounded completely by city territory (from which self-serve operation is banned). Gilmore, incidentally, buys its gasoline from Olympic Refining Co., which in turn acquires its supplies from General Petroleum under a rebrand arrangement—but Olympic may not in turn sell to rebranders. Thus, *Olympic* gasoline is the product of General Petroleum and presumably is the same as the G. P. brand. (This is one of the agreements that was made when the majors feared a postwar oversupply because of expanded wartime facilities.) The policies of Olympic are such that dealers are completely free to do whatever they please in matters of price or any other operating procedure, except that they may not rebrand the gasoline, which has already been rebranded once.

[8] Hane operates full-service stations (see below, p. 135) but also a self-serve station under the name Tide Oil Company in county territory.

[9] Rothschild provides most, if not all, of its gasoline requirements from its own refinery.

[10] Like Rothschild, Urich operates a refinery which supplies, in part at least, the gasoline requirements of his stations. Before Urich went into the self-serve business he served twenty-five conventional stations, which sold 250,000 gallons of gasoline per month. In November, 1947, his six self-serves and two conventional stations were selling a total of 2,000,000 gallons per month.

[11] Within ninety days after the opening of the first Urich station, it was pumping 450,000 gallons per month, or as much as 45 average-size service stations.

[12] The manager of one of the large self-serve stations reported great disappointment in the sale of tires, batteries, and accessories (TBA as they are known in the trade). He stated that his offer in batteries and tires was as good as anybody's in town, but that he did not sell as many tires as a conventional station located near-by, whose sales averaged 10,000 to 15,000 gallons of gasoline per month. He felt that one reason for this was that customers patronized self-serve stations, in part at least, to avoid selling pressure. This suggests that while a self-serve station has a large potential market for automotive items in addition to gasoline, the attempt to realize on such a potential might cause patrons to go elsewhere for their gasoline requirements!

[13] A recent survey conducted in the San Francisco Bay area (*National Petroleum News*, April 26, 1950, p. 17) indicated that the "better price" is by far the most important reason given by customers of such stations in that part of the state for patronizing self-serve outlets, but that "faster service" is of considerable importance also. However, some of the self-serve operators feel that the importance of price has been overstated (see footnote 28, below).

TABLE 15

LEGISLATIVE RESTRICTIONS ON SELF-SERVE GASOLINE OPERATIONS IN THE 45 CITIES
COMPRISING LOS ANGELES COUNTY, SUMMER, 1948

Proscription by ordinance: (no person except owner or regular employee may dispense
motor fuel)

1. Los Angeles[a]	3. San Fernando
2. Monrovia	4. San Gabriel

Regulation of sale by ordinance: (requiring "no smoking" signs, automatic shut-off valves,
fire extinguishers, employee supervision, water lines, telephone, etc.[b])

1. Alhambra	3. Monterey Park
2. Montebello	4. Pomona

Combination: (proscription in certain areas and regulation in others)

1. Burbank[c]

No special regulatory action by city ordinance[d]

1. Avalon	13. Glendale	25. Pasadena
2. Arcadia	14. Glendora	26. Redondo Beach
3. Azusa	15. Hawthorne	27. San Marino
4. Bell	16. Hermosa Beach	28. Santa Monica
5. Beverly Hills[e]	17. Huntington Park	29. Sierra Madre
6. Claremont	18. Inglewood	30. Signal Hill
7. Compton	19. La Verne	31. Southgate
8. Covina	20. Long Beach	32. South Pasadena
9. Culver City	21. Lynwood	33. Torrance
10. El Monte	22. Manhattan Beach	34. Vernon
11. El Segundo	23. Maywood	35. West Covina
12. Gardena	24. Palos Verdes Estates[f]	36. Whittier

[a] This refers to the city of Los Angeles. Self-serve stations are allowed in unincorporated county territory when
provided with proper safeguards.
[b] Some of the ordinances, especially those of Monterey Park and Pomona, have much more extensive regulations than others. These include the requirement that buildings be isolated, public address systems be installed,
limiting the number of pumps to be handled by each attendant, requiring metal containers for the dispensing of
waste material, the prohibition of roller skates being used by attendants unless rollers are made of fiber, etc.
[c] Among its regulations is a requirement that there be not less than one attendant for every 3 pumps.
[d] The Fire Chief may, however, require special safeguards in connection with the issuance of a permit. Moreover, there is opposition to self-serve operation by the city councils of several of these cities. For example, the
City Clerk of Hermosa Beach reported that the City Council had passed a resolution against self-serve stations.
[e] However, Beverly Hills' regulation that pumps be limited to 6 per station (and storage capacity to 10,000
gallons) in effect excludes self-serve outlets.
[f] But the city has only one service station and no other lots are zoned for this type of business.
Source: Survey by the authors by means of mail questionnaires and telephone check.

2. Self-serve stations must be located on a heavily traveled thoroughfare, but on space whose valuation is not so high that the total
cost will be prohibitive.[14]

---

[14] An executive of one of the very successful self-serve firms stated that his company
sets up stations according to the following principles:
(1) The location must be on a major traffic artery. He thinks it would be fine to
make a traffic count but that this is a little too scientific for him. He is of the
opinion that one can easily tell whether a street is a major traffic artery. Another self-
serve operator puts it as follows: "I check the traffic on a street which I know is

3. Self-serve stations must have a spacious area for two reasons: (a) they must have room for a large number of cars—sometimes as many as one thousand per day and (b) spaciousness is in itself attractive to patrons.

4. Self-serve stations rely heavily (usually exclusively) for publicity on large and often expensive promotional price signs[15] which

---

heavily traveled, say Wilshire, and then check the traffic on the street I am considering and compare the results. If the street under consideration is as heavily, or nearly as heavily traveled as the one it is compared with, I know it is o.k." (This operator mentioned a traffic-count figure which was found by the authors to be impossibly high.)

(2) There must be a concentration of population contiguous to the location, or at least near-by. This company has not yet gone into a town of less than 15,000 population. This might be considered as a minimum. Moreover, the company would not set up a station in a community at all if there were already two self-serve stations there. The other successful self-serve operator to which reference was made above, first investigates if there is any self-serve competition in the area, and if not, will consider the location.

(3) While there must be a population concentration and heavy traffic, this self-serve operator would *not* want to be in the business area; he would prefer to be four or five blocks out from the center of town where rents are lower and foot traffic lighter. Foot traffic, states our informant, makes property expensive, and while it would be desirable, for example, for a shoe store, a self-serve station not only would not require it but could not afford it.

[15] Many of the promotional price signs are large, steel-constructed, neon-lighted, and represent a considerable investment. By the terms of Section 20880 of the California Business and Professions Code the use of promotional price signs in the sale of motor fuel or gasoline is restricted in this state. While it is lawful to publicize a low-priced offering, the law requires that in advertising the price of the commodity in such signs one must show the actual price per gallon including taxes, as well as the word or words "gasoline" or "motor fuel," and the trade name or brand of the product. A recent amendment to the law requires that no one shall post a sign which by the use of such terms as "Save 5" or "5 ¢ off" indicates a reduced price ". . . unless there is posted . . . in letters of equal size and as part of the same sign, . . . the total price, including all taxes, at which . . . [the] fuel is being . . . offered for sale, designating the price for each brand or trade name of . . . fuel being sold or offered for sale."

Before the amendment, the law had little actual restrictive effect on the use of promotional signs by price cutters. In the city of Los Angeles, for example, literally hundreds of such signs publicized discounts, most of which did not provide the information specified in the law. As mentioned below, there were only three cases in the entire state, of which the authors are aware, that arose out of violation of the original legislation. All were lost by the government. Of the several disadvantages with which the prosecution was faced—the poorly drawn legislation, inadequate enforcement, and sympathy of the jurors for those offering lower prices—the most important was the faulty legislation. Thus, a defendant might argue with some success that a sign carrying the designation "Save 5 ¢" was not in fact a price sign, and therefore was not within the scope of the law. (Ironically enough, a seller who, in addition, honestly attempted to publicize his prices but failed to give, for example, the name of the gasoline, would be in violation because the sign *was* technically a price sign.) The legislation, as amended, seems to take care of this difficulty (see above). The Serve-Yourself Gasoline Stations Association, Inc. in October, 1949, sought an injunction against the enforcement of the amended law on the grounds that the legislation deprived the prominently publicize the type of operation and the discount offered.[16]

5. The number of pumps in self-serve operations varies from nine to twenty-four. They are easily operated by the motorist and equipped with "dead-man" nozzles and automatic shut-off devices to prevent overfilling, thus reducing fire hazards. There are usually three pumps to an island.[17]

6. Pump islands are usually placed perpendicularly to the street with the result that (a) only one turn needs to be made in entering the station, and (b) traffic flows one way. (There is a trend toward the use of diagonal islands in recently constructed superstations.)

7. The product offered by self-serve stations is usually good quality and often sold under the retail dealer's own brand name.[18]

---

operators of property without due process of law, that the edicts were an arbitrary and unnecessary exercise of police power and, hence, that the regulations were unconstitutional. The Superior Court of Los Angeles in late 1950 found for the government. (*Serve Yourself Gasoline Stations Assoc., Inc. v. A. A. Brock*, No. 565,702, L.A. Super. Ct., December 7, 1950.) From what the authors have seen of misleading and dishonest promotional price signs in this market, it would seem that the law is a reasonable and not an arbitrary regulatory effort.

[16] Pending the outcome of the case the authorities were conducting with considerable success a campaign in May, 1950, against the use of misleading promotional price signs in the Los Angeles gasoline market area; at least four complaints had been issued and convictions obtained on each complaint. The law which was being invoked, however, was Section 17500 of the California Business and Professions Code which proscribes untrue or misleading statements made by any means in connection with the offers of products and services for sale to the public. The reasons for the invocation of Section 17500 in place of Section 20880 (which restricts the use of promotional price signs in the sale of motor fuel) were: 1. The latter was being tested in the courts, and the Bureau of Weights and Measures felt it should "pass muster" before relying on it generally. 2. The retaliatory efforts of major-company stations during the pending price war made the price signs of those advertising big savings so flagrantly untrue that the invocation of this law was practicable. (*Automotive Dealer News*, April 3, 1950, and May 15, 1950; also *National Petroleum News*, April 12, 1950, p. 15, and April 19, 1950, p. 13.)

[17] One expert in the field thinks that six islands with eighteen pumps is the optimum size, since with fewer the peaks cannot be handled adequately and more prevents intensive utilization of facilities. An organization (Sav-Mor Oil Company) which is in the business of promoting the establishment of self-serve outlets, favors the use of only three islands of three pumps each. However, one should not underestimate the importance of spaciousness even in small units.

[18] Suppliers do not control the policies of the self-serve operators except Rothschild and Urich who operate their own self-serve stations. Few if any have a contract, except possibly a straight-purchase contract for gasoline with no brand specified.

Self-serve gasoline comes from: (1) self-serve operators' own refineries (e.g., Rothschild and Urich), (2) minor companies (e.g., Hancock, Sunset), and (3) major companies (e.g., General Petroleum, Standard Oil). One minor-company official thinks that 90 per cent of the gasoline used by self-serve people comes from the major com-

8. The service facilities for windshield cleaning, battery and water replenishing, oil checking, etc., which are operated entirely by the customers, are relegated to the back of the lot.[19] These facilities are plentiful, handy, and usually well kept.

9. Self-serve stations have wash- and rest-room facilities but seldom canopies.[20] In front of the station is a "control tower," containing a public address system, switches for shutting off each pump, fire-extinguishing equipment, and a cashier's booth.

10. Self-serve stations must have large supplies of gasoline available at "rock-bottom" prices.[21] They must have supplies in prospect as well as in their tanks for their immediate requirements.

11. Minimum storage capacity for a successful self-serve operation has been put at 30,000 gallons (three or four days' supply for some serviceless operations). One of the large ones (Gilmore) reportedly operates with 40,000-gallon capacity, another (Rothschild) has a reported 60,000-gallon capacity.[22]

---

panies indirectly; Serve Yourself Gasoline Stations, Inc. claim 75 per cent of their gasoline is from major-company refiners.

[19] The separation of gasoline dispensing from servicing has two important aspects: (1) the conservation of frontage space and dispensing equipment when the use of driveways between islands is confined to the sale of gasoline; the use of this high-cost area for non-revenue purposes is avoided; (2) specialization of effort—some employees, possibly less experienced, hence paid at a lower rate, concentrate on tire and windshield service, where provided, others on sales of merchandise.

[20] In the abstract, one might feel that self-serve operations would experience substantial seasonal business declines in areas where winters are severe, because of (1) the discomfort of getting out onto the wet, slushy driveways and having to handle the damp, cold, and often messy hose, and (2) the disadvantage of driving out of one's way under conditions which make driving anything but a pleasure. In at least one instance, this seasonal decline was not as great as anticipated. One station, in La Crosse, Wisconsin, reported a decline of 37 per cent during the depth of the winter from the summer peak, although a 50 per cent drop had been expected. This station keeps its driveways clear of snow constantly, which may be an offsetting factor. (*National Petroleum News*, January 18, 1950, pp. 7 and 8, and April 26, 1950, p. 9.) One wonders if supplying work gloves to customers might not prove to be an effective device tending to attract trade in cold weather.

[21] A dealer's ability to buy gasoline at lowest prices is due in part to the fact that he usually is free from tie-ups with any company and can buy gasoline from the most advantageous source at the moment; and also, because such a dealer buys in truck-and-trailer lots, which saves money.

[22] The existence of large storage facilities (1) protects the operator from running out of gasoline, (2) allows the dealer to acquire supplies of the product whenever the opportunity presents itself, and (3) makes possible large-quantity deliveries. In short, it facilitates procurement of supplies and makes for a certain amount of independence on the part of the self-serve operator.

12. Since the customer dispenses the gasoline himself,[23] self-serve stations are operated with a minimum of personnel.[24] While there is usually one male employee on duty on each shift, the rest of the force is composed of a relatively small number[25] of attractively garbed young women, whose duties consist primarily of collecting for the gasoline. The typical 18-pump self-serve station is open 24 hours a day and requires three girls and two men during daytime.[26]

To conclude: The key to the success of self-serve gasoline stations is very probably the lower-than-market price charged by them which attracts custom from competitors. The self-serve device provides what appears to be a logical basis for lower prices, and thus tends to dispel doubts concerning the quality of the product.[27] However,

---

[23] One, at least, of the Sav-Mor self-serve stations displays a sign soliciting the patronage of women by offering them the services of an attendant in dispensing the gasoline. However, a 1950 survey in San Francisco (*National Petroleum News,* April 26, 1950, p. 17) indicated that men constituted the bulk of the patrons of self-serve stations in that area (98 per cent).
Some self-serve stations may serve customers when attendants are not busy, although this may make for complications. One self-serve operator reported that he had served a customer twice because the attendants were not busy at the moment; the next time this patron came into the station they were busy, but he expected service and was angry when it was explained to him that this was a self-serve station.

[24] However, some of the restrictive legislation governing self-serve operations is so devised as to prevent the full realization of such gains. For example: (1) Monterey Park has a clause in its ordinance regulating self-serve stations which requires not less than one attendant on duty for each two-pump island. (2) The ordinance for the city of Burbank requires at least one attendant for every three pumps in a self-serve station.

[25] As was mentioned earlier (chap. vii, p. 97, n. 27), the Teamsters' Union opposes self-serve operations because of the effect they have on the employment of "retail clerks."

[26] One independent supplier who is informed about self-serve operations feels that self-serves should be small enough to be operated by one man—perhaps three islands of three pumps each. He reports that one such unit has pumped as much as 165,000 gallons per month. Even assuming this is an ideal arrangement, union regulations and legislative restrictions might render it impracticable.

[27] Like the low rates of self-serves, the price-cutting of "trackside" stations would appear to have a reasonable basis. Trackside stations—found in the Middle West— are outlets which have large storage facilities and are located contiguous to spur tracks, thus allowing an operator to purchase gasoline in tank-car lots at a considerable saving. This saving enables the operator to offer his product at a discount from the market price. Indeed, in most instances he must sell at a discount if he is to obtain a large volume of sales because of (1) an inferior location (determined not by consumer convenience but the accidental intersection of track and highway) and (2) the offering of a little-known, often private, brand. Many track sellers do not seem to recognize the opportunity they have of sacrificing unit margin to maximize dollar margin. A recent rough check indicates that of the track stations in the Twin Cities, few, if any, sell the brands of major companies, and that their prices are only a cent or so below the prices charged by other stations.

spaciousness, ease of entrance, and reduction of time required to service a car should not be underestimated as factors attracting custom.[28] Undoubtedly some consumers prefer to patronize self-serve stations, and presumably would do so even without the existence of a price differential. The large-volume self-serve operation thrives on a low-price, narrow-margin policy because low price produces large volume, which in turn creates a favorable relationship between costs and margins. The success of self-serve operations is based not so much on the cost aspect of the operation, as on the enhanced dollar margin created by the large volume despite a relatively narrow per-unit margin. Obviously, the self-serve gasoline station could not be as successful if all sellers adopted its policies.

Actual study[29] has shown that self-serve customers are largely (1) not former customers of major-company dealers, but former customers of other cut-rate dealers,[30] and (2) bargain hunters, as indicated by their patronage habits with respect to the purchase of other types of merchandise (groceries, etc.). This suggests strongly that self-serves have only a limited market from which to draw

---

[28] One independent-company official, an expert in self-serve operation, is of the opinion that, in the first place, a self-serve station requires size—from one to two acres of ground with a frontage of 150 to 200 feet. However, he does not believe that it is necessary to be on a corner; in fact, it is an advantage not to be located on a corner, because a "good" corner is likely to have a traffic light; entrances to stations are then blocked at peak traffic hours, which materially cuts into the business.

This person also feels that the self-serve driveways must be invitingly wide. He believes, furthermore, that the reduction in the time required to service a car is also a prime factor in the increasing preference of consumers toward self-serve operations. He was formerly associated with one of the large major companies which used a figure of nine minutes per car to do a first-class job of serving a customer; he states that a car can get in and out of a self-serve station in one and a half minutes.

This official feels that he has "definite proof" that these factors of space, ease of entrance, and speed are more important than price. To prove this, he reports having purposely raised the price of gasoline in his stations with no resulting reduction in volume. The difficulty with this experiment is that while the posted price was raised, thus reducing the differential to only four cents, the "5 cents off" signs remained up. Thus, the absence of evidence of a drop-off in business may be due in large part to the fact that consumers did not realize that prices had been raised. One cannot help but comment, also, that such tactics by a seller are ethically at least questionable, if not actually dishonest.

[29] Reported verbally to one of the authors by the former marketing research director of one of the major companies (early March, 1950).

[30] This conclusion is supported by the findings of a recent survey conducted in the San Francisco Bay Area (*National Petroleum News*, April 26, 1950, p. 17) which indicates that 70 per cent of those patronizing self-serve stations in that part of the state formerly purchased their requirements from cut-rate stations.

custom,[31] and that an increase in the number of such stations is bound to have a serious effect on the average volume of each of them.[32] It may well be, however, that more consumers will be forced to consider price when business activity recedes, in which case the future of self-serves will be somewhat brighter than has been suggested. It might even be that a fully automatic operation has some possibilities.[33]

Semi-Self-Serve Stations. As was mentioned earlier, self-serve stations are outlawed in many places, including the city of Los Angeles. Anti-self-serve laws, it will be recalled, require that none but the owner of a service station or his paid attendants may dispense motor fuel.[34] In some communities, therefore, semi-self-serve stations have been established. These outlets are operated like self-serve stations except that customers are limited in serving themselves.[35]

---

[31] To the question "Has any member of your family patronized a self-service gasoline station during the past month?" posed by representatives of the *Los Angeles Times* "Continuing Home Audit Los Angeles County" in the fall of 1949 to Los Angeles area householders, only 25.5 per cent of the respondents replied in the affirmative; however, the percentage answering "yes" showed the following results: July, 1948: 17.3; January, 1949: 19.7; June, 1949: 24.2; January, 1950: 26.1.

[32] According to one of the large self-serve operators, the average business of self-serve stations has fallen off, generally speaking, because of competition; whereas, they were averaging 300,000 to 400,000 gallons per month when they started (summer, 1947), the average by summer, 1950 was nearer 100,000, he estimates. He feels that in time it will level off to perhaps 80,000 or 90,000. It is not unlikely, he adds, that the self-serve station may settle down to a three- or four-island operation, that is, a total of nine to twelve pumps against the present eighteen to twenty-four.

[33] Coin-operated service stations exist in some localities, but none are reported in the Los Angeles area. According to a competent observer in the Denver area, some stations of this type are in operation there. According to this informant, these generally fall into two categories which may be designated as old and new types: (1) The older operation has the outmoded globe or bowl pumps into which the gasoline is pumped when coin-activated, and fed from there to the gasoline tank of the car by gravity. (2) The new type is adapted from the standard Wayne pump. Though the latter was not entirely satisfactory at first, it reportedly operates fairly well now. While a station might be operated entirely by a coin in the slot (in the absence of a legal proscription), coin operation might better be used as a supplementary device. Several concerns in the Denver area are reportedly experimenting with this new type of coin-operated pump as an adjunct to normal service-station operation. That is, they are installing one pump which is not in operation during regular business hours, but lighted and available for use after the station has closed. The coin-operated station would have been ideal during the war to conserve manpower, but was impracticable because of its inability to collect coupons during the period of gasoline rationing.

[34] See p. 124, table 15.

[35] Instead of signs reading "Serve Yourself" or "Self-Serve," they may read "Save Yourself" or "Help-Serve."

As in any mass-selling gasoline operation, typically, the semi-self-serve station is located on a heavily traveled thoroughfare, is ostentatiously spacious and easily accessible from as many directions as possible. It usually concentrates its efforts on the sale of motor fuel (possibly only premium grade), offers the product under its own brand name, sells at a stubstantial discount, and publicizes its offerings by large and advantageously placed price signs.

Unlike self-serve stations, its attendants (usually young women) not only accept payment and make change but also dispense gasoline and oil. In such stations, while the customer may not dispense gasoline himself,[36] he must fill his own radiator, check his own tires, clean his own windshield, and check his own oil. Thus the gasoline is dispensed by an attendant, but any other requirements must be met by the customer's own effort through the use of unattended service facilities in the rear of the lot; consequently, this is a partial- or semi-self-serve operation. The cost of operating a station of this type is likely to be more than that of a self-serve station, while the appeal is likely to be considerably less.

An interesting operation of this kind was one owned by Gilmore Oil Company on the northwest corner of heavily traveled Third and Fairfax streets (only a few blocks from the 24-pump Gilmore self-serve station located in county territory). This station had 21 pumps on a fairly spacious Gilmore-owned city lot, across the street from the heavily patronized Farmers' Market. As in the self-serve station, the attendants were attractively garbed young women, but unlike the attendants in the self-serve station, they dispensed the gasoline as well as accepted payment and made change. They offered no other service, except supplying oil, but, as in self-serve stations, convenient facilities were available in the back of the lot for those who wished to check their tires, radiators, and batteries, clean windshields, etc. This Gilmore semi-self-serve station offered regular-grade gasoline and what were supposed to be two qualities of premium-grade gasoline, and the prices when last observed were fractionally

---

[36] The pumps in some instances must be wound up with a key to set the transaction meter back to zero before the gasoline will flow. To insure against the possibility of attendants leaving this little key in the pump, enabling customers used to self-serve stations to serve themselves and possibly becoming involved with the law, the attendants are required to carry the key on a chain around the wrist. Thus, they are never without the key, hence no one but the attendants can dispense the gasoline.

higher than those featured by the Gilmore self-serve outlet except on the "super quality" motor fuel.[37] The general manager of the Gilmore service stations estimated that the operating costs of the "help-serve" station would be about 25 per cent higher than in the service-less operation. This appears to be reasonable since personnel costs are likely to be double those expended in the self-serve operation (assuming equal gallonage), and since in most retail enterprises personnel expense is approximately one-half of total operating expense.

Full-Service Superstations. There is a considerable number of stations operating in the Los Angeles area largely on the same basis as self-serve and semi-self-serve stations, except that the patron is offered full service by a station attendant. Such stations attempt to compete on a narrow-margin, large-volume basis while offering full service to patrons.

Much the same requisites to successful operation exist in this as in the self-serve type of business, except, of course, for the serviceless feature—gasoline is offered below the market price, the location is easily accessible to a large number of motorists, the station is laid out so as to present a spacious appearance, the capacity of the plant, including storage facilities, is large, the outlet has a low-cost source of supply, and ordinarily low-priced offerings are publicized at the point of sale (the promotional price signs often overstating the savings).[38] In addition, merchandise is usually offered either under the distributor's own label (e.g., Hane's *Magnum*) or under the brand

---

[37] The following table is a comparison of prices in the two stations on July 25, 1949:

	Regular grade	Premium grade	"Super Quality"
	(in cents)	(in cents)	(in cents)
Gilmore self-serve...........	19.9	21.6	22.6
Gilmore semi-self-serve.......	20.3	21.9	22.6

On June 4, 1950, the comparison was as follows:

	Regular grade	Premium grade	"Super Quality"
	(in cents)	(in cents)	(in cents)
Gilmore self-serve...........	18.9	20.6	22.6
Gilmore semi-self-serve.......	19.3	20.9	22.6

[38] This is not to say that the savings are not substantial, merely that the amount of the savings usually is exaggerated in the price sign. (See chap. xiii, footnote 9.)

name of the independent supplier (e.g., Eagle Oil & Refining Company's *Golden Eagle*).

Full-service superstations of this type are Hane Bros.,[39] Mark Bloome,[40] and Craig Oil Company, among others (see table 14). Two of these operations seem to justify special comment:

1. Among the most interesting of the large-scale service station operations in the Los Angeles area is the Craig Oil Company. Included in its several outlets is a large 24-pump superstation located on heavily traveled Wilshire Boulevard.[41] The special interest in this firm, for our analysis, derives in part from the fact that the company operates its stations on a coupon rather than a cash-discount basis. The company supplies full service and offers its product at a substantial reduction[42] (but from a "jacked up" price). For several years Craig displayed a large promotional price sign which carried the amount of the purported saving, but latterly no price figure appears on the sign.[43] Craig obtains part of its gasoline from Hancock Oil Company (which in turn obtains part of it from General Petroleum on a crude-for-gasoline agreement) and part from Signal Oil & Gas Company.[44] The product is sold under the *Craig* brand name.

---

[39] As was mentioned earlier, Hane Bros. also operates a self-serve station under the name Tide Oil Company.

[40] Mark Bloome is an aggressive price-cutter in the Los Angeles area selling through six not exceptionally attractive stations. Some of the Mark Bloome stations operate on a split-pump basis; they sell *Macmillan* gasoline as well as *Golden Eagle*, in addition to Bloome's private brands. Recently the company has switched from coupons or premiums to a cash-discount policy. All its stations carry a full line of tires, batteries, and accessories. Recently (early 1950), Bloome has been aggressively promoting the sale of tires on a two-for-one basis.

[41] The islands, interestingly enough, are laid out parallel instead of perpendicular to the boulevard, despite the fact that the lot has sufficient depth to accommodate the latter type of layout.

[42] When the station first opened, the purported discount was only 2 cents, but was increased to a purported 5 cents when a giant self-serve station was opened on another boulevard about a mile north (Beverly). This suggests that the market is somewhat thin but extensive. Craig operates a chain of large-volume superstations in other parts of California also. He has stations in Oakland and Berkeley which offer somewhat smaller discounts. It would appear from this that competition is not as intensive in Oakland as in Los Angeles. This may be due to the fact that the former is a deficit area and the latter a surplus area for gasoline, and that "sloppy" conditions are more likely to develop in the Los Angeles market.

[43] The sign now reads: "Save Craig Premium Coupons." This change very possibly was due to pressure from the State Bureau of Weights and Measures on retail distributors displaying misleading and fraudulent promotional price signs.

[44] Which reportedly owns a 50 per cent interest in Craig and obtains its gasoline from Standard Oil of California.

Craig coupons are not usable on the day issued. Those customers who do not return, therefore, pay the posted price for their gasoline, which means that the pricing scheme is to this extent discriminatory. This coupon system has at least two noteworthy aspects: (a) it acts as a sort of "come on" for many patrons, since the customer must return in order to realize any saving on his purchases,[45] and (b) even if the advertised saving is completely accurate, the average reduction per gallon is not nearly as great as it first appears because some of the patrons do not redeem their coupons.[46] (Some fail to return, others lose their tickets, etc.)[47] If the reduction is based on a "jacked up" posted price,[48] some patrons of Craig stations not only fail to obtain a reduction on their purchases but pay a higher price for gasoline than they would if they patronized major-company dealers.

The Craig Oil Company has been experimenting with the offering of a choice between cash and coupons in three of its stations (those in Glendale, Monterey Park, and Washington Boulevard and Santa

---

[45] One of the authors patronized the Craig station a number of times and found it difficult to resist going back because he always had 10 or 12 tickets, worth 5 cents each, which could be used in partial payment of his purchases the next time. He discussed with one of his sons in a semi-humorous vein the problem of just how one could use up the tickets without accumulating more, for example, buying tins of oil, getting a car wash, or simply going in, handing the man the tickets, and leaving in a hurry!

[46] When the discount was only 2 cents and the denomination of the coupons 5 cents, another advantage accrued to the seller, unless sales were in multiples of two and a half gallons, because there was always gallonage on which no discount was given. Interestingly enough, Hane Bros. issued coupons in 1 cent as well as 5 cent denominations, and as a result no such gain could be made except on fractional gallonage sales.

[47] An operator of a competitor station estimates that only 25 per cent redeem their coupons. This, of course, is a mixed blessing since it represents potential volume which has been lost.

[48] One day when the Craig-posted price was 27.9 cents and 26.4 cents for premium-grade and regular-grade gasoline (excluding the value of 5 cent coupons), competitors' prices were 27.1 cents and 24.1 cents at one Union station; 26.5 cents and 24.5 cents at one Shell station, one General Petroleum station, one Richfield station, one Associated, and two Signal stations; and 26.1 cents and 24.1 cents at one Standard Oil station. While competitors reported some effect on their operations after Craig opened the superstation, for a long time no competitive station openly adjusted its prices, although two reported that they offered discriminatory discounts to regular customers, that is, those coming into the station at least twice. Some months later, the neighboring Shell station reduced its prices a purported 3 cents. Actually, the posted price was "jacked up" to meet the higher-than-average price posted by Craig, so the actual discount offered by the Shell station was only 1.7 cents on premium grade and 0.7 cents on regular grade.

Fe Avenue in Los Angeles).[49] According to the manager of one of the stations: (a) the introduction of this scheme has had little, if any, effect on the volume of business done in these stations and (b) the division between those choosing cash and those choosing the coupons is about half and half. Some persons seem to prefer to postpone the advantage of a price cut until some later time and, therefore, choose to receive the reduction in the form of coupons rather than cash.[50]

2. Frank Hane runs a number of large-scale, mass-selling gasoline stations in the Los Angeles market under the two company names— Hane Bros. and Tide Oil Company. Hane, who operates his stations on a price-cutting basis, formerly had a coupon arrangement (similar to Craig's) but now has switched to the use of a straight cash-discount plan which he claims is more satisfactory.[51] The especially interesting aspect of the Hane operation is that, in addition to its full-service stations, it runs one large self-serve unit.

One of the Hane full-service superstations occupies the whole front of a short block facing heavily traveled Olympic Boulevard. The station is canopied and has 22 pumps although the lot is very shallow, possibly 40 feet; hence, islands are laid out parallel instead of perpendicular to the street, and services like tire checking or wind-

---

[49] The actual mechanics are as follows: The customer enters the station and asks for 10 gallons of gasoline. The attendant dispenses the number of gallons requested and then asks the customer if he wants the discount in cash or in coupons redeemable in merchandise. If the preference is for cash, then the attendant simply charges the customer the discount price registered on the pump; if the customer prefers the coupons, the salesman adds the discount to the price and gives the customer the equivalent in coupons. Should the customer not ask for a certain number of gallons of gasoline but specify the amount of money, such as $2.00 worth, the attendant fills the tank with the corresponding gallonage at the non-discount rate. He then gives the customer coupons or change depending upon his preference.

[50] Some persons indicated a preference for coupons because they make possible the purchase of gasoline at a time when the customers are short of cash. That is to say, for some consumers the coupons serve as a kind of budgeting device. One station on Santa Monica Boulevard, which operates on a coupon discount basis, attempted to do away with the system because of the bookkeeping problems which it involved, but found that its customers would not stand for it.

[51] At one stage in our study the operator of this station openly admitted that the practice was to "kick up" the price 1 cent before computing the discount. However, he pointed out that Hane Bros. gave the same discount on both premium grade and regular grade in contrast with the usual practice of giving a smaller discount on regular grade. Upon examination it was discovered that in this station the posted price on regular grade was "kicked up" 2 cents, instead of 1 cent, before computing the discount. So the net result was the same. Latterly, the discounts offered by Hane stations are among the most accurate observed in the Los Angeles market area.

shield cleaning must be performed at the pumps. Although Hane is a mass distributor of gasoline, he has never done any advertising to speak of, except at the point of sale.

Hane super-service stations provide the customer with full service. While the operation conducted by Hane under the name of Tide Oil Company is the serviceless type,[52] the large service and non-service stations are similar in many respects. For one thing, the physical plants are essentially the same (except that Tide has perpendicular islands while the others have parallel islands). Besides, the gasoline prices at the self-serve station differ only fractionally from those at the full-service stations.[53] While the Tide self-serve station on Santa Monica Boulevard employs a total of eight girls and five men, and the Hane Bros. full-service station on Olympic Boulevard thirteen or fourteen men, the self-serve station does about 50 per cent more business than the full-service station.

Hane obtains his gasoline from various sources and sells it under his own brand for cash at deep-cut prices.[54] He displays giant point-of-sale signs which advertised (until recently) the amount of the saving per gallon.[55] He also displays signs reading, "You can't buy

---

[52] The Tide Oil Company is in county territory and thus may be operated legally on a self-serve basis.

[53] The prices of these two stations were surveyed on December 3, 1949 with the following results:

	Hane Bros. (service)	Tide Oil Company (serviceless)
	(in cents)	(in cents)
Regular grade.............	19.9	18.9
Premium grade.............	21.6	20.9

But on June 4, 1950, the results were as follows:

	Hane Bros.	Tide Oil Company
	(in cents)	(in cents)
Regular grade.............	18.9	18.5
Premium grade.............	20.9	19.9

[54] Compared with prices of major-company dealers before the 1950 price break.

[55] Because of the present market conditions, combined with the current legal activity regarding misleading statements of supposed "savings," the Hane promotional price signs now read "Save ?" instead of their former wording "Save 6¢." Incidentally, some aggressive operators, reportedly, have substituted a dollar sign for a numeral, for example, "Save $."

a better gasoline at any price." [56] While Hane stations stock accessories and perform lubricating and oil-changing service, they appear to concentrate on the sale of gasoline.

A number of large, aggressive price-competitive stations in the Los Angeles area are supplied by one company—the Eagle Oil & Refining Company (although most of this company's dealers are small-rather than large-scale aggressive competitors). Eagle Oil & Refining Company sells gasoline under the *Golden Eagle* brand and condones, if not actually encourages, price advertising by dealers.[57] This policy appears to be profitable since the company has managed to establish a reputation for a good product at a low price. However, many of the Golden Eagle stations are not properly situated or laid out to employ aggressive price-competitive tactics with maximum success. It should be noted, incidentally, that once the low-price reputation of a brand of gasoline, such as Golden Eagle, is established, stations selling it would have difficulty offering it at the market price.

Five concluding points might be made here:

1. The self-serve device is not necessary for the success of mass retail operations in gasoline, although a successful large-scale service outlet might be more successful if operated on a self-serve basis.

2. The large-scale service station operation seemingly calls for aggressive price tactics regardless of the price policy contemplated before the station was established. It must obtain large volume to remain in business, and must therefore attract customers from a wide area through price concessions.

---

[56] He not only displays signs but has attached to each pump a metal plate carrying the words: "Warranty—You can't buy a better gasoline at any price."

[57] Until June, 1949, Golden Eagle had an agreement with Standard by which Standard supplied Golden Eagle's gasoline requirements. According to one of the company officials, the contract had a clause prohibiting Eagle from selling at cut rate and displaying price signs. When this official came into the picture the company was abiding by the contract and "rapidly going broke." The company soon changed its policy, despite the terms of the contract; it quit selling its dealers at a narrow margin and supervising all of their activities; instead, it began to sell its dealers gasoline at whatever margin was necessary to get business (6–8 cents perhaps), allowing them to dispose of the product in any way they pleased. Thus, Eagle dealers typically sell at cut prices and display price signs. This shift by Eagle Oil & Refining Company from a conservative to an aggressive price policy seems to have paid off well; the sales of the company reportedly increased from 2½ million gallons per month to 10 million gallons per month in about a year. Recently, however, the company seems to have shifted back to a more conservative type of operation. (See chap. xiii, p. 193.)

3. A price-induced, large-volume operation cannot be conducted in this market without assurance of an adequate supply of gasoline, either from an indirect source or from major companies on a rebrand basis.

4. Some stations have attempted aggressive price tactics without success because of cramped and uninviting facilities.[58] Actually, such an attempt is more futile than it at first appears, since it would be physically impossible to accommodate the number of cars required to obtain the volume necessary for the success of this type of operation.[59]

5. Recently several large-scale, major-company dealer stations have appeared in the area, indicating perhaps that certain of the large supplier concerns are willing to experiment with mass-selling outlets after the independents have shown them the way.

Small- and Medium-Scale Aggressive Price Competitors. Aggressive price competition in the retail gasoline business is by no means confined to large-scale establishments (although they are at once evidence[60] and a cause[61] of aggressiveness). There are many aggressive small- or medium-size stations, having three to six pumps and occupying a small lot. Since they are not equipped to pump the large volume distributed by super- and self-serve-type stations, their sales will range from 20,000 to 60,000 gallons per month.

Stations in this group usually are conventional-looking and actually are conventional in many operating aspects. They generally do not have the requisites for mass-selling—large-volume location, spaciousness of plant, scientifically planned layout (including separation of free and revenue-producing service facilities) and large storage capacity. Such stations offer average or a little better than

---

[58] According to an executive of one of the companies having a great deal of experience with self-serve stations, the conversion of a station designed for a service operation to a self-serve station has not been successful; it lacks the functional advantages and psychological appeal of originals, due in part to limitation of space and improper layout.

[59] This suggests that much of the price cutting in the Los Angeles area is not for aggressive purposes at all, but rather for defensive purposes, that is, merely an attempt to offset some competitive disadvantage by a price inducement. This will be discussed in detail in the following chapter.

[60] However, a chain of smaller price-cutting stations might be considered just as indicative of aggressiveness.

[61] Price reductions are most often used as a means of providing the volume necessary for profitable large-scale operations.

average service, and place considerable stress on service-station items other than gasoline. However, they obtain their business primarily through aggressive price cutting, which they usually publicize by promotional price signs. (These often overstate the savings, as do the signs of other aggressive price competitors.)

The aggressive price-competitive policies of smaller stations are conditioned by: (1) the position of the seller, in the sense that he is free to formulate his own price policy[62] and can cut price without inevitable retaliation—indeed, *must* cut in order to attract volume; but not in the sense that his facilities lend themselves to large-volume operations and (2) the attitude of the seller, in the sense that he does not mind engaging in vigorous competition[63], in fact often prefers it, and that he has confidence in price cutting as a means of enhancing volume.

Among those operating in this fashion in the Los Angeles market are Parks' Service Stations,[64] Victory Petroleum Company, Sears, Roebuck & Company,[65] Coöp,[66] and many, if not most, of the stations

---

[62] Generally speaking, such operators control the station property and facilities, by ownership or lease. Under these conditions they are free to buy wherever they please and to set their own prices. However, some without control acquire supplies from distributors who exert little if any influence on the retailers' policies.

[63] These dealers are usually aggressive by temperament and are the type of persons who want to be free to do as they please in operating their businesses.

[64] The twelve Parks outlets are medium size (six pumps) and give full service. Parks started his first service station in 1932 and operated on a deep-cut price basis for seven or eight years. He now has his own brands (Parks' *Airway* and *XL*) of gasoline, which he procures from Richfield. At the time the Parks operation was surveyed the product was offered at a modest (2 cent) discount in the form of a coupon. In addition to the discount, the stations also were giving away a Buick automobile every two months in a drawing. At that time the stations displayed no price signs.

[65] Sears, Roebuck operates nine medium-size, full-service, cut-rate stations in connection with its retail stores, thus deriving the advantages of the goodwill of store customers in addition to the business obtained from passers-by. Sears sells its gasoline (procured from Standard Oil Company of California) under the *Allstate* label at a discount from the price posted at Standard Stations, Inc. The company, which offered its product at 2 and 2½ cents less than market price before prices broke, offered it at 2 cents less than the major-company outlets following the break in major-company prices, and in July, 1950, reduced the differential to 1 cent. Until late October, 1949, Sears did not use promotional price signs; even then its signs were not very large, appeared to be temporary only, and were of the informative type, giving Sears' price quotations for the regular-grade and premium-grade gasoline.

[66] Special mention might be made of the Coöp Service Station in Santa Monica— now under new ownership. This station was painted an unattractive yellow and green, the Coöp colors, and did not look too inviting. At the time this part of the investigation was made (November, 1948), the regular-grade gasoline was selling at 19.9 cents and the premium-grade at 21.9 cents. Both grades were sold under the brand name

selling Eagle Oil & Refining Company's *Golden Eagle* brand of petroleum products.[67] It is difficult to say what percentage of the stations
of the Los Angeles market area operate in this manner because the
classification of stations in this category is not clear cut.

Gasoline marketed by these smaller aggressive dealers usually falls
into one of four categories: (1) a private brand which the dealer procures from an independent supplier, for example, *Lightning*; (2) a
private brand which the dealer acquires from a major-company supplier, for example, *Allstate*; (3) an independent brand, not restricted with respect to price advertising, for example, *Golden Eagle*;
or (4) the "secondary" brands of one of the independent companies
on which price-cutting is allowed, for example, Century's *Mascot*.[68]
It should be recalled that much of this gasoline, though acquired
directly from independent vendors, *originates* from major-company
suppliers.

The really aggressive dealers establish their service station business
on the principle of price cutting. They realize at the outset that they
must cut price to operate at all, and that in order to do a sizable
volume they must cut substantially. Price cutting by aggressive price
competitors (in contradistinction to defensive price competitors) is
designed not merely to offset the disadvantage of handling a little-
known brand, but to attempt vigorously to acquire a "healthy slice"
of the market.

It is the opinion of the authors that the price-depressing effect of
the small aggressive price competitors is not as great as that of large-
scale aggressive price cutters. This is so because (1) some small competitors do not practice deep cutting (Sears, for example) and (2)

Hy Grade. At the same time, the Coöp was obtaining gasoline for private branding
purposes from the General Petroleum Company. In addition to these pumps, the
station operated a couple of others through which *Mohawk* gasoline was sold, and
posted these pumps at the regular major-company prices, several cents higher than
the prices on its own brand. Anyone could buy gasoline at the Coöp station, and
there was no difference in price to members of the coöperative as against non-members.

[67] Recently, Eagle Oil & Refining Company changed its policy from that of condoning
or even encouraging deep-price cutting to that of suggesting that its dealers resell the
Golden Eagle brand at only a moderate discount from the price posted by major-
company dealers. In order to implement this policy Eagle Oil has advertised its net
prices in the Los Angeles press—"21.9¢ for *Super* and 23.9¢ for *Radar 91 Ethyl.*"
This, note, is the third distinctly different price policy followed by the company
in the last three years.

[68] As was pointed out elsewhere, some dealers selling secondary brands of gasoline
offer both the primary and secondary brand, and some offer the secondary brand only.

some have unattractive or poorly located facilities (such as Victory). It should be noted, in conclusion, that much of the price cutting by the small stations is defensive rather than aggressive; that is, much of it is designed merely to offset competitive disadvantages rather than to create a positive advantage in favor of the price cutter.

X

NATURE OF RIVALRY:
DEFENSIVE PRICE COMPETITORS

In previous chapters we discussed (1) the type of rivals which stresses competitive devices other than price in attempting to acquire custom and (2) the type which uses aggressive price cutting tactics in its competitive activities. There is in addition to these a type of competitor in the retail gasoline field which uses price as a major competitive device but does so for defensive rather than for aggressive reasons.

Thus, defensive price competitors are those who make active use of price as a device for protecting themselves against the inroads upon their business caused by superior competitive weapons. These competitors are made up of retail sellers who (1) are operating at a disadvantage in the market and whose suppliers exert little control over their policies (small independents), (2) though controlled take matters into their own hands when their business is adversely affected by aggressive sellers, or (3) enjoy the coöperation of their supplier companies in taking defensive price action when serious inroads have been made on station volume.

Nature of Defensive Price Competition

It is sometimes difficult to distinguish between aggressive and defensive price competitors. This is not usually so with large-scale outlets which are almost bound to be aggressive in price because of the large volume, which has to be drawn from a wide area. The difficulty arises with the small unit whose aims may be anything but clear cut. Defensive price competitors, it should be added, usually operate small, three- to six-pump conventional-type stations which provide free service and depend to a considerable extent on sales other than gasoline as a source of additional revenue. Such outlets usually publicize their offerings by promotional price signs which often over-state the savings.

While aggressive and defensive price competitors may be difficult to distinguish in practice, theoretically such competitors are distinguish-able. Whether a seller is aggressive, depends on what he is attempt-ing to do, which, in turn, may be inferred from his actions in rela-tion to his market position. The purpose underlying the price-cutting policy differs considerably in the two instances. The aggressive seller plans for, and has reason to expect, large volume. The defensive price competitor, on the other hand, either is not primarily interested in volume operations or, though interested, is in no position to handle them; he is so situated that he can not attain large volume even when cutting price drastically;[1] the best he can do is to protect himself against the encroachment of competitors.

Such operators give away a large part of their unit margin without having any chance of greatly augmenting volume, and hence of en-hancing dollar margin. As a matter of fact, under certain circum-stances deep price cutting may result in *smaller sales volume* because of consumer suspicion of low product quality accompanying the low price; in such instances the demand curve curls back toward the ver-tical axis, thus causing a reduction in amount taken as price declines.

We doubt whether some of the sellers in this category have any real notion of what strategy they are trying to follow. Curiously enough, defensive price cutting, designed to *retain* business which tends to be drawn off by rivals, inadvertently becomes offensive price cutting in part of the market in so far as it results in *gains* in business at the expense of those who have not cut.

---

[1] In this position is, for example, the small station on heavily traveled Olympic Boulevard which advertises "7¢ off" but has neither the space nor the facilities to pump a large volume of gasoline. One might conclude by inference, therefore, that its price cutting is designed to prevent loss of volume to others rather than to sell a larger volume of gasoline.

Independent-Company Dealer Defensive Activities

Many hundred small independent stations in the Los Angeles area
—more in some communities than others—have little chance of successful volume operations because of certain market disadvantages.
Some of these are: (1) the brand of gasoline may not be well or
favorably known; (2) the station may be located in a thinly populated
area; (3) the plant may be in the middle of the block, set back, and
difficult to see; (4) the station and equipment may be dirty or otherwise unattractive; (5) the service may be poor; (6) the service, while
good, may not be given promptly because the station is operated by
one man.

These are only examples of competitive disadvantages requiring
compensating price concessions or some other offsetting competitive
device. Most stations not selling major-company brands of gasoline
are faced with one or more of these disadvantages.

Perhaps the most common disadvantage requiring defensive price
action is the selling of a brand of gasoline that is not readily acceptable to any substantial number of consumers. If, in such instances
the station operator is free to choose, he has the alternative of attempting to sell the product at market price and thus retain the
larger margin or of "giving away" a part of the margin to customers
in exchange for patronage he could not otherwise obtain.[2]

One independent station operator stated that it is useless for an
independent dealer to try to compete with majors unless he cuts
price.[3]

One fairly common type of defensive price cutting in the Los
Angeles market area is the offering of a discount by a retail dealer on

---

[2] Actually, a seller so situated may (1) offer his product at a discount as a direct
offset to the good-will advantage enjoyed by competitors selling major-company
products, (2) hold the line on posted prices but provide regular customers with an
"under the canopy" discount (from the posted price), (3) offer the product at
market price but be reconciled to a lower volume at a wider margin (possibly
depending upon the station to provide the operator with supplementary income
only), or (4) sell at market price but strive to offset the disadvantage by giving the station an attractive appearance and concentrating sales effort on personal service, thus
attempting to obtain the total business of station customers (oil and accessories sales,
washing, lubrication).

[3] Another said the prestige of the major companies is such that the independent
station does not have a chance without cutting price. It might be, however, that the
independent operator has other alternatives to reducing his posted price. See footnote
2, above.

a secondary brand only. This is not practiced by those representing major concerns or subsidiary companies,[4] but has been adopted by some dealers selling the products of several large independent suppliers (see table 8) such as Sunset (*Air King*) or Douglas (*Spitfire*). The purpose of this device presumably is to allow the seller to make concessions in order to retain, and possibly even to attract, the custom of price-conscious patrons, while at the same time holding the line on the price of the company's principal brand.

Normally, most if not all defensive price competitors in the retail gasoline field are dealers representing independent-supplier companies. However, this is not true at the present time. By June, 1950, most major-company dealers in this market were employing defensive price-competitive tactics. This is discussed in detail in the next section.

Major-Company Dealer Defensive Activities

The disadvantages which the seller faces may be due largely to the existence of a price differential between his own and a competitor's product which is equally acceptable to consumers. In such instances, evidences that price action by a competitor is primarily defensive are: (1) the amount of the cut (it might be expected to be smaller than for aggressive purposes); (2) the time of the cut (defensive action might be expected to take place after similar action by others).

There is a difference between a normal price adjustment by major companies and a defensive-competitive price reduction. For one thing, the defensive cut is likely to be larger than the normal competitive price adjustment; for another, the former is likely to be publicized by promotional price signs, while the normal adjustment is likely to be announced without fanfare in the form of a news item appearing in the newspapers.

Conditions Underlying the Shift in Competitive Emphasis. Mention was made earlier of the price cutting by dealers selling major-company products (above, pp. 116–119). Most such dealers are defending themselves against any change in the *status quo* (as the

---

[4] Occasionally, however, a station will distribute the product of a subsidiary company and sell the product of an independent concern on a split-pump basis at a discount. For example, in 1949 one small Signal station on Slauson Avenue was found to adhere to the market price on *Signal* gasoline but offered *Operators* gasoline at a substantial price cut.

major-company retail vendor who adjusts his price to prevent the siphoning of his volume by a large mass-selling price cutter). In some such instances, however, the dealer has taken the offensive; thus the operator must be classed as aggressive (as an aggressive-minded retailer having a large-capacity station which requires large volume for successful operation).

There is normally in this market very little open price cutting by major-company dealers. Most of it is practiced secretly ("under the canopy"), because of the make-up of operators of stations selling major-company products, the considerable degree of influence over policies by suppliers, and the realization by major-company dealers of the nature of their competitive position. It would seem obvious that the bulk of secret price cutting is defensive.

Until early 1949, all price cutting in the Los Angeles gasoline market (except "under the canopy" concessions) was confined to the large-scale, private-brand promoters and the dealers representing independent-supplier companies. At that time began a progressive development toward the use of price as a defensive weapon by major-company dealers. If one examines the brand-preference data compiled periodically by the *Los Angeles Times,* it is possible to get some idea as to whether a particular company has or has not been maintaining its volume in this market, and thus discover an important cause of the shift in competitive emphasis by major-company suppliers and their dealers. These figures, which represent the percentage of respondents purchasing various major-company brands,[5] are:

Company brand	Jan. 1947	Jan. 1948	Jan. 1949	Jan. 1950
Standard..................	20.2	20.8	18.3	16.7
Union.....................	9.3	14.2	10.9	10.5
Mobilgas*.................	8.9	9.8	9.3	8.5
Texaco....................	9.9	10.2	7.2	8.3
Richfield.................	6.1	4.2	5.8	7.7
Shell.....................	11.8	7.4	6.9	7.1
Associated................	3.2	1.6	2.0	1.9
	69.4	68.2	60.4	60.7

* General Petroleum Corporation's brand name.

[5] The data are from the *Los Angeles Times* "Continuing Home Audit Los Angeles County." The question asked was: "What brand [of gasoline] do you usually purchase?" The monthly data given above have the advantage of "pin pointing" changes in

Major companies were unquestionably hurt by aggressive operators in this market during 1947–1949. This not only was reported to the authors by various major-company officials, but is confirmed by the preference data given above. It may be inferred that this was the reason for their making substantial adjustments in their prices in late 1949 and early 1950.[6] Under the circumstances, it was inevitable that a general adjustment would take place sooner or later.[7]

While the data given above reveal the competitive loss suffered by major companies in the Los Angeles area (about 13.0 per cent from January, 1947 to January, 1950 according to the preference figures), they show that the loss differed greatly among companies and, in-

---

patronage. They are, however, not entirely reliable because they are based on only 600 interviews each month. That this disadvantage is not serious in the present instance is indicated by the following figures, which are based on three-month experience (1,800 interviews):

Company brand	First quarter			
	1947	1948	1949	1950
Standard..........................	17.4	17.3	17.0	15.3
Union.............................	11.5	13.2	12.6	11.9
Mobilgas..........................	7.8	9.8	8.1	8.1
Texaco............................	7.9	8.8	7.2	8.6
Richfield..........................	7.5	7.4	6.7	6.4
Shell..............................	11.6	8.2	8.2	7.8
Associated........................	3.4	2.1	2.8	2.2
	67.1	66.8	62.6	60.3

[6] Declines in the share of the market by major-company dealers are not as great in the state as a whole as indicated by the following taxable gallonage figures:

Company	Per cent of total Calif. distributions[a]		
	1947	1948	1949
Standard Oil..	24.4	21.7	20.3
General Petroleum....................................	12.5	12.9	12.0
Union Oil..	11.5	11.0	11.0
Shell Oil...	10.7	10.3	10.4
Richfield Oil...	6.7	6.8	7.2
Tide Water Associated................................	7.3	7.4	7.2
Texas	7.2	6.7	6.5
Total, major companies..........................	80.4	76.8	74.6

[a] Basic data obtained from California State Board of Equalization reports on taxable distributions of gasoline

[7] High officials of two major concerns reported to the authors that the impact of price cutting by competitors is an accelerating phenomenon. An affected company, which might have been hopeful that the tide would turn, finally concludes that the loss has gone far enough and decides to adjust its prices.

deed, that some companies suffered little or no loss. For example, the figures suggest that Standard Oil [8] and Shell lost considerable custom between January, 1947, and January, 1950; on the other hand, Union appears to have held its own for the period.

Just one more point: The timing of relative losses by companies also is significant in interpreting competitive behavior. For example, the *Los Angeles Times* figures indicate that Shell began to lose position early in the period (January, 1948); Standard Oil's loss, on the other hand, appears to have started somewhat later. This variation in individual company experience may explain the sequence of competitive developments which took place in the Los Angeles market between 1948 and 1950; they are described in some detail in the following subsection.

Stages in the Development Toward a Shift in Competitive Emphasis. The increasing trend toward the use of price as a competitive device can be traced in six time periods as follows:

1. The period of World War II and shortly thereafter, when little if any price cutting existed in this market.
2. Shortly following World War II until February, 1949, when moderate price cutting was practiced by some independent-company stations but no major-company gasoline dealers in the Los Angeles area openly cut prices.[9]
3. February, 1949 to June, 1949, when only a few scattered major-company dealers[10]—chiefly those distributing Shell and Tide Water Associated products—were offering gasoline at moderate discounts (two to three cents at most),[11] in addition to the independents.
4. June, 1949 to October, 1949, when the handful of price-cutting major-company dealers multiplied several times, as evidenced by signs (but still probably totaled less than a hundred).

---

[8] According to the *Los Angeles Times* data, Standard Oil's loss in the share of the market was 3.5 percentage points or about 17 per cent from January, 1947 to January, 1950; Shell's loss was even greater with a reduction of 4.7 percentage points or almost 40 per cent in the share of the market. This of course does not indicate the amount of loss of business because of the partially offsetting growth of the market during this period.

[9] A study of the 53 Sawtelle district stations in October, 1948, revealed identical prices in all except two major-company outlets. One of the authors observed a sign on an Associated station in late December, 1948, which read: "Save 2 to 10 cents a Gallon with our Dividend Plan." In February, 1949, a Texaco station tried openly selling at a discount but shortly thereafter the dealership was discontinued. (See above, chap. viii, p. 117, n. 25.)

[10] There were only a dozen or so in the Los Angeles area.

[11] The actual net saving to consumers was often less than this, however, because the discount was based on a "jacked-up" posted price.

5. October, 1949 to late January, 1950, when rapidly increasing numbers of major-company dealers representing mainly Shell Oil, Tide Water Associated, and The Texas Company (but excluding those selling the goods of General Petroleum, Richfield, Standard Oil, and Union Oil companies)[12] were offering gasoline at less than prevailing prices, using promotional price signs.

6. Late January, 1950, and immediately thereafter, when increasing numbers of representatives of all major and subsidiary companies (including those formerly excluded) were cutting price[13] until most dealers of such companies were selling at cut rates.

---

[12] One reason for the spread of price signs among the stations of the same supplier companies (Shell and Associated, for example) may be the existence of a high degree of cross elasticity among stations offering the same brand of gasoline and in close proximity to one another.

[13] It was interesting to watch the spread of the price war into the Westwood Village shopping district (contiguous to the University of California, Los Angeles campus). There are in the Village eleven major-company owned-and-operated or dealer stations representing all seven major concerns and one subsidiary-company dealer station; the one other outlet in the Village is operated by Sears, Roebuck. There was no price cutting in this area—except by Sears, which normally operates on a moderate price-cutting basis—until shortly after March 1, 1950. Most of the stations reported serious losses of business to dealers outside the Village prior to the price adjustment. The first station dropped its prices and posted price signs about noon on Thursday, March 2,—about a month after similar cuts had been made by competitors elsewhere in the market, and by the following Tuesday all major- or subsidiary-company dealer stations (excluding the two Standard Oil outlets and one Union Oil station which are company-owned and -operated) were displaying price signs advertising gasoline at cut prices.

The first to display a sign offering gasoline at cut prices was the General Petroleum dealer, who stated that he cut his prices to compete with the other General Petroleum dealers in the area surrounding the Village. He also told the interviewer that the size of his operation required that he maintain his volume and that a considerable part of his business was done on the General Petroleum credit-card system, but that some of this credit business disappeared when other General Petroleum dealers outside the Village began cutting their prices. Since changing his prices, five days prior to the interview, he had not missed any more of his regular customers.

Beginning with the opening of business on Friday (the morning after the General Petroleum station cut its prices), the Associated dealer, across the street to the west, dropped his prices and a few hours later the Shell station, across the street to the north, lowered its prices for gasoline. The Associated dealer located at the other end of the Village dropped his prices Friday morning upon the recommendation of the company salesman, who told him that the other Associated station would be selling at the lower prices and it would be foolish for him to try to compete at a higher price level with a dealer of the same supplier company. In approximately the following order, the other stations in the Village lowered their prices during the next three to four days: the second Shell dealer, the Richfield outlet, the Union Oil dealer station, and the Signal and Texas Company outlets. Standard Stations, Inc. was the last of the major-company stations to cut prices.

The Standard Oil Company station managers reported that before approval was given for them to lower their prices they had to wait until directly competing dealers posted signs. The company then sent photographers to take pictures of the competitors' price signs which were submitted to the home office in San Francisco. Simi-

Thus by late January, 1950, the "price war," [14] which was about two years in the making, finally broke out in various parts of California,[15] including the Los Angeles area.[16] A few pertinent facts concerning this price disturbance would seem to be in order here:

To begin with, while hundreds of scattered skirmishes were taking place in this market in early 1950, the action of Standard Stations, Inc. of dropping its prices[17] in certain communities[18] in late Janu-

---

larly, the manager of the company-operated Union Oil station reported that he could initiate no price action. Sears, Roebuck had made no change in prices at the time of the interview but stated that the head office was going to make an analysis of the price situation and then determine if its station should lower its prices. A subsequent check disclosed that several weeks later Sears lowered its prices and posted new price signs.

[14] This may not be a price war in the technical sense but the term is used here for want of a better designation. The difficulty is to distinguish a price war from ordinary price competition. Technically, a price war may be thought of as temporary downward price action on the part of competitors, without regard to cost, in an effort to wrest business from rivals or protect one's business from inroads by rivals.

In their early stages price wars appear to be, and indeed may be, nothing but the exercising of normal price competitive tactics. But as in real war—where submarine activity may require first secrecy of departures and zig-zag tactics, then the equipping of merchant vessels with antisubmarine guns (still largely defensive), and finally all-out offensive action—so in price wars raids by aggressive competitors result first in better service and the use of other non-price or semi-price competitive devices followed by moderate price adjustments in particular areas (still defensive), then, as in the present instance, sharper-than-normal price adjustments by major-company dealers over a wide area, and finally, if necessary, the actual meeting of the aggressive sellers' prices.

[15] According to one Standard Oil Company official, the critical price competitive areas have been Sacramento, Seattle, San Francisco Peninsula and East Bay, San Jose (city limits), Los Angeles basin, and San Diego. When asked if it was true that self-serves were operating in all these areas, he said it was, except Seattle, although they surround that city. He feels that it may have been that self-serves caused the other major companies to cut prices; Standard Oil Company, however, lowered its price because the other major companies did and not because of the actions of self-serves.

[16] The long period of time (many months) in which the wide differential—as much as 5 cents—between major-company stations and aggressive price competitors prevailed caused one to wonder whether major-company dealers were vulnerable to price competition by dealers handling private and independent brands. Since then these doubts have been dispelled, to some degree at least.

[17] It is interesting to ponder the possible reasons for the Standard Oil action in abstract terms: (1) Sales of certain stations might definitely have been adversely affected by the price cutting of competitors, (2) the company might have felt that sales would fall off in time and wanted to forestall such an eventuality (a corollary of the first reason), or (3) customers might have been loyal enough but were complaining about the difference in prices of the company's and competitors' offerings. The price cutting might even have had an emotional basis, that is, the seller being stampeded into it, as it were. Actually, an executive of Standard Oil reports that some of its stations had lost from 5 to 30 per cent of their business and thus were forced to cut.

[18] California has a law which proscribes selling at lower prices in one section of

ary, 1950,[19] finally resulted in open price cutting by practically all rivals. Standard's defensive action was followed by many Chevron dealers (non-company-operated stations selling Standard Oil products) and stations selling General Petroleum, Richfield, and Union Oil Company products as well as increasing numbers of stations distributing the products of companies which had already allowed their stations to cut.[20] At this writing (June, 1950) probably 95 per cent of all major stations in the area are selling at cut rates, as compared with the prevailing price in major-company dealer stations in early January, 1950.

Characteristics of This "Price War." Perhaps the most interesting developments in the so-called price war are these:

1. The tankwagon (wholesale) price of gasoline has not changed in this market since November 18, 1949, thus in the absence of any special adjustments by major-supplier companies the dealers would have to carry the major impact of the war themselves.[21]

2. Reportedly, allowances have been provided dealers as a partial subsidy for competitive price action by retail dealers. Evidently there

---

a community or city than in another with the intent of destroying or preventing competition of any regularly established dealer of any article in general use or consumption (including gasoline). (*Bus. and Prof. Code of Calif.*, Secs. 17000 to 17101.) Thus, such locality-discrimination measures outlaw intrastate geographical discrimination for the purpose of injuring competition.

This type of legislation was originally designed to prevent what were thought to be opportunities for destructive competitive tactics in the form of local price cutting, and in some states the laws were specifically directed against oil companies. For example, a 1907 Minnesota law (after making due allowances for possible differences in quality and cost of transportation), was directed at those discriminating among different localities in the sale of petroleum and its products for the purpose of destroying competition. This was upheld in *State v. Standard Oil Co.*, 126 NW (Minn.) 527 (1910), on the ground that powerful corporations selling this product are in an unusually favorable position to stifle competition through the use of local price discrimination.

It is pertinent to note that locality discrimination laws require intent of injury; therefore, discriminatory price cutting may be justified on the grounds that the vendor is meeting the lower prices of a competitor.

[19] The "shooting" seems to have started in Oakland, California. (*Automotive Dealer News*, January 30, 1950, p. 2.)

[20] A reduction in price by Standard Oil makes it mandatory for others to follow—because of the fact that this company's product is unusually well and favorably known and the company's coverage of the market is very intensive, with the result that it would make serious inroads on the business of major-company competitors if its prices were not met.

[21] There seemed to be a feeling in the trade that because tankwagon price had not changed this was a "retailers' price war." It might be mentioned, incidentally, that many of the retailers were angry about this. (*National Petroleum News*, March 15, 1950, p. 13.)

are several types of propositions being made to dealers[22] who are in a position requiring defensive price action:[23] (a) The supplier company offers a small rebate (1 cent on regular-grade and 1½ cents on premium-grade gasoline) [24] to dealers in "critical" areas[25] who elect to meet competitors' prices. This has the effect of reimbursing dealers only partially, since the cut usually exceeds the allowance. (b) The supplier company offers a small rebate to those who meet competitors' prices, and dealers in certain localities are required to cut. Thus mandatory price cutting at the retail level is partially subsidized by suppliers. (c) The supplier company offers dealers no rebates but advises dealers in "critical" areas to compete pricewise. This means, of course, that the dealer carries the full impact of the competitive struggle (except to the extent that sales volume is reduced, which loss is shared by both parties).

3. Many major-company dealers initially rejected [26] the "sugges-

[22] Reported by research assistant from discussion of the subject at a mass meeting called by the Los Angeles Service Station Dealers' Association, which was held in Hollywood Legion Hall on February 15, 1950.

[23] One of the major companies reportedly introduced this plan of offering rebates to dealers who meet competitors' lower prices in extremely keen competitive situations in Oakland, California, long before price cutting became general; however, it had to rescind the offer because of the protests of dealers who were not offered the rebates.

[24] One company reportedly offered a 1½-cent rebate if the dealer posted a 3-cent-cut sign. Latterly some suppliers base the rebate on the amount of the cut but have a maximum allowance.

[25] There is no question but that cut-price competition is more effective in acquiring custom in some localities than others. This may be due to the proficiency of aggressive competitors or to the ineffectiveness of the efforts of dealers who are losing volume. Whatever the cause, some dealers simply do not lose much volume even to deep price cutters. One Chevron dealer, for example, argued that the better dealers are not hurt by self-serves—that while his own business was adversely affected at first by competition from such outlets, he had more than made up the loss in the past year despite three such stations in his immediate vicinity.

However, normally, given time (see p. 22–23), some custom is likely to be lost, especially if the price cutting is engaged in by competitive major-company dealers. As one major-company official said: "The customers we have to look out for are those who never complain but who silently fold their tents and leave." Therefore, he advises, the dealers in highly dynamic competitive situations must watch sales "like hawks"; he feels that up to a certain point increasing service is effective in holding custom, but beyond that point price adjustments must be made.

[26] The following is a resolution which was sent to major oil companies by dealers protesting cuts in their "fair margin of profit": "The service station dealers of Los Angeles as of February 8 unanimously resolve to maintain our present fair margin of profit on petroleum products. We further resolve not to accept cuts in our margins in order to effect retail price cuts, agreeing that if these retail price cuts are necessary, such reductions in price must be brought about by the major oil companies by lowering their wholesale price." (*Automotive Dealer News*, February 13, 1950, p. 11.)

tions" by suppliers that they cut price to meet competition,[27] largely on the ground (one suspects) that such action involved cuts in margins.[28] One could not expect such refusal by a few hundred service station operators to be effective in the face of price cutting by thousands of competing dealers.

4. Despite the efforts of the Los Angeles Service Station Dealers' Association, price cutting had extended to most major-company dealers by mid-March, 1950; in fact it would seem that most if not all of those who so strongly voiced their support of the association's resolution to maintain "a fair margin of profit" finally succumbed to the price-cutting method of competition.

5. By mid-March, 1950, little if any counteraction had been taken by the large independents.[29] Reportedly, self-serve operators received a warning from their trade organization against becoming involved in this price war. They were advised not to make retaliatory price reductions since this might precipitate "a wild melee of price cutting" that would prove costly to such outlets.[30] However, by June, 1950, some minor price adjustments were made.

Prospective Developments. One cannot safely predict future developments in the Los Angeles retail gasoline market. The following possibilities may be of interest, however:

1. Aggressive price competitors might reduce prices further[31] (al-

---

[27] Actually, the price of competitors may not be met but only the differential reduced by a downward price adjustment.

[28] Some dealers have stated that by these cuts of 1–3 cents the retail vendor cannot increase his gallonage sufficiently to make up for the loss in margin revenue. Actually, however, a retail vendor no longer has the alternative of maintaining the status quo by failing to cut; if he chooses not to cut prices he may lose the bulk of his volume.

[29] Two high officials of oil companies operating in this area expressed the opinion that the self-serves cannot reduce prices from their present level because their costs will not justify any reductions. (The tankwagon price of gasoline has not been reduced, hence the cost to self-serves, which is based on the tankwagon quotation, has remained the same.) One questions the reasoning leading to this conclusion, however, because self-serves might expect that enhanced volume resulting from further cuts would offset the narrower per-unit margins, or, indeed, self-serves might cut without regard to cost if reductions appeared to be indicated in order to stop this siphoning of volume. The point here probably is that the operators of self-serve stations are foresighted, and feel that since major companies have already reduced prices in order to maintain what they consider to be their share of the market, they would not hesitate to do it again. Therefore, a reduction in price by self-serves would cause further reductions by major-company dealers; hence such reductions would simply result in lower prices without any gain in volume.

[30] *National Petroleum News*, March 8, 1950, p. 11.

[31] There is reason to believe that now the self-serves are being seriously affected.

though there are limits to this).[32] If so, major companies—one leading off and the others following—might decide to abandon their
defensive position and take the offensive by dropping their prices
even further. Aggressive price competitors might thus be given a les-
son in genuine hard competition. While further cuts by aggressive
price competitors as a group might be clearly unwise, individual
operators might feel that they could reduce prices without retaliation; actually, however, in time such moves would make for competitive adjustments by others, and result in general price cutting.

2. Aggressive price competitors might, as a result of forethought,
decide to operate their stations at a less drastic discount in the hope
that major companies would recognize the opportunity of restoring
balance in the market between the conservative and aggressive
forces.[33] Some of the major-company officials expressed the opinion
that with a 2- or 2½-cent differential between major and independent companies they can both "get along fine." Just how such an adjustment would take place, however, one cannot say in view of the
aggressive attitude of many price cutters and the fact that rivalry
among aggressive price competitors is extremely keen.

3. Individual major-company dealers (without the sanction of
supplier companies) might cut prices further in order to obtain
an advantage in their particular segment of the market. There seems
to be some evidence of such a softening of the market at present, with
dealers of certain major companies undercutting the prevailing
major-company dealer price. While cases of such further cutting are
not very common at this writing (July, 1950), they do exist in this
market. Such price shading is bound to spread if left to continue over
a period of time.

The present conditions might continue indefinitely, assuming a
continuation of the large stocks of crude and products of the mid-
1950's. If so, the price war, which has spread to all subareas within
the market, may be accepted as a normal condition in this market
for some time. On the other hand, if the international situation

---

[32] See footnote 29, above, regarding the opinion of two major-company executives on
this matter.
[33] An official of one major concern stated that this might actually happen. A top-
level executive of one of the major companies stated that in Sacramento, California,
the dealers had come to an agreement with the result that prices were raised and
promotional signs removed.

were to develop into a genuine emergency which would call for all-out mobilization, the price war would very likely come to a sudden end.

It is interesting to speculate which side will ultimately emerge the victor[34] in this present price war and what changes (if any) in the competitive situation will take place. While one cannot foresee detailed developments one may safely predict that, when the price war is over, stations selling major-company products will once more return to conservative competitive methods with stress on service rather than price.[35] Moreover, the aggressive competitor will not be eliminated as long as (1) there is an adequate supply of gasoline in this market, and (2) competition exists among suppliers so that each is attempting to unload as much of its supply as possible. This means, then, that any change which takes place will affect the division of the market among types of competitors rather than the types of competitors which will be found in the market.

---

[34] As far as recovery of lost volume is concerned, a top executive of one of the major companies, which had suffered serious losses, states that his company has recovered the business that had been lost.

[35] As one former major-company executive put it, the retailer has full say as regards price policy but the company salesman has a great deal of influence over him, and the company will try to persuade the dealer to act in the best interests of the company and himself.

XI

RETAIL DEALER MARGINS

One of the ways in which competition in the market expresses itself is in dealer margins. Dealer margins are in considerable part a product of commodity prices, which will be discussed in detail in the following two chapters. In their simplest form "dealer margins in gasoline" may be defined as the difference between the tankwagon (wholesale) price and the dealer's posted (retail) price per gallon; from margins must come expenses and profits, if any.[1] In most other fields the margin is expressed as a percentage of sales; the margin in gasoline is expressed in cents per gallon. "Unit margin"—the differential per gallon—must be distinguished from "dollar margin"—the differential times the number of gallons.

Meaning of the Term "Margin"

If all gasoline were acquired at the same tankwagon (wholesale) price and all sales were made at a uniform retail price, the margin concept would be simple enough. Actually, however, the posted tank-

---

[1] Margins, of course, should not be confused with net profits, which are the residual after expenses. It might be mentioned, that some of the concessions made by suppliers to their retail distributors in individual instances have an effect on net profit but not on margins. Examples of such concessions are low interest rates on money borrowed from the company, or free painting and paving jobs.

wagon (buying) price as well as retail (selling) quotations vary.[2] Therefore the "theoretical" margin must be distinguished from the "effective" margin. Moreover, while major companies may maintain their prices, differences may be expressed in terms of rent of facilities; hence adjustment covering rental payments made by either or both parties should be considered also. While supplier companies may frequently apply standard rental figures, variations from these are common. Thus, margins actually realized by retail dealers may vary widely among individual operators.

It is useful, therefore, to distinguish three different meanings of the term "margin" in connection with sales of gasoline:

Theoretical or Indicated Margin. This margin is the difference between the supplier company's tankwagon price and the major-companies' posted retail price.[3] It makes possible a comparison of margins between independent and major companies (for example) whose tankwagon prices differ. Thus, if an independent dealer acquires his product at a price which is 2 cents under the major-companies' tankwagon quotation, the independent-company dealer's theoretical margin may be referred to as 2 cents wider than the major-company dealer's, regardless of his selling price.

Realized or Actual Margin. This margin is the difference between the supplier company's tankwagon price and the individual dealer's retail price. Since the independent-company dealer often sells at retail at a discount approximately equal to the tankwagon differential, the realized margin of major- and independent-company dealers may be identical.[4] A major-company dealer's theoretical margin and his realized margin may be identical, also.

---

[2] Especially since the posting of the retail price at the home office was discontinued by most major companies operating in this market in November, 1948.

[3] While the posting of retail prices at the home office has been discontinued by most of the major companies in this market, one may still properly—though ordinarily less accurately—speak of the theoretical margin as the difference between the tankwagon price and the price at which gasoline is quoted at Standard Stations, Inc. outlets (i.e., the retail market price).

The "theoretical" or "indicated" margin is the meaning of the term as used in the trade. Up to the time when Standard Oil ceased posting retail prices, no one in the trade referred to the price at which gasoline was being purchased—only to the margin obtained; the margin was universally used as a means of price quotation.

[4] An independent-company dealer may have a 6½-cent theoretical margin as compared with a 4½-cent margin for the major-company dealer (as a result of the lower supply price for the little-known brand), but because he sells his product at a discount, the effective margin may be the same or even less than that of the major-company dealer.

Realized Margin Adjusted for Rent.[5] As mentioned earlier, many major companies attempt to adhere strictly to the posted tankwagon price but make adjustments by individual negotiations for the amount of rent to be paid by the operator (if company owns station) or by the company (if operator owns station) or both (in case of lease and lease-back).[6] While the rental transaction is separate from the transaction that involves the wholesale price of the gasoline, both must be taken into account in any realistic consideration of margins. Any rent advantage enjoyed by the dealer is in effect a discount from the tankwagon price.[7]

Indicated Margin in Los Angeles as Compared with Other Areas

Reference was made above to the indicated margin (i.e., the difference between the tankwagon price and the retail market price). In-

---

[5] Offhand, one would feel that the term "net realized margin" would serve more effectively in this circumstance than the term "realized margin adjusted for rent." The use of the former term would be confusing, however, in cases where the realized margin is increased by the *receipt* of rent by an owner-operator from a supplier.

[6] The *paying* of rent to a supplier-owner by an operator and *receiving* of rent by an owner-operator from a supplier appears odd at first glance. To illustrate: One man operates a service station for a supplier-owner. He buys regular-grade gasoline for 19.6 cents and thus earns 4.5 cents, assuming the retail price is 24.1 cents. However he *pays* rent of 1 cent thus "netting" 3.5 cents. Another man owns his station and buys regular-grade gasoline for 19.6 cents, thus earning 4.5 cents. However he *receives* 1 cent for rent, thus "netting" an aggregate margin of 5.5 cents. If the two men are equally skilled and astute and the facilities are similar, the second is gaining an advantage over the first; in order to be on the same basis as the first, he would not receive any rent but would merely not pay any. (Actually, the second man should as landlord charge himself, as station operator, 1 cent to keep the records straight.)

It would seem, therefore, that if an advantage accrued to the owner from such transactions companies would tend strongly to own their properties rather than rent them. Actually, however, while an owner-operator usually does receive rent from the supplier, he also normally pays rent on the lease-back. Thus the individual receives rent as landlord *and* pays rent as operator.

Standard Oil reports that if a dealer owns the property and leases to the company, it is subleased back to the dealer at the same price. Owner-operators in such instances have the advantage only of not having to pay rent. Some companies report, however, that dealer-owners may sublease at a lower price than that called for in the base lease, thus giving property owners an advantage. An example of this is given in the following footnote.

[7] An example of a lease providing for such an advantage is that allegedly given by Shell Oil Company to an owner-operator. (*Complaint, Raymond L. Myers v. Shell Oil Co.*, Civil No. 11260–C, S.D. Cal., March 17, 1950.) The contract required the lessee (Shell) to pay the lessor-owner (Myers) a rental of 1 cent per gallon of gasoline delivered by lessee but the property was subleased by Shell to Myers for a consideration of only $1.00 per year.

dicated margin figures are given in table 16 for various representative cities in the United States including an estimated figure for Los Angeles. Varying widely among cities margins range from 6.8 cents in Casper, Wyoming, to 4 cents in Omaha, Nebraska.

TABLE 16

INDICATED DEALER MARGIN[a] FOR REGULAR-GRADE GASOLINE IN 51 REPRESENTATIVE
CITIES OF THE UNITED STATES, SEPTEMBER 1, 1949

City	Margin (cents/gall.)	City	Margin (cents/gall.)
Casper, Wyo.	6.80	Detroit, Mich.	5.03
New York, N. Y.	6.40	Portland, Maine	5.00
Charleston, W. Va.	6.20	Buffalo, N. Y.	5.00
New Orleans, La.	6.20	Houston, Texas	5.00
Norfolk, Va.	6.10	Reno, Nev.	5.00
Vicksburg, Miss.	6.10	Phoenix, Ariz.	5.00
Charleston, S. C.	5.90	San Francisco, Calif.	5.00
Memphis, Tenn.	5.80	Spokane, Wash.	5.00
Portland, Ore.	5.80	Los Angeles, Calif.	4.90
Dover, Del.	5.70	Providence, R. I.	4.90
Birmingham, Ala.	5.60	Hartford, Conn.	4.90
Newark, N. J.	5.60	Philadelphia, Pa.	4.80
Twin Cities, Minn.	5.60	Huron, S. Dak.	4.80
Manchester, N. H.	5.50	Fargo, N. Dak.	4.70
Washington, D. C.	5.50	Des Moines, Iowa	4.70
South Bend, Ind.	5.50	Denver, Colo.	4.70
Tulsa, Okla.	5.50	Boise, Idaho	4.70
Charlotte, N. C.	5.50	Jacksonville, Fla.	4.60
Baltimore, Md.	5.40	Chicago, Ill.	4.60
Atlanta, Ga.	5.40	Milwaukee, Wis.	4.50
Albuquerque, N. Mex.	5.40	Butte, Mont.	4.50
Little Rock, Ark.	5.40	Wichita, Kans.	4.30
St. Louis, Mo.	5.30	Lexington, Ky.	4.00
Burlington, Vt.	5.10	Youngstown, Ohio	4.00
Boston, Mass.	5.10	Omaha, Nebr.	4.00
Salt Lake City, Utah	5.10		

[a] Difference between dealer (tankwagon) and service station prices.
Source: *National Petroleum News*, October 5, 1949, p. 51 (adapted). Prices quoted were A.P.I. figures as reported by the Texas Company, except the Los Angeles figure which was computed by the authors on the same basis as that used in other cities.

While no attempt will be made in this study to present a definitive explanation of the differences in indicated margins among cities, one might suggest a few possible explanations. Different margins may be a reflection of the different retail costs in different areas. On the other hand, they may in some communities be due to the activities of a strong retail association or union not subject to antitrust action, which have the effect of creating a higher margin. They may arise, conversely, from differences in the degree of development of strong cut-price outlets which provide pressure on retail margins in some communities but not in others.

It should be clear from the discussion in the preceding section that indicated margin figures are somewhat artificial since variations from them are normal, especially among independent operators.[8] Indicated margins do have some significance in relation to major-company dealers, however, because realized margins often are identical with indicated margins. The indicated margin of gasoline retailers in the Los Angeles market is considerably below the median margin of the 51 cities listed in table 16; 35 of them have higher, 14 lower indicated margins, and 2 have the same indicated margin as Los Angeles. Assuming the figures reflect normal conditions and that similar service requirements prevail in the various communities, this indicates that Los Angeles retail service stations were operating at better-than-average efficiency.

Factors Affecting Width of Realized Margins

Realized margins differ considerably among individual dealer-sellers, even within the same class. Each transaction is unique, involving different amounts of the commodity purchased, different degrees of ownership and control of vastly different facilities, and different amounts of skill among individual buyers and sellers. The following are the key factors affecting the width of individual dealer margins in the gasoline field:

1. Ownership of facilities.—If the operator owns the facilities, he may have bargaining power superior to one who doesn't, when considering the terms offered by different supplier companies.[9] Even if

---

[8] Because posted tankwagon prices, upon which indicated margins are in part based, usually apply to major-supplier companies and not to their independent counterparts. Actually, the tankwagon quotations of the independent suppliers are usually lower than those of the major concerns.

[9] Variations may occur also depending on what the specific facilities are. For example, the station might have a wash-rack or even a little restaurant as part of the property. The supplier company leases the whole installation from the owner and subleases it to the operator at a figure he can afford to pay; he in turn subleases the special facilities and thus reduces the rent.

no concession from the tankwagon price[10] is made by a supplier, variations in the rental agreement may create margin differences in the broad sense of the term.[11]

2. Control of facilities by operator.—An operator may retain control over the service-station facilities instead of relinquishing it to a supplier company through subleasing. By so doing he remains independent of any supplier company and merely purchases gasoline from the most advantageous source. The margin on such purchases may vary considerably depending on the competitive conditions existing at the moment, but such an operator ordinarily has an advantage because of the availability of alternative sources of supply.[12]

3. Ability of the operator.—The operator may be (1) unusually effective and recognized as such in the industry and (2) a tactician who knows what he might be able to obtain through bargaining and gets what he goes after.[13]

4. Conditions in the industry at the time the operator signs the contract.—Since different operators sign at different times, their margins may vary. There may be substantial differences from one time to another in the need for operators or facilities by supplier com-

---

[10] Standard Oil, General Petroleum, and Union Oil indicated to the authors that they "held the line" on tankwagon price with few if any exceptions, but would meet competition by negotiations on the basis of rent of facilities. Richfield, Shell, Texas Company, and Tide Water Associated indicated that they may have to vary the tankwagon price from time to time to meet competition.

The executive of one major company reports that while his firm tries to keep the tankwagon price inviolate, it is not able to do so actually in all instances. He reports one case of the company weakening when an operator with six stations offered to shift his custom to the company from his previous source, in return for a contract calling for a 2-cent discount off the tankwagon price. This executive now wonders whether this was a wise move.

[11] A major-company executive reports that the tankwagon price does not vary one penny from dealer to dealer, but variations occur in the rent of facilities, which are quite separate transactions. Factors which affect rent are the same as in any real-estate contract ("horse trading" with variations according to what the operator has to offer and the intensity of the company's need for the property in the particular community).

[12] Variations may be carried a step further on a basis of control of facilities. For example, some companies pay dealers for the privilege of putting up signs on the property.

[13] Since operators in southern California ordinarily buy gasoline at a higher temperature than they sell it (because the gasoline is warm when dumped from the truck and cool when pumped from the underground tanks), an allowance for temperature correction is made by suppliers to some buyers. Allegedly, one company—and perhaps others —provides an arbitrary $\frac{1}{4}$ cent per gallon to some purchasers and not to others to offset the difference in temperature.

panies, particularly in certain areas;[14] moreover, there may be variations in the pessimism or optimism of supplier companies as to the future supply situation. As of June, 1950, variations in realized margins existed because of the different allowances made by suppliers to dealers engaged in the price war.[15]

5. The brand of gasoline.—Major-company brands of gasoline are more desirable than those of independent companies because they are preferred by consumers and therefore usually bring a higher tankwagon price, that is, yield a lower (theoretical) margin.

6. The quantity of gasoline.—Some supplier companies offer discounts based on the quantity of the product purchased. One company's plan is as follows: (1) ordinary delivery of 40 gallons or more —tankwagon price; (2) delivery at the seller's convenience to dealers having a storage capacity of at least 2000 gallons (with an average dump of a 1000 gallons or more)—tankwagon price minus 1 cent; (3) purchases of truck-and-trailer lots (6000–6500 gallons)—tankwagon price minus 1½ cents.

7. The activities of dealers in manipulating retail prices.—This includes the raising as well as the lowering of prices. In Oakland, in December, 1948, the major-company retail dealers reportedly took action in raising retail prices one cent. As this was done without any change in the tankwagon price, it of course had the effect of widening retail margins.[16]

Differences in Realized Margins Among Major-Company Dealers

As has been seen, many factors account for the differences in realized margins among dealers in the Los Angeles area. Margin vari-

---

[14] An executive of one of the major companies reports that margins may not vary among L.O. (lessee-operated) stations but variations in other types of control situations depend on the competition for outlets by suppliers and the facilities offered by the station operators.

[15] One of the complaints made by the plaintiff in *Myers v. Shell* (see footnote 7, above) is that rebates in prices of gasoline are being made to some operators and not to others during the present unsettled price conditions.

[16] Reportedly, enough members of the association increased their prices to make the action effective. Moreover, according to the reports, they did not lose much volume to dealers in independent-company gasoline who still sold at the lower figure. However, according to one of the officials of the Northern California Service Station Operators' Association, the situation had by mid–1949 become quite serious because price cutting had developed among major-company dealers. There is always a temptation under wide-margin conditions for an individual seller to give away part of the unit margin, in order to increase volume sufficiently to offset the cut and maximize dollar margin; but such action leads to general price cutting in the long run.

ations may manifest themselves, however, only in a limited number of ways. Probably the most important device through which special arrangements may be made to particular major-company dealers is the rental allowance. It might be helpful to analyze the effect of varying rental arrangements on dealer margins.

Margins differ for premium-grade and regular-grade gasoline—the margin for premium grade typically is ½ cent higher than that for regular grade in this market.[17] If deductions or allowances are made for rent (assuming a rental figure of 1 cent per gallon), adjusted margins for regular-grade and for premium-grade gasoline would be:

	Approximate margin	
	Regular grade	Premium grade
	(in cents)	(in cents)
Indicated margin (differential between tankwagon and retail market prices)	4.9	5.4
Station owned by company but rented by dealer (rent assumed to be 1 cent per gallon)	3.9	4.4
Station owned by dealer and leased back on the same terms called for in original lease (1 cent each way)	4.9	5.4
Station owned by dealer and leased back on terms which are favorable to the owner-operator (to the extent of an assumed 1 cent per gallon)	5.9	6.4

As can be seen from the figures shown, individual adjusted margins may vary as much as 2 cents among dealers distributing major-company gasoline, even without any difference in buying or selling prices (although a part of this difference should not be assigned to the service station operation but to the property owner). As mentioned above, the figures illustrate the typical situation only—margins of individual dealers may vary from these.[18]

According to an executive of one of the major companies, the average independent company's tankwagon price normally is 1½–2 cents lower than that of major companies.[19] His opinion is, furthermore,

[17] Based on the prices at Texaco stations in this market area. (The table giving indicated dealer margins for various cities in the United States [table 16] was drawn up from prices reported by the Texas Company.)

[18] Actually, however, the ranges found in the market are not likely to be wider than those shown since individual major-company dealers seldom receive a discount on gasoline purchased on top of a rental advantage, although this is quite possible.

[19] An executive of one independent company states that independent concerns do not at present offer markedly better margins than major companies on ordinary transactions (although an official of another independent company stated recently that the tank-

that the independent companies have a rack price[20] which is 2–2½ cents below the tankwagon quotations of major companies. If the independent supplier distributes his product through controlled outlets, rental adjustments may be available to dealers also, so that the independent-company dealer's potential margin may be very wide. However, much if not all of this must be passed on to consumers in the form of lower service-station prices, which of course has the effect of narrowing the realized margins of such dealers.[21] Generally speaking, it is doubtful whether independent-company dealers actually realize wider margins than their major-company counterparts.

Retail Margins Among Volume Distributors

As mentioned, dealers distributing non-major-company brands of gasoline normally operate on a considerably wider theoretical margin than those selling major-company brands. This is due to the fact that distributors of brands from non-major companies usually acquire the gasoline from suppliers at a considerably lower price. The favorable position of those buying at lowest prices is based on: (1) a product which is unbranded and can therefore be acquired from alternative sources, (2) freedom from any restrictions so that one may trade with those offering the most advantageous terms, (3) storage capacity which makes it practicable to buy in large quantities, and (4) astuteness and aggressiveness of operators in recognizing opportunities and pressing for advantage.[22]

---

wagon price of his firm is 2 cents lower than that of the major oil companies). If major and independent companies are so close in terms of margins, one wonders how independent concerns find dealers. It has been suggested that independent suppliers possess the following advantages: (1) Speed in completing negotiations, in contrast to major companies; negotiations may be completed as soon as inspection can be made of the station facilities. (2) Availability of improvement contracts; independent concerns more often than major companies will agree to such improvements as putting in tanks or black-top paving. (3) Willingness to co-sign notes; major companies would not participate in this kind of financing but it might be an important factor in acquiring a particular dealer by an independent-supplier company. One might add that independents also have the advantage of allowing dealers freedom of action; moreover, such dealers have a traditional dislike of majors.

[20] Independent companies generally sell at a "rack price" (i.e., f.o.b. loading rack) and at a "delivered price" as well. A rack price is probably the best available. The general opinion in the market seems to be that this would be the absolute outside quotation.

[21] The alternative would be wide margins per unit but on little or no volume.

[22] The fact that some dealers have wider margins than others would not necessarily make the supplier company vulnerable under the Robinson-Patman legislation for the following reasons: (1) The margin of one seller may be wider than that of another but

But the effective margin maintained by independent-company dealers is likely to be as low or even lower than that of major-company dealers, because concessions have to be made to consumers to induce them to purchase little-known brands. It should be noted that most large-scale dealers are independent of supplier control; hence, margin variations result not from rental adjustments but directly from the relationship of buying and selling prices.

At first glance a wider theoretical margin would appear to have little significance for the dealer if the "premium" is passed on to the consumer. But much depends on the responsiveness of consumers to price concessions. If the demand for the price-cutter's product is sufficiently elastic, the passing on of the advantage derived from the supplier may result in greatly enhanced dollar margin; hence, a larger-than-average theoretical margin may be extremely important for the retail dealer from a competitive point of view.

Major-company dealers could not meet the low prices of aggressive sellers (without help from major-supplier companies), because in

---

involve entirely different (and even different types of) sellers, for example, independent companies as against major concerns. (2) Wider margins may be due not to a lower buying (wholesale) price but to a higher selling (retail) price. (3) Wider margins *may* be provided by the seller but may be based on an individually negotiated rental figure (traditional practice in real-estate transactions) which is favorable to the operator. (4) Wider margins may be due to a lower supplier price to one than to another but the purchases may involve different quantities of the product which *may* demonstrably affect costs in such a way as to provide a legal justification for the differences. (5) Wider margins for one dealer may result from the purchase of the product unbranded from the supplier for sale under private label. (6) A wider margin may actually result from discriminatory pricing by a supplier but with no resulting effect upon competition as required by the law. (7) A wider margin may have resulted from a discriminatory supplier price but the transactions were in intrastate, not in interstate commerce. (8) A lower price might be justified by a momentary market situation favorable to the buyer at the time the contract was consummated (as provided for in Section 2 (a) of the law).

One of the most recent decisions arising out of the Robinson-Patman legislation— *Standard Oil* v. *Federal Trade Commission*, 173 F.2nd 210 (1949)—concerned the sale of gasoline by a major company to certain semijobbers in the Detroit area at a price lower than that charged retail customers, with these distributors reselling to price cutters. The court found for the Federal Trade Commission, on the grounds that such sales caused "substantial damage" to other service station operators. This finding ignored a rebuttal of the *prima-facie* case which showed that the company made its low prices to the favored ones "in good faith to meet an equally low price of a competitor." In its review of this decision the United States Supreme Court reversed the finding of the lower court (*Standard Oil Company* v. *Federal Trade Commission*, 19 U.S.L.Week 4073 [Jan. 8, 1951]) thus affirming the right of an individual seller to discriminate among his customers where such discrimination results from a meeting in good faith of competitors' prices.

making such an attempt many would have passed on their whole margin. As one reduces his margin in the hope of inducing volume he must obtain larger amounts of business in order to offset the reduction of margin per unit.[23] When he reduces prices to the extent of eliminating the margin entirely, obviously no amount of volume would offset the reduction.[24]

Before the price war, effective margins of large-scale aggressive competitors often amounted to 4–4½ cents, although some were undoubtedly less;[25] these margins compared favorably with those of some major-company dealers. Such margins very likely have contracted to some extent since the price war. However, the basic reason for the lower retail prices of such sellers has not been the acceptance of narrower per-unit margins[26] but rather the acquisition of supplies at favorable buying prices. Given sufficient volume, large-scale retail distributors could operate profitably on a much narrower margin than this.[27] The fact that the mass distributors have been able to do business with a substantial margin per unit and at the same time do from six to ten times the volume of orthodox outlets has made for enormous profits;[28] this in turn has resulted in a tremendous rush

---

[23] A seller with a 4-cent margin who reduces his prices by 1 cent must have one-third more business in order to offset the reduction per gallon—assuming expenses remain the same and that non-gasoline sales are not enhanced. If prices were cut 2 cents, however, the amount of business would have to be doubled, if the reduction were 3 cents it would have to be quadrupled.

[24] If one seller has a 6-cent margin (including rent received) and another a 3-cent margin (after payment of rent) it is obvious that a 3-cent cut made by the former cannot be met by the latter without incurring out-of-pocket losses.

[25] The lowest rack price the authors heard quoted was 17 cents, including tax, for premium-grade gasoline. This figure probably would be available only to large-volume units. A retail price of 21.5 cents would yield a retail margin of 4.5 cents. Typically, the margin on the regular-grade product would be slightly narrower, perhaps 4 cents.

[26] This in a sense vitiates a statement made earlier. It was argued (above, p. 129) that despite narrower per-unit margins the self-service outlet was able to maximize dollar margins through the enhancement of unit sales. However, this is still theoretically true. The fact simply has been that the self-serve station in this market, for a considerable period of time, has been able to "have the cake and eat it too."

[27] Despite a contrary opinion (chap. x, p. 153, n. 29), the authors feel that the aggressive sellers have not reached "rock-bottom" in retail prices. The authors do recognize the fact, however, that such sellers very likely have felt, and probably correctly, that while they could cut further, such a cut if effective would bring on further retaliatory measures by major-company dealers, hence would result in less rather than more profit.

[28] This suggests that aggressive price competitors could reduce prices if they cared to. They very likely choose to retain a wider margin on a reduced volume than to trade part of their margin for a temporarily expanded volume, only to end up eventually with a smaller margin *and* a smaller volume.

into this type of business, particularly the serviceless variety, with a resulting reduction in profitability.[29]

Margins in Gasoline as Compared with Other Fields

As mentioned earlier, margins in gasoline are expressed in cents per gallon while margins in most other retail fields are expressed as percentages of sales. This makes it somewhat difficult to compare margins among fields. It can be done, however, by translating the cents-per-gallon figures for gasoline into percentage figures.

A typical per-gallon margin figure for gasoline in the Los Angeles market prior to the price war would be 4½ cents for regular grade and 5 cents for premium grade. Regular-grade gasoline sold at that time for about 24 cents and premium-grade gasoline at about 26½ cents. Therefore the margin was less than 19 per cent of sales[30] (assuming no inventory losses). Actually this figure perhaps should be higher—closer to 25 per cent—because the gross sales prices would be reduced by the amount of the gasoline tax, 6 cents, to net sales figures[31] of approximately 18 cents and 20 cents respectively.

This 19–25 per cent margin in gasoline (depending upon whether tax is included) compares with typical margins of 15–20 per cent in groceries[32] and 30–35 per cent in drugs,[33] both of which are

---

[29] According to one observer in the market (Frank Breese in *National Petroleum News*, March 29, 1950, p. 13): "In the early days of self-serves two years ago, there were so few of them and they were situated so far apart, that they had no apparent effect on one another. In some areas now they have popped up in small clusters of two to five in a square mile area. Their gallonage potential is so great [however] that they inevitably come into direct competition when they are that close. . . .

"What this means is that serve-yourself proprietors are required to hustle like almost everyone else these days to get their share of the motorists' dollars. . . .

"The gasoline price war has pulled conventional station prices down to the self-service range. Frequently, conventional prices are lower than those at serve-yourself stations. The nickel differential between self-service and conventional premium gasoline, which was the keynote of early self-service merchandise and which caught public fancy, is gone. . . .

"In the early months, the self-serve pumped fabulous quantities of gasoline, some claims by individual stations running as high as 500,000 gallons a month. Proprietors looked upon 200,000 gallons a month as a good average and expressed disappointment at anything under 100,000 gallons. Now, however, that 100,000 figure looks good to self-service proprietors. And 200,000 is easier to dream about than count on."

[30] 4.5 divided by 24 = 18.8 (per cent) and 5.0 divided by 26.5 = 18.9 (per cent).

[31] Posted price minus gasoline taxes.

[32] Paul D. Converse and Harvey W. Huegy, *The Elements of Marketing*, 3rd revised ed. (New York: Prentice-Hall, Inc., 1946), p. 515.

[33] *Lilly Digest of the 1948 Statements of 1,122 Retail Drug Stores* (Seventeenth Annual Edition published by Eli Lilly and Company, Indianapolis, Indiana), p. 10.

also classified as convenience goods. Considering the high degree of convenience provided consumers by gasoline outlets and the narrow merchandise line carried by service stations—both of which affect volume and hence expense percentages—the gasoline margin would appear to be reasonable, although this is not to say that the figure could not be reduced. Interestingly enough, because of the considerably lower base price and an only slightly narrower margin, aggressive price competitors may retain as wide if not a wider percentage margin than conventional operators.[34]

---

[34] For example, an aggressive seller offers regular-grade gasoline at 20 cents, tax included. If his effective margin is 4 cents, his margin as a percentage of sales is 20 –28 per cent (depending on whether tax is included).

XII

RETAIL GASOLINE PRICING
AND PRICE BEHAVIOR: I

Price is only one of the several competitive devices used by gasoline vendors in striving for custom. Among the others are location, a differentiated product, customer service, and clean facilities. However, price has certain special aspects that set it apart from other competitive devices. For one thing, price directs attention to the payment for the product-service, rather than to the item the buyer obtains (or thinks he obtains) in exchange for the payment. For another, price usually provides a sharper cutting edge than is available in other competitive weapons, which makes it a more effective instrument for acquiring custom from rivals. Price is such an important factor in gasoline competition and there is so much interest in actual price behavior that detailed treatment of this topic is desirable.[1]

The following discussion in chapters xii and xiii presents an analysis of the prices resulting from the competitive situation in the Los Angeles retail gasoline market. As will be seen, retail price behavior is a multi-dimensional phenomenon and must be so considered if a complete picture of the price structure is to be obtained. Thus, retail gasoline price behavior in the Los Angeles area is examined in subsequent paragraphs in relation to (1) different periods

---

[1] Although admittedly the other factors—for example, location, demand manipulative effort, product differentiation, station layout—would warrant detailed treatment also, if space permitted.

of time, (2) retail prices charged in other areas, (3) tankwagon (wholesale) and crude petroleum prices, (4) different types of dealers in the market, and (5) various quality levels at which the product is offered.

Behavior of Retail Prices in Time

Logically, perhaps the first approach to an analysis of price behavior should be the observation of price changes over a period of time. The following subsections deal with analyses of the number and extent of price changes, cyclical price variations, and trends of prices over a period of time; retail gasoline prices do not appear to vary seasonally so that no discussion of seasonal behavior will be necessary.

This phase of the analysis relies on published price quotations and disregards for the moment variations from them.[2] Therefore, it should be borne in mind that the prices shown in tables and charts in this section represent only those of retail sellers who adhered to the posted prices—generally speaking, largely the major- and subsidiary-company dealers. That is, the prices of the price cutters are not included in these data but will be separately analyzed later.

Number and Extent of Price Changes. Figure 5 shows monthly changes in Los Angeles retail gasoline prices for 1923–1949. Two points should be noted: (1) Prices are shown both with and without tax. (The present total tax of 6 cents in this state—1½ cents federal and 4½ cents state—is included in the price of a gallon of gasoline.[3]) The effectiveness of competition as well as the impact of gasoline prices on the consumer may thus be judged. (2) Because of the excessive space required for recording daily changes, prices are shown as of the 15th of the month.[4]

---

[2] The analysis is based on published price quotations in trade papers and on announcements of price changes appearing in newspapers.

[3] Each of the 48 states has a sales tax on this product in addition to a federal tax of 1.5 cents. State levies range from a high of 9 cents (in Louisiana) to a low of 2 cents (in Missouri); the modal rate is 4 cents and the median tax 5 cents. For certain cities, tax rates are increased by city and county levies on the sale of gasoline. For example, Birmingham, Alabama, and St. Louis, Missouri, have a 1 cent city gasoline tax.

[4] A chart showing daily price changes at both the retail and wholesale level, as well as changes in crude prices, was prepared by the authors to be in a better position to detect relationships among the several levels. This chart covers only 19 years (since it excluded the 7 years during which no changes took place) but is still more than 14 feet long.

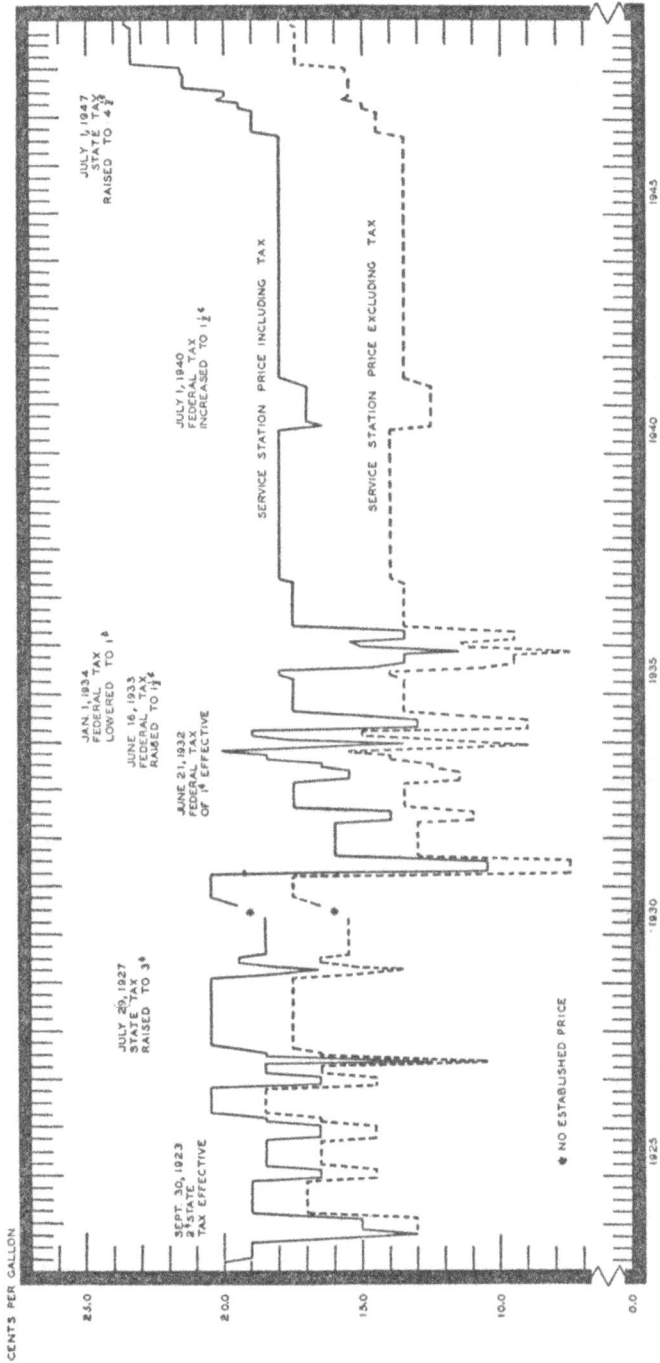

Fig. 5. Service-station price of regular-grade gasoline excluding and including tax in the Los Angeles market as of the 15th of each month, 1923–1948. Basic data from *Petroleum World Annual Review, 1949* (pp. 271–273), supplemented by announcements of price changes in the newspapers; tax information from the California State Board of Equalization and the U. S. Bureau of Internal Revenue.

Although figure 5 is not detailed enough to show them all, there was a total of 82 retail price changes from 1923 to 1949; 40 of these were increases and 42 decreases. The highest and lowest posted prices for this period were 18½ and 7½ cents, excluding tax.

Two other characteristics of the behavior of gasoline prices should be mentioned:

1. Gasoline prices are extremely active at times and very inactive at other times. For example, in the year 1933 the posted price moved 15 times (with a range of 6½ cents), while in 1928, 1938, 1939, 1942, 1943, 1944 and 1945 there were no changes at all.

2. The reasons given by the firms announcing price changes[5] indicate that the price adjustments in gasoline are largely competitive rather than cost phenomena. Thus, most price *decreases*[6] and well over half of the *increases* were explained as the result of competitive adjustments.[7]

It appears, from the data under observation, that gasoline is a commodity which is subject to periodical serious price disturbances; that is, supply and demand conditions are such that price wars[8] seem to occur from time to time.[9] In 26 years more than half a dozen such

---

[5] Reasons reported for announced changes in the price of gasoline from 1923 to 1949:

Price increases[a]		Price decreases	
Attempt to restore price after price war	10	Meeting competition	12
Rise in price of crude	7	Price war	8
Supply not equal to demand	3	Surplus stocks	6
Save federal conservation program	1	Seasonal adjustment	3
Heavy summer demand	1	Excess stocks and sporadic price cutting by	
Attempts to increase dealer margins	1	independents	1
Increased cost of doing business	1	General weakening of the market	1
First rise authorized by O.P.A.	1	Reversed act of previous day	1
No reason reported	15	Gifts by competitors blamed	1
	40	Interest of improved national economy	1
		No reason reported	8
			42

[a] From announcements in the *Los Angeles Times* and, where necessary, the *Los Angeles Evening Herald & Express* on or about the dates on which price changes were found in the *Petroleum World Annual Review*.

[6] While these did not involve cost changes in the cost-to-manufacture sense, they may have resulted from weakened tankwagon prices, which in turn resulted from "sloppy" supply conditions.

[7] Moreover, increases which were reported as resulting from a rise in the price of crude may have been rationalizations.

[8] See definition of "price wars" given above, chap. x, p. 150, n. 14.

[9] Influenced by such factors as "sloppy" supply conditions making for occasional bargains in gasoline, enough elasticity in the demand for the product of an individual firm to assure sales for price-cutters (but not enough to bring on immediate reprisals), the existence of aggressive-minded sellers in gasoline retailing, and others.

disturbances are discernible from the daily price-change chart prepared by the investigators. When the authors attempted to probe this matter of price wars in discussions with some industry spokesmen, the consensus was that little if anything is accomplished by such disturbances and that they are costly to all concerned.

Industry spokesmen to the contrary, price wars may actually achieve certain competitive results.[10] Moreover, one may not necessarily be able to avoid such disturbances simply because they are costly. It appears from the evidence that gasoline price wars usually are not planned; rather, the participants become involved through the heat of everyday rivalry. That is, in striving for patronage the tactics of one group (such as certain independent sellers) may be especially successful; consequently competitors may make moves designed to prevent further inroads on their custom or even to recapture that which has been lost. They may possibly cut price secretly at first. Finally, the participants may find themselves in the midst of a struggle which no vendor really wanted and from which no individual seller can withdraw until the heat of battle subsides.[11] Assuming

---

[10] Theoretically, price wars could have three possible results:

(1) The price war might have the effect of correcting the basic factors giving rise to the war—excess supplies, aggressive competition, and so on—and thus competitive conditions would be restored to normal (including the share of business which the participants formerly had); as a result no further price flurries would occur, at least for a time.

(2) Assuming surpluses to be the cause of the price war, the war might have little or no effect—both sides might suffer losses during its duration but afterwards surpluses might still overhang the market. Competitors who precipitated the war still might be in business and still determined to continue to strive aggressively for a larger share of the market.

(3) The price war might have little effect in changing basic physical factors but one or both of the participants may have learned important lessons, at least temporarily (especially those hurt most). As a result *attitudes* of competitors may have been altered, i.e., the change might be psychological. This change in attitude might apply to (a) the major companies, who may now have decided that they will be satisfied with a smaller share of the market, or (b) the aggressive independent companies, who may now accept a live-and-let-live philosophy and will henceforth avoid *drastic* price-cutting.

[11] Attempts to bring a price war to an end often fail. For example: In mid-November, 1933, the posted price of regular-grade gasoline in the Los Angeles market had declined to a low of 9 cents excluding tax (13 cents including state and federal levies) by a series of reductions over a period of a little over a month. Within two weeks a raise of 2 cents was announced and a couple of days later another 2-cent advance was made. One month later another increase of 2 cents was posted. But less than two months following the last increase, prices were reduced 1½ cents; seven days later another drop occurred, this time 2 cents per gallon (one firm reduced top grades 3 cents). Within a little over a week, two more drops took place, the posted price slipping

the existence of competition, however, the participants might feel forced to make the same decision again with the full realization that they are running a risk of becoming involved in another price war, that is, assuming a calculated risk.

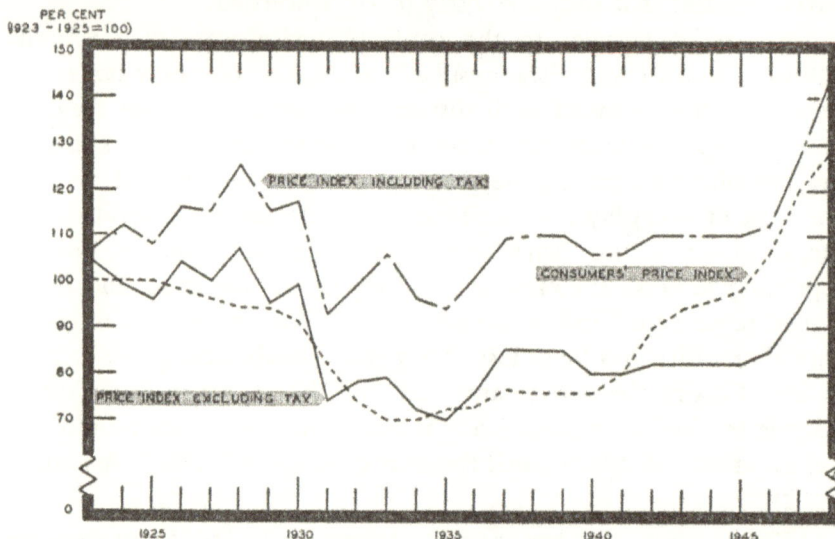

Fig. 6. Indexes of service-station prices of regular-grade gasoline excluding and including tax, and index of general retail prices (Bureau of Labor Statistics, Consumers' Price Index), Los Angeles, 1923–1948. Basic data from *Petroleum World Annual Review, 1949* (pp. 271–273); U. S. Department of Labor, Bureau of Labor Statistics, *Handbook of Labor Statistics* (ed. 1947, pp. 110–111); and *Monthly Labor Review,* LXVIII (February, 1949), 261.

Cyclical Behavior. The price data in figure 5 show a cyclical behavior pattern. The chart reveals that retail gasoline prices dropped

back to 9 cents. Elapsed time from 9 cents to 15 cents and back to 9 cents was 3½ months.

About 2½ months later the major companies started "inching up" again—the first raise amounted to 2 cents, a second, a month later, to 2½ cents; a little over two months later the price increased another ½ cent. Almost immediately (after a lapse of only one day) the price dropped back fractionally to 13½ cents and remained there for over seven months. The first change following this period of temporary stability was a 2-cent reduction followed ten days later by an increase of 2½ cents. This increase lasted less than two months when the price declined first to 11½ cents (from 14 cents) and then almost immediately to 10½ cents, followed within a few weeks by a drop to 9 cents. A few months later the price fell to 8½ cents and then to a low of 7½ cents.

sharply in 1931 and continued to be weak during the depressed business conditions of the early 1930's; they did not show any evidence of permanent recovery until after 1935. Figure 6, which depicts the movements of posted retail gasoline prices in the form of indexes of annual averages, presents a somewhat clearer picture of the ups and downs in the 1930's. In this chart, price indexes, including and excluding taxes, are shown in comparison with an index of general retail prices[12] (both based on 1923–1925).[13] (The annual prices on which the indexes are based are weighted averages of the daily price quotations.) This chart reveals a remarkable similarity in the direction of gasoline and general price movements,[14] although the former lags considerably behind the latter.

If the experience of the great depression is any criterion, it appears that gasoline prices move closely with the cyclical fluctuations in business activity—declining when business becomes inactive and increasing when it improves. In view of the degree of inelasticity of demand for the generic product and the prompt meeting of one major-company seller's changes by his major-company competitors, loss of revenue almost inevitably results from a price reduction in gasoline by such sellers. Thus, assuming that major vendors are well informed and foresighted, they would not choose to drop prices; it follows that competition must force them to do so.[15]

---

[12] Bureau of Labor Statistics index, formerly known as the Cost of Living Index, now the Consumers' Price Index.

[13] The years of 1923–1925 seemed to represent best the "normal" price situation in gasoline (not too high and not too low). Both gasoline price series were based on prices excluding tax. The base for the general index of retail prices was shifted from 1935–1939 to 1923–1925 to match the gasoline price index.

[14] The extent of the deviation below and above the base will depend, of course, on the base used.

[15] This may work in several ways: (1) Major companies may display forethought in the pricing of the segment of their product sold under their own brand, and still cut prices on the segment sold unbranded to independent distributors. And this in turn may make for price cutting by independent dealers, which in turn would exert a pressure on the prices charged by major companies for the product sold under their own brand. (2) Even without a price change on the part of the independents, the degree of elasticity of demand for the individual seller's product tends to increase in time of depression so that shifts might occur from major standard-price outlets to independent cut-rate outlets; as a result the "balance of market power" would be disturbed and a downward pressure on major-company prices would be created. (3) A major-company competitor striving for volume may inadvertently become involved in a price skirmish by authorizing or condoning secret price concessions, which then develops into open price reductions by dealers, which in turn may lead toward reductions in the posted price.

Price Trends. The trend of posted retail gasoline prices (as shown in figure 7) differs considerably for prices including and excluding tax. (The trend lines in the chart were fitted by inspection.) As was mentioned before, the price excluding tax should be used when determining the effectiveness of competition in the industry, the price including tax when considering the viewpoint of the consumer. Thus: (1) The trend of posted retail prices *excluding* tax is down-

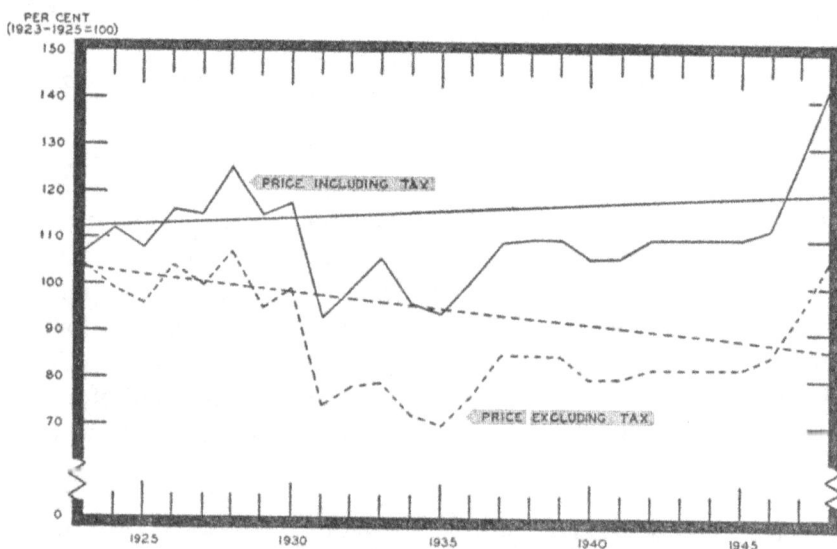

Fig. 7. Trend of service-station prices for regular-grade gasoline excluding and including tax, Los Angeles, 1923–1948. Basic data from *Petroleum World Annual Review, 1949* (pp. 271–273).

ward from 1923 to 1949, even taking into full account the more recent postwar-announced price increases. But (2) the trend *including tax* is slightly upward. It should be noted in passing that judging from the published data, gasoline prices were much more effectively controlled during World War II than retail prices in general.

We may conclude from the data immediately above, combined with those in an earlier section, that (1) the petroleum industry has provided an increasingly higher-quality product at a decreasing price over a period of time (although not necessarily as low as it could have), but (2) the gasoline price the consumer must pay has increased over a period of time because of the application of a state tax (beginning at 2 cents and now 4½ cents) and later a federal tax (beginning at 1 cent and now 1½ cents).[16]

Leadership in Gasoline Pricing. A detailed study of price behavior in a particular industry over a period of time may reveal the pattern of leadership in pricing, if any, in that industry. The following table, based on a study of the public announcements of price changes in the Los Angeles market from 1923 to 1949, gives the identity of the price leader or leaders, where available, in connection with each of the 82 changes in posted retail prices during that period.

Price Increases		Price Decreases	
Standard Oil	25	Standard Oil	16
Standard Oil and Union	2	Texas	3
Union and Associated	1	Shell Oil	2
Union and Richfield	1	Union Oil	2
Shell, Union and Texas	1	Shell and Union	1
Calpete	1	Shell, Union and Standard	1
All majors	3	Union, General Petroleum, Shell, Texas, Richfield	1
Majors	2	Gilmore (independent) followed by Richfield (major)	1
Los Angeles majors	1	Pan American	4
Majors and independents	1	All majors	2
Station operators	1	Majors	4
Not stated	1	One major	2
	40	All majors except Standard	1
		Four major oil companies	1
		Not stated	1
			42

We might draw the following conclusions from the data given in the table.

1. The major companies have taken the lead in publicly announcing price changes in the Los Angeles market in almost all instances.

2. *All* major firms have assumed leadership at one time or another (although some do not appear to have been very active in this regard).

3. Standard Oil Company of California has assumed leadership much more often than any other firm.

---

[16] At least two major companies in this market were in May, 1950, displaying signs indicating the tax burden from the point of view of the motorist. For example, the Standard Oil Company sign read: "Do you know you pay 33% tax on every gallon of gasoline?" General Petroleum Corporation displayed a similar sign: "Taxes add 33% to your 'gas' bill."

4. Standard Oil has taken the lead in price increases more often than in decreases.[17]

It can be seen from the foregoing that despite the dominant position of Standard Oil Company of California in this area, price leadership in the area has not been entirely a one-company proposition as has been generally thought, but has been shared to a considerable extent by several major concerns. It should be pointed out, in any case, that price leadership as used in this connection is something of a misnomer—especially as related to downward movements—because to a considerable extent the changes in price publicly announced by the major firms have simply been moves in response to changes that had already been made by independent retail vendors.[18] (See footnote 5, above.) Thus, in most instances the leader concern, while taking the lead in the moves by major companies, is actually a follower of previous price reductions made by independent dealers.[19]

---

[17] There is some evidence that, from a public relations point of view, a major company prefers to assume the responsibility of taking the lead in raising rather than in lowering prices. According to the vice-president in charge of sales of the Standard Oil Company (Ohio): "We find that as a practical matter we can lead the market up under certain conditions, but that politically it is not wise to lead it down.

"Economically, in theory, there might be times when a marketer should lead a market to lower and sounder levels. . . . It promotes good industry relations to follow the market down belatedly [however], thus sharing with others the responsibility for achieving lower levels. Politically, we should not be the spearhead which drives uneconomic distribution out of the market. These levels having been set by others, however, we can follow to realistic economic levels.

"On the other hand, in our own interest we must usually take the lead in attempting higher price levels when we believe that conditions will permit. Having a substantial distribution in our market we are confronted with the fact that few marketers, especially those with a lesser consumer acceptance, can take the lead in increasing prices. Upward moves in our market are made by us only when, in our opinion, general prices and the economic pressure from industry costs are such that our competitors in their own interest will follow." (Edmund P. Learned, "Pricing of Gasoline—A Case Study," *Harvard Business Review*, November, 1948, p. 731.)

[18] This is not necessarily so, of course, because under certain circumstances a shift in patronage might take place from those selling "at market" to cut-price dealers without any change in prices, due to changes in income or increases in other prices.

[19] That is, the leader's price reduction may have been precipitated by a reduction in the major company's share of the market resulting from a previous cut by independent dealers. This suggests the importance of the horizontal aspects of price cuts (existing cuts spreading over a large area) as against the vertical aspects (deeper cuts at localized points).

Apropos of this is a statement by a Standard Oil Company official, mentioned earlier, concerning a previous price war. That war, it will be recalled, "grew out of price decreases made here and there throughout the Pacific Coast;" various sellers "followed

Los Angeles Retail Gasoline Prices Compared with Those in Other Communities

In a study of retail gasoline prices it would seem advantageous to provide a basis for orientation by showing the relationship between Los Angeles prices and those of other markets. There are, of course, limitations to the success of carrying out such a plan. The most important difficulty is that the price data which prevail are the posted prices of major companies, and do not reflect any variations from them by (1) major-company dealers who may offer secret or open concessions from the prevailing price, or (2) independent-company dealers who usually must offer their product at a discount if they are to compete successfully.

The extent of such variations from the prevailing prices of major-company dealers will vary from time to time and, even more important, from community to community. Thus, while valuable, this intermarket price analysis by no means fully reflects actual price differences among the various communities; it reflects at most differences in prices among communities for the product of major- and subsidiary-company dealers (totalling from two-thirds to four-fifths of the number of retail vendors).

Having established these reservations, we now turn to the intermarket gasoline price data. Two types of relationships can be shown: (1) that between the Los Angeles retail price and prices in other California communities (which should give some idea of the geographical price pattern, if any, among communities within the state), and (2) that between the Los Angeles retail price and prices in other markets throughout the United States (which should provide a rough standard by which one may judge the reasonableness of the price of gasoline in the Los Angeles area). Looking at these two types of relationships more closely we find:

1. The data[20] in table 17 show the price of regular-grade and premium-grade gasoline in Standard Oil stations in 14 widely scattered California communities. As can be seen, Los Angeles retail prices are as low or lower than those in any other California com-

---

the downward trend of . . . competitive price reductions until, at some points, suppliers and dealers were selling gasoline at or below cost." The result was that the product was being sold at a low price throughout a wide area.

[20] Provided by the company.

munity shown in the table. This is to be expected because Los Angeles is the main source of supply for other communities in the state. The pattern seems clear that retail prices increase roughly with the distance from the Los Angeles market, although differences in the type of transportation required to haul the gasoline seem to have some influence on the price. Thus, the price in Oakland, 400 miles away from Los Angeles, but accessible by tanker, is only 0.8 cent higher than in Los Angeles, while the price at Bishop, 270 miles

TABLE 17

SERVICE STATION PRICES, TANKWAGON QUOTATIONS, AND INDICATED RETAIL MARGINS
FOR GASOLINE AT STANDARD STATIONS, INC. IN 14 SELECTED
CALIFORNIA TOWNS, SEPTEMBER 13, 1949

Town	Chevron Supreme			Chevron		
	Retail	Tankwagon	Margin	Retail	Tankwagon	Margin
Bishop............	32.5	25.3	7.2	30.0	23.3	6.7
Truckee...........	30.6	25.1	5.5	28.1	23.1	5.0
Redding..........	30.4	25.1	5.3	27.9	23.1	4.8
Blythe...........	30.1	24.7	5.4	27.6	22.7	4.9
Eureka...........	29.5	24.2	5.3	27.0	22.2	4.8
Salinas..........	29.2	23.8	5.4	26.7	21.8	4.9
Sacramento.......	28.8	23.5	5.3	26.3	21.5	4.8
Fresno...........	28.8	23.5	5.3	26.3	21.5	4.8
Santa Barbara.....	28.4	23.0	5.4	25.9	21.0	4.9
San Diego........	27.9	22.7	5.2	25.4	20.7	4.7
San Francisco......	27.4	22.1	5.3	24.9	20.1	4.8
Oakland..........	27.4	22.1	5.3	24.9	20.1	4.8
Bakersfield........	27.5	22.1	5.4	25.0	20.1	4.9
Los Angeles........	26.6	21.6	5.0	24.1	19.6	4.5

Source: Standard Oil Company of California.

away, but accessible only by truck, is almost 6 cents higher. The data presented suggest that retail gasoline prices in other California cities are based on the quotation in the Los Angeles market and vary from it roughly according to transportation cost.

2. Table 18 shows the prices of regular-grade gasoline in Los Angeles and in 50 markets scattered throughout the United States. At least two conclusions may be drawn from the data: (a) The net retail price of gasoline received by the vendor in the Los Angeles market (as evidenced by the prices, excluding tax, in major-company stations) is with only two exceptions the lowest of any of the listed

markets. (b) The gross price of gasoline to the consumer in the Los Angeles market (as evidenced by the prices, including tax, in major-company stations) is with only three exceptions the lowest of the markets considered.

TABLE 18

MAJOR-COMPANY SERVICE STATION PRICES WITH AND WITHOUT TAXES FOR REGULAR-GRADE GASOLINE IN 51 REPRESENTATIVE CITIES OF THE UNITED STATES, AUGUST 1, 1949[a]

City	Price		City	Price	
	(Excluding tax)	(Including tax)		(Excluding tax)	(Including tax)
Boise, Idaho.........	24.00	31.50	Detroit, Mich........	20.43	24.93
Spokane, Wash.......	22.60	30.60	Lexington, Ky........	20.30	28.80
Casper, Wyo.........	22.50	29.00	Manchester, N. H.....	20.10	25.60
South Bend, Ind......	22.50	28.90	Burlington, Vt........	20.00	26.50
Milwaukee, Wisc......	22.10	27.60	New Orleans, La......	20.00	30.50
Twin Cities, Minn.....	22.00	28.50	Charleston, S. C......	19.80	27.30
Phoenix, Ariz.........	21.90	28.40	Buffalo, N. Y........	19.80	25.30
Fargo, N. D..........	21.90	27.40	Omaha, Neb.........	19.70	27.20
Reno, Nev...........	21.80	28.80	Denver, Colo........	19.50	27.00
Huron, S. D.........	21.70	27.20	Washington, D. C.....	19.50	25.00
Charleston, W. Va.....	21.60	28.10	Norfolk, Va..........	19.50	27.00
Salt Lake City, Utah..	21.50	27.00	Tulsa, Okla..........	19.50	27.50
Atlanta, Ga..........	21.00	29.50	Jacksonville, Fla......	19.50	28.00
Birmingham, Ala......	21.00	29.50	Hartford, Conn.......	19.30	24.80
Vicksburg, Miss......	21.00	28.50	Newark, N. J........	19.30	23.80
St. Louis, Mo........	21.00	25.50	Boston, Mass........	19.20	23.70
Albuquerque, N. M....	21.00	30.00	Portland, Maine......	19.10	26.60
Chicago, Ill..........	20.50	25.00	San Francisco, Calif...	19.10	25.10
Des Moines, Iowa.....	20.50	26.00	Philadelphia, Pa......	19.00	25.50
Dover, Del...........	20.50	26.00	Baltimore, Md.......	19.00	25.50
New York, N. Y......	20.50	26.00	Youngstown, Ohio....	19.00	24.50
Memphis, Tenn.......	20.50	29.00	Providence, R. I......	19.00	24.50
Little Rock, Ark......	20.50	28.50	Los Angeles, Calif.....	18.50	24.50
Charlotte, N. C.......	20.50	28.00	Wichita, Kan........	18.40	24.90
Butte, Mont.........	20.50	28.00	Houston, Tex........	18.00	23.50
Portland, Ore........	20.50	28.00			

[a] Prevailing prices in Texaco stations in the several markets; Los Angeles figure obtained from the Texas Company office in that city.

Source: *National Petroleum News*, Sept. 7, 1949, p. 58.

The fact that the price of gasoline in Los Angeles is low in comparison with other markets in the United States is not an unexpected phenomenon. The reason is the same as that pointed out when the gasoline price in Los Angeles was compared with that in other California cities: Los Angeles is a major production area, and many of the markets with which comparisons are made must "import" supplies from some production center with a resulting higher cost of transportation.

We must again remember that we are dealing with published price quotations in this analysis. Such prices, as we have said, are by no means representative of all sellers—the market variations from the published prices are common phenomena in most, if not all, markets and these differ greatly among communities. Such variations occur in accordance with the nature of the demand—in both its psychological and income aspects—and the aggressiveness of the competition in each market, as well as with the cost-supply aspects of each area. Because of the proximity of supplies, the number of aggressive vendors,[21] and the price consciousness of a segment of the consumer market, gasoline may be obtained by consumers in the Los Angeles market at prices at least as low as (and very likely considerably lower than) in other markets. This will be discussed in detail in the next chapter.

Retail Gasoline Prices in Relation to Tankwagon and Crude Petroleum Prices

Another interesting and possibly profitable area of investigation into the behavior of gasoline prices lies in probing relationships between retail prices and tankwagon prices on the one hand, and retail prices and crude petroleum (raw material) prices on the other. As an aid to the detection and measurement of these price relationships, daily price changes for the three series—retail, tankwagon, and crude quotations—from 1923 to 1949 were recorded on graph paper. Summary statements of relationships were then drawn from this presentation.

Figures 8 and 9 (segments of the long work chart mentioned above) are presented (a) to provide a graphic picture of the price relationships described in this book verbally and statistically, and (b) to show

---

[21] There are two aspects of the influence of aggressive price competitors in any market: (1) the availability of offerings at low-price levels, and (2) the pressure on major-company price levels (which may actually reduce the differential between aggressive and conservative vendors).

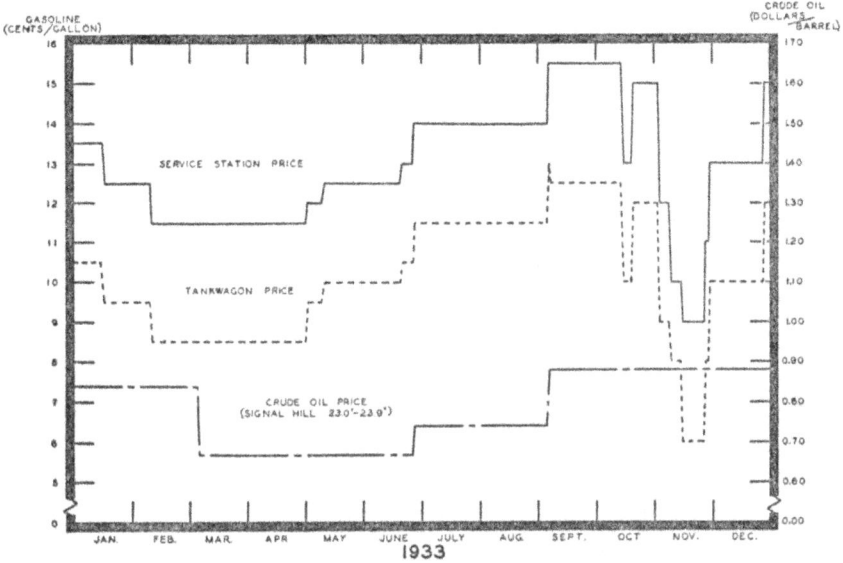

Fig. 8. Service-station prices and tankwagon quotations for regular-grade gasoline excluding tax, and the prices of crude oil (Signal Hill 23-23.9°), Los Angeles, 1933. From *Petroleum World Annual Review, 1935* (p. 67).

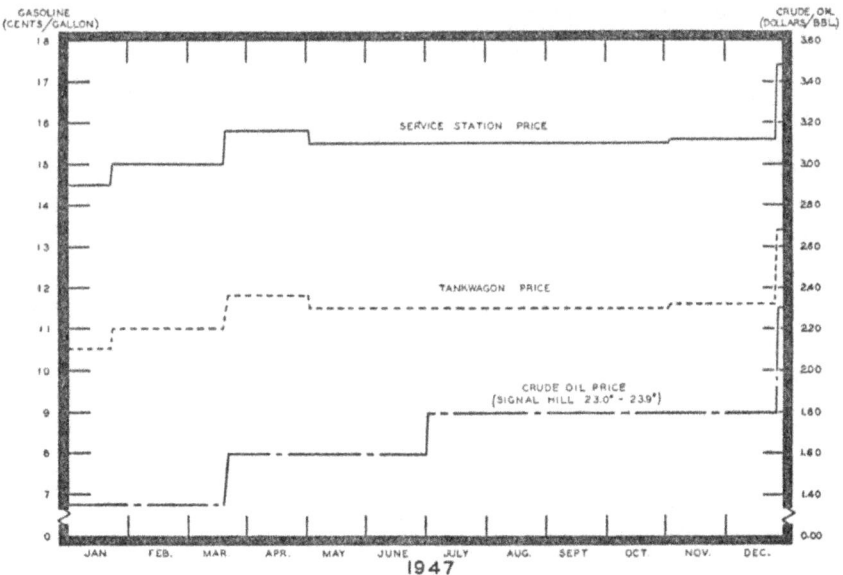

Fig. 9. Service-station prices and tankwagon quotations for regular-grade gasoline excluding tax, and the prices of crude oil (Signal Hill 23-23.9°), Los Angeles, 1947. From *Petroleum World Annual Review, 1948* (p. 258).

two contrasting price behavior patterns. Figure 8, covering 1933, depicts a period in which the price of gasoline fluctuated violently with little regard to the price behavior of crude oil; Figure 9, covering 1947, depicts a much more stable period with a somewhat closer relationship between retail and crude prices.

The retail, tankwagon, and crude relationships prevailing during the 26-year period are:

1. Retail and tankwagon price movements in gasoline in the market under observation are closely related. There were, in the 26 years between 1923 and 1949, 87 changes in the Los Angles tankwagon price as against 82 changes in the retail price.[22] These may be broken down as follows:

Number of changes in posted retail price and tankwagon price occurring on the same
  day... 150[a]
Number of changes in tankwagon price without an immediate change (within two
  weeks) in posted retail price... 8
Number of changes in posted retail price without an immediate change (within two
  weeks) in tankwagon price.. 5
Number of changes in tankwagon price without an established retail price........... 2
Number of changes in tankwagon price followed by a change in posted retail price in
  two weeks or less.. 2
Number of changes in posted retail price followed by a change in tankwagon price in
  two weeks or less.. 2
  Total number of price changes... 169

  [a] In 89 per cent of these simultaneous movements the posted retail price and the tankwagon price changed by the same amount.

It is apparent from these figures that most changes in the posted gasoline price—89 per cent—were simultaneously made at the wholesale and retail levels. A few additional changes, while not immediate, were made within a few days, which would indicate an even closer relationship between tankwagon and retail price movements.

However, the statistical presentation, in a sense, overstates simultaneity of movement of retail and tankwagon prices because of the potential significance of some non-simultaneous movements. The failure to move together in a specific instance may create a sustained

---

[22] This discrepancy between the number of changes at the wholesale level as against the number at the retail level may come about as a result of (1) piecemeal changes in the tankwagon price as contrasted with a single change in the retail price, or (2) a change in the tankwagon quotation unaccompanied by a change in the retail figure.

change in margin;[23] hence, absence of simultaneity in a particular instance may be much more significant than a particular datum suggests.

It may be, on the other hand, that an absence of simultaneity in the retail and tankwagon price movements is more apparent than real, since supplier companies might prefer to subsidize dealers who are forced to meet competition, by cutting prices rather than by reducing tankwagon prices (as at present, in June, 1950). All in all, however, the breakdown based upon the relationship of published tankwagon and retail prices presents a fairly accurate picture of the situation. In sum, it would seem that a close correlation exists between the movement of tankwagon and retail prices in the Los Angeles market.

2. On the other hand the relationship between retail gasoline prices and crude petroleum prices appears to be rather remote. The following tabular arrangement, based upon detailed study of the fluctuation depicted in the work chart described above, indicates the nature of that relationship.

Number of changes in the posted retail price without a change in the crude oil price within one month... 53
Number of posted retail price and crude petroleum price changes in the same direction on the same date.. 20
Number of price changes represented by posted retail price changes preceding changes in crude oil prices within one month... 18[a]
Number of price changes represented by crude oil price changes preceding changes in posted retail prices within one month.. 13[a]
Number of changes in the crude oil price without a change in the posted retail price within one month... 9

Total number of price changes... 113

[a] Price changes are sometimes more numerous than movements in price because several individual price changes might be involved in one price move. For example, in a period of only one month in early 1931 five changes in the retail price were followed by only two changes in the crude price. When this occurs it has the effect of overstating the relationship between retail and crude price movements.

The foregoing figures indicate that the relationship between crude oil and retail gasoline prices is considerably less direct than between

[23] While somewhat unusual, such a situation is not unheard of. For example, on May 23, 1934, the tankwagon price of gasoline in the Los Angeles area was increased 1 cent (to 9 cents net) while the posted retail price remained the same (at 11 cents net). This reduction in margin from 3 cents to 2 cents remained in effect for a year and a half!

tankwagon and retail prices. The price of crude oil changed much less often than the retail price of gasoline; during the period 1923–1948, the crude price moved only 33 times while the retail price moved 82 times. In approximately 55 per cent of the total price changes occurring in the 26 years under observation either (1) retail prices changed without any apparent relationship to crude prices or (2) crude prices changed without any apparent relationship to retail prices. Of these the majority were in the former category.

In only about 45 per cent of the instances was there any apparent relationship between retail gasoline and crude petroleum prices. But this figure should not be interpreted as representing the degree of influence of crude prices on retail gasoline prices in the Los Angeles market area. The data suggest that crude petroleum prices are of minor importance as a factor influencing retail gasoline prices. To begin with, even where a relationship between crude and gasoline price movements exists, the causal relationship often runs from retail gasoline to crude[24] rather than the converse.[25] Moreover, the price of one product may have little influence on the other; rather both prices may depend on a common factor; for example, a heavy demand for motor fuel, and therefore for crude petroleum, causes a rise in the price of both products. This situation would seem to be indicated when the price movements are simultaneous.[26] But even where the price movement seems to proceed from crude to retail gasoline, the change in the price of crude petroleum may merely be a rationalization for a change in the retail price. The foregoing seems to confirm an earlier conclusion that market influences are more important in

---

[24] Such a relationship under certain circumstances might even be inverse. It is claimed by some independent operators that the control of crude prices is a powerful weapon which may be used by the majors to "discipline" the independents in case of a price war. That is, when the retail price is low a raise in the price of crude would "squeeze" the independent refiner between the new high crude price and his low gasoline price, with the result that he would be forced to raise the latter. It should be noted that any raise in the crude price affects the major company in its role of crude buyer just as it does the independent company. The difference may be that the independent is selling gasoline at a lower price; also, the major company might be willing to withstand a temporary loss in order to bring about order in the market.

[25] There may be some significance in the fact that in most cases of posted retail price changes which preceded changes in crude prices, the movement was down rather than up.

[26] It may be significant that in most instances where the posted retail price and the crude petroleum price moved together the movements were upward.

determining gasoline prices than the cost of the raw materials which make up the product.[27]

---

[27] This relationship between gasoline prices and crude prices was probed by Professor Learned in the Middle Western market (E. P. Learned, *op. cit.*, p. 734) and while his findings are similar, his interpretation differs to some extent from that of the authors. Learned states: "There is no constant or necessary relationship between the amount of a price advance in crude and the amount of a price advance in gasoline. . . .

"Moreover, the timing of gasoline price moves has been neither automatically nor precisely tied to changes in crude prices. All the increases in crude prices, however, brought about eventual changes in gasoline prices, as is only to be expected in view of the fact that this company is a large net buyer of crude. The reaction time varied from immediately to a lag of as long as three months. . . . The one decrease in the price of crude during this period was preceded by a reduction in product prices.

"Gasoline prices are much more sensitive than crude prices. The statewide posted S.S. and dealer prices changed fourteen times in the years 1937 through 1941, whereas the price of crude oil changed only four times."

XIII

RETAIL GASOLINE PRICING
AND PRICE BEHAVIOR: II

So far we have used published gasoline quotations in our analyses of retail gasoline prices. The figures given in previous sections, although useful, present as we have said a somewhat artificial picture of gasoline prices, because they imply a uniformity in the market price in each area which actually does not exist. Because of this absence of uniformity, no one quotation can adequately represent price conditions in any market. Lack of intra-market price homogeneity is particularly true of gasoline, and especially at the retail level (where imperfections in consumer information and differentiations among offerings prevail). In this chapter we recognize the fact that variations from the published quotations exist. The chapter analyzes the market prices actually observed in the Los Angeles area (1) among types of sellers and (2) between products of different qualities.

While the retail price structure of gasoline in any market appears to be simple at first thought, consumers undoubtedly find it difficult to compare intelligently alternative offerings because of the multiplicity of brands, the several grade levels, the publicizing of discounts which may or may not be correct, and particularly the use of decimals or fractions in pricing. When, in addition, various dealers change their quotations from time to time, consumers are indeed likely to become confused. The choice of sources of gasoline by consumer-buyers, therefore, is apt to be made on considerably less than rational grounds.

Prices Within the Los Angeles Area

Since the end of World War II competitive conditions in the Los Angeles market have vastly changed. Retail prices in any market vary greatly from time to time as market conditions change. The conditions may range from considerable uniformity in the prices of rival sellers, including the independent-company dealers (as during and immediately following World War II) to wide variations in prices (as now, July, 1950).

Retail Price Structure in Late 1949. Actually one can expect a fair degree of uniformity in the prices of gasoline at major-company outlets in any particular market. This expectation is based on several factors: (1) the absence of preference on the part of a large segment of the consuming public toward the brand of any one major company (even though they prefer major-company gasoline to that sold by independents); (2) the "follow the leader" tradition which has prevailed in this business (in part due to this absence of strong preference among major-company brands); and (3) the attempt by most major companies to keep prices in line by some type of resale price maintenance activity.

Company	Cents per gallon	
	Regular grade	Premium grade
General Petroleum Corporation.	24.5	27.0
Richfield Oil Company.	24.5	26.5
Shell Oil Company.	24.2	26.6
Standard Oil Company of Calif.	24.1	26.6
Texas Company.	24.5	27.0
Tide Water Associated Oil Company.	24.5	27.0
Union Oil Company.	24.1	27.5

While there is a substantial degree of uniformity in the quotations of pump prices, they may vary to some extent among dealers of various major companies, even where price cutting is not practiced. The table above shows representative prices of non-price-cutting dealers of the seven major companies in the Los Angeles area in December, 1949[1]—before the general decline of major-company retail prices.

As can be seen from the table on page 189, the retail prices of the non-price-cutting dealers of the several major concerns in this market were by no means perfectly uniform at the time the observations were made.[2] This indicates a certain degree of independence in pricing by the major-companies' dealers. However, differences among such vendors were largely fractional. Thus, the difference between the highest and the lowest quotations for regular-grade gasoline was only 0.4 cents in late 1949. As to premium-grade gasoline, except for Union (whose price was 1 cent higher than the lowest quotation for that grade of gasoline and 0.5 cents higher than the nearest quotation) the price spread was only 0.5 cents.

Actually, the difference in prices among non-price-cutting major-company dealers was less than is indicated by the foregoing figures. That is, the price differential among all such dealers for the *average* of regular-grade and premium-grade gasoline was less than half a cent per gallon as of December, 1949 (specifically, 0.45 cents).[3] While absolute uniformity of retail prices was absent, then, a high degree of uniformity did prevail. A careful observation of this market over a period of time indicates that the condition of close, but not absolute, uniformity of price quotations among non-price-cutting major-company dealers is typical of the market area.

The retail prices of subsidiary-company dealers show somewhat the same relationship as that prevailing among the major-company dealers, although prices are, perhaps, a little less uniform. The table on the next page shows representative prices[4] for the subsidiary-company dealers in this market during early 1950—just before the general price break.

---

[1] Based on quotations found in Westwood Village, Los Angeles, and supplemented by observations in other parts of the market as a check.

[2] Since Standard Oil of California ceased posting its retail prices in the Western market in November, 1948, there is not as much uniformity among prices of individual dealers selling major-company products. However, as one aggressive independent distributor said, "Standard Oil still posts its prices in its company-operated outlets [Standard Stations, Inc.] hence other firms may follow Standard Oil prices as before."

[3] A company might charge a higher price for premium-grade gasoline than its competitors, but offer its regular-grade product at a lower-than-average price.

[4] Based on observations in the Pico-Robertson and Westwood Village sections of the Los Angeles market, supplemented by prices in other areas as a check.

Company	Cents per gallon	
	Regular grade	Premium grade
Petrol Corporation[5]	—	—
Rio Grande Oil Company	24.5	27.0
Seaside Oil Company	24.1	26.1
Signal Oil Company	24.0	26.6

These figures show that the prices of gasoline at non-price-cutting subsidiary-company stations in this area closely approximated those found in non-price-cutting major-company stations, although there is a little more variation among the offerings of the subsidiaries.

While there has been a high degree of uniformity in the pump prices of major-company and subsidiary-company dealers in this market, two types of variations may exist, which are not revealed in the figures given above:

1. "Secret" ("under the canopy") concessions to favored patrons. There is no question that pump prices are not always firm, even where the service station is ostensibly offering its product at the market price without advertising any discount. Reports indicate that discounts to favored customers were common in the trade during the period under study; that is, selective price cutting was practiced by those who were ostensibly not price cutters.[6] This checks with common experience in this market. The authors believe that, generally speaking, if a motorist in the Los Angeles market had cared to shop around a bit at the time under consideration, he would have been able to obtain discounts from the posted price of those ostensibly selling at market price in the majority of non-company-operated stations,[7] majors as well as independents, in most if not all neighborhoods.

2. Open price cutting by major-company dealers. At the time this phase of the survey was made, a substantial and increasing percentage of the stations selling Shell, Tide Water Associated, and Texas Com-

---

[5] Petrol stations no longer exist. The corporation became a Standard Oil Company subsidiary in January, 1948. Subsequently, its stations were converted into either Signal Oil Company outlets (also a subsidiary of Standard Oil) or Chevron outlets (Standard Oil dealer stations).

[6] Most companies evidently have "winked" at the practice over the years.

[7] Typically, price "chiseling" is not practiced by company-operated stations.

pany products publicly offered some sort of discount from the prevailing price in the market. Unquestionably some of the major companies became increasingly tolerant of price cutting by their dealers (and of displaying promotional price signs)[8] during the two-year period 1948–1949. As was mentioned in an earlier chapter, Standard Oil, Union, General Petroleum, and to a large extent Richfield outlets adhered (at least publicly) to the prevailing price level. Price cutting by major-company dealers, where it existed, was moderate, however; it seldom amounted to purported discounts of more than 3 cents and actual discounts in excess of 2½ cents.

As might be expected, most independent-company dealers offered gasoline at prices considerably below those of most major-company dealers, although as mentioned there was a discrepancy between savings advertised and those actually realized.[9] Such discounts amounted to from 2 to 3 cents, perhaps more, in late 1949.

It is interesting to note that some independent companies (Douglas and Sunset for example), which for a time seemed to be attempting to hold the line on prices, began to offer a second brand at a considerable discount,[10] evidently to avoid "spoiling the market"

---

[8] This is probably due to a combination of circumstances: (1) caution induced by Department of Justice action against Standard Oil and Richfield in connection with exclusive agreements with dealers, (2) the increasing intensity of competitive conditions, and (3) the cessation of the posting of retail prices by the market leader, Standard Oil of California.

[9] There is no question that promotional price signs exaggerated savings—and this applies to major-company outlets as well as independent-company outlets. Generally speaking:

1. The price signs which publicized the specific prices of the gasoline were accurate.

2. On the other hand, the signs which advertised the amount of the discounts only (e.g., 5 cents off) usually were inaccurate in some particular.

3. Such inaccuracies were due (a) to the higher-than-market posted price on which the discount was based or (b) to the fact that the discount mentioned did not apply to all grades of gasoline.

4. A spot check of 16 stations displaying signs was taken on November 26, 1948. The same stations were rechecked on July 5, 1949, before amendment of the legislation. (See chap. ix, p. 125, n. 15.) The results indicated that signs had become more, rather than less accurate during the period.

This does not mean, however, that all misleading signs have disappeared. Some of the price signs found lately are amusing but nonetheless dishonest. Two examples will suffice: (1) One promotional sign observed in the Pasadena area features a giant figure "6" with the word "pumps" appearing in very small letters just below the figure. (2) Another observed in Pasadena, had the usual "Save 5" but with the word "minutes" printed in small letters where the "cents" mark was formerly found.

[10] At times gasoline sold under the primary and secondary brand is reportedly identical (e.g., Sunset and Air King; Harbor and Bonded or 5 Star); in at least one case, the premium-grade gasoline sold under primary and secondary brands, reportedly, is differ-

for their principal brand.[11] One wonders whether the principal brand enjoyed sufficient goodwill to justify the measure.

Aggressive price competitors provide the most vigorous competition in the Los Angeles market. As can be seen from the figures in table 19 these competitors offered actual discounts from the retail prices posted in Standard Stations, Inc.[12] ranging from 1 cent to 5.7 cents for premium grade and from 1 to 4.2 cents for regular-grade gasoline.[13] Discounts by aggressive price competitors, which averaged approximately 2 cents a year following the war, increased to close to 4 cents[14] by late 1949 (at least for premium-grade gaso-

ent but the regular-quality gasoline is the same under both brands. In one instance where the gasoline sold under the two different brands is the same, the dealers pay more for the product sold under the primary brand than for that sold under the secondary brand. In this case, incidentally, the truck driver is charged with the responsibility of seeing that the product is run into the proper tank so that the product purchased by the station operator at the lower price to be sold under the secondary brand, is not actually sold under the primary brand.

[11] There are three courses that may be taken in the sale of the secondary brand. 1. Retain the name of the company on the station but distribute only the secondary brand, on which the price is cut—one station was observed which carried a banner reading "Wilshire Products" but whose pumps dispensed *Radio* (secondary) brand only. 2. Offer both brands and maintain a price differential between the two—in one Sunset station displaying a "Save 5 cents cash" sign, *Air King* (secondary brand) was offered at 22.9 cents, while *Sunset Ethyl* and *Sunset De Luxe* were sold at 27.0 and 24.5 cents. 3. Offer both brands and maintain a differential at one quality level but not at the other—one Hancock station offered *Trojan* (a secondary brand) at 20.9 cents and 22.9 cents for regular grade and premium grade, while *Hancock* gasoline was offered at 20.9 cents for regular grade and 25 cents for premium grade.

[12] Table 19 is based on Standard Oil retail prices which were slightly lower than those of some of the other major companies, hence may provide a higher standard of accuracy than is justified. Moreover, for our purposes, a price sign purporting to provide savings to consumers is assumed to apply to *all* grades of gasoline unless a statement to the contrary is made, for example, "5¢ off on Ethyl."

[13] Much of the gasoline, though sold under independent-supplier or private (distributor) labels, originates from major-company refineries as was indicated earlier (chap. ix, p. 121, table 14). The result is that gasoline originally from the same refinery may be offered under different brands in stations in close proximity to one another, at greatly different prices. Thus, for a long time Golden Eagle stations were selling Standard Oil gasoline for as much as 4 cents below Standard Oil dealer prices.

[14] The savings given in table 19 average 4.1 cents for premium-grade and 3.3 cents for regular-grade gasoline.

Eagle Oil & Refining Company evidently has been attempting to reverse this trend toward deeper price cutting. In a large advertisement appearing in the *Los Angeles Times* on May 22, 1949, it was indicated that *Golden Eagle Radar* gasoline (treated with thermo-lube) was available from Golden Eagle stations at a saving of "up to 5¢ a gallon." This suggests that retailers had *carte blanche* in pricing matters, which is substantiated by reports to us by company officials made about that time.

However, in an advertisement in the *Los Angeles Times* of December 14, 1949, *Golden Eagle Radar Ethyl* was advertised at 23.9 cents per gallon and *Golden Eagle*

TABLE 19

DISCOUNTS OFFERED BY REPRESENTATIVE AGGRESSIVE PRICE COMPETITORS IN THE LOS ANGELES RETAIL GASOLINE MARKET, LATE FALL, 1949

	Brand of gasoline	Single unit or chain	Premium — Advertised saving	Premium — Saving from S.O. price	Regular — Advertised saving	Regular — Saving from S.O. price	Other — Advertised saving	Other — Saving from S.O. price	Form of discount — Cash	Form of discount — Other
Aggressive Retailers:										
Consumer's Coöperative[a]	HyGrade Special	Single	—	4.7	—	4.2	—	—	X	
Craig Oil Company	Craig	Chain	—	3.7	—	2.7	—	—	X	Coupon
Foster Oil Company	Community	Chain	5.0	4.7	5.0	3.2	5.0	4.7	X	
Gilmore Self-Serve	Olympic	Single[b]	5.0	5.0	5.0	4.2	—	—	X	
Hane Bros.	Magnum	Chain	6.0	5.0	6.0	4.2	—	—	X	
Hutton's Shell Service	Shell	Single	—	2.7	—	2.5	—	—	X	
Mark Bloome	Golden Eagle Mark Bloome Macmillan	Chain	—	3.7	—	4.2	—	—	X	
Muller Bros.	Flying A	Single	—	1.0	—	1.0	—	—		Coupon
Parks Service Stations	Parks	Chain	—	1.7	—	0.2	—	—		Coupon
Rothschild Service Stations	Poverine Save 6	Chain	6.0	5.0	6.0	3.5	—	5.6	X	
Sears, Roebuck & Company	Allstate	Chain	—	3.0	6.0	2.5	—	—	X	
Tide Oil Company	Tide	Chain[c]	6.0	5.7	6.0	4.2	—	—	X	
Urich's Self-Serve	Ben Hur	Chain	5.0	4.6	5.0	4.2	—	5.1	X	
Victory Petroleum Company	Military, Victory	Chain	7.0	5.7	7.0	4.2	—	—	X	
Supplier-Brand Promoters:										
Eagle Oil & Refining Company	Golden Eagle	—	5.0 Average	5.4	5.0 Average	4.3	—	—	X	
Olympic Refining Company	Olympic	—	5.0 Average	5.4	5.0 Average	4.3	—	—	X	
Rothschild Oil Company	Poverine	—	5.0 Average	5.4	5.0 Average	4.3	—	—	X	

a No longer in business.
b Gilmore Oil Company also operated a semi-serve unit at the time of this survey.
c Hane Bros. self-serve station.
Source: Field survey by the authors.

line). As shown in table 19 purported savings by station operators were as high as 7 cents,[15] with a mode of 5 cents.

Several interesting aspects of price cutting in the Los Angeles retail market prior to the price break of late January, 1950, deserve special mention.

1. As was said, the most commonly advertised discount in the Los Angeles market was 5 cents. The preponderance of "Save 5¢" signs suggests some special significance in the use of this particular figure for promotional purposes. Field investigation disclosed that the selection of 5 cents was not mere happenstance but rather the result of a rational choice. Interviews with leaders among aggressive vendors revealed a feeling that psychological and economic reasons were underlying factors in the use of this figure.[16]

2. The behavior of competitors of price cutters seemed to differ materially in different submarkets. One explanation of this is that cross elasticity differs in various locations within the metropolitan market. As may be recalled (chapter ix, footnote 48, above), the impact on competitive outlets of the price cutting of the large 24-

---

Super Premium (regular grade) at 21.9 cents, which represented savings of only 2.7 cents and 2.2 cents under Standard Stations' prices in this market. This suggests two things: The company decided to (1) try operating under a moderate, in place of a drastic, discount policy, and (2) attempt to maintain the retail price (which runs counter to their previous policy and which they may find difficult to effect under these circumstances).

[15] Signs advertising as much as "9 cents off" have been observed in this area. One station with such a sign—an eight-pump unit of a small independent chain which reportedly is supplied by one of the major oil companies—offered regular-grade gasoline under a private brand for 18.9 cents and the premium-grade for 19.9 cents. The actual savings, while substantial, were somewhat less; based on Standard Stations' prices of that date, this vendor's prices actually provided savings of 5.2 and 6.7 cents for regular-grade and premium-grade gasoline.

[16] The question whether there is any particular significance to the nickel discount was asked several of the leaders in the field. The answers may be classified as follows: (1) Originally self-serves had to price the product attractively enough to give the distinct impression of a real saving. Five cents seemed to be enough below the price of the majors to be attractive and yet sufficiently higher than invoice cost to provide an adequate realized margin. (2) Five cents has a psychological advantage—it is a unit of exchange and not "just pennies"; moreover, five cents is a round figure, easily computed and thus more practicable than four cents or six cents. (3) The 5-cent discount is close enough to the dealer margin of the conventional station to preclude the meeting of such a cut by such stations. (4) The "5¢ off" has become almost standard as the advertised reduction. Thus, one man when questioned as to why he chose a 5-cent discount rather than some other replied: "I have to give what the rest give to stay in business." Another said: "Everyone else gives 5 cents." Still another stated: "Because it is the customary discount given by self-serve operators."

pump cut-rate Craig station on Wilshire Boulevard was relatively
slight. No open price cutting was observed for a long period after
the establishment of the Craig stations.[17] On the other hand, competitors in the immediate vicinity of the large Hane Bros. superstation
on Olympic Boulevard (which was operating on a "6¢ off" basis)
had adjusted their prices to those posted by this aggressive competitor.[18] Differences in competitive behavior in these two instances
may be due to (1) the impact of the efforts of aggressive vendors
on the competing sellers[19] and (2) the amount of aggressiveness of
those so affected and the influence of the supplier-company policies
on their thinking.

3. Self-serve stations were by no means the only price cutters in
this market, although with few exceptions their cuts were the
deepest. The deep price cuts of the self-serve stations seem to have
resulted from unusually efficient operation with the savings being
passed on, at least in part. But what is even more striking, the
smallness of the price differentials between mass distributors providing service and self-service operations, suggests that cost differences

---

[17] There is a strong tendency for stations to meet (or move in the direction of meeting) prices of aggressive competitors, if only to satisfy customers who claim they
can do better elsewhere. This probably results in at least "secret" price concessions.
(See chap. x, p. 144, n. 2.)

[18] Including dealers distributing major-company products (Texas Company and
Tide Water Associated), although most stations found it unnecessary actually to *meet*
Hane Bros. prices, particularly the major-company dealers. On the other hand, one
independent station advertising a 7-cent discount, while the same as Hane on regular
grade, actually was 0.7 cents below Hane on premium grade. The prices of Hane
Bros. and their immediate competitors just before the major-company price break
were as follows:

Station	Premium grade	Regular grade
	(in cents)	(in cents)
Hane Bros.	21.6	19.9
Lightning	20.9	19.9
Lees'	22.9	21.6
Tide Water Associated	23.6	21.6
Texas Company	24.0	21.5

[19] This may be very different in various areas, because of differences in the amount
of transient custom available and in the expansion of the market contiguous to the
trading area in which the stations are located, as well as differences in the location of
competitor stations (on the same side or on the opposite side of the street).

are not as great as one might suppose.[20] That is, stations giving full service seem to be able to compete almost as effectively, if not as effectively as self-serve stations.[21]

Price Structure in Mid-1950. Conditions changed drastically from the time this study was started, when little open price cutting was in evidence in the Los Angeles market (and *none* in the major-company stations), to mid-1950 when price cutting—from the prevailing level of January, 1950—had become almost universal, and promotional price signs were displayed by most sellers. This trend toward a break in the price structure of major-company dealers resulted from (1) an extremely wide gap between the prices of major-company dealers and aggressive price competitors,[22] and (2) the piecemeal cutting by individual major-company dealers (especially those selling Shell, Associated, and Texaco products), which undoubtedly was due, in large part, to the aggressive price-competitive efforts of the mass vendors.

By mid-1949 the trend toward open warfare[23] in the Los Angeles market area was unmistakable. This result would appear to have been almost inevitable, in view of the increasing demand elasticity[24]

---

[20] One man operating a self-serve as well as service outlets (but under a different company name) offered his product in the superservice station at 19.9 for regular grade and 21.6 cents for premium grade and at the self-serve station for 18.9 and 20.9 cents, while advertising gasoline at a 6-cent saving in both types of establishments!

[21] The self-serve aspect of motor-fuel retailing seems to be a much less important cost factor than the self-serve phase of other pursuits, such as grocery retailing. Indeed, one doubts whether a supermarket could actually be operated on a service basis. For one thing, assembling each consumer's order is a time-consuming task if performed in the tradition of service establishments where the consumer gives his order orally to a clerk, one item at a time. For another, the concentration of customers at a counter, being served and waiting to be served, would require considerably more space than is needed in self-serve operations where patrons distribute themselves throughout the establishment in such a manner as to avoid concentration at any one point. One has only to experience the difficulty of being served in a meat department of a large market to appreciate the difficulties. Even here the difficulties are not as great as they might be, because customers may shop for themselves in other departments if congestion becomes too great at the meat counter, and, in any case, the assembly problem is relatively simple. It should be noted that both of the foregoing arguments are vitiated to some extent when applied to establishments operating on a telephone-order basis because of the possibility of filling customer orders systematically.

[22] This was possibly the widest gap between independent- and major-company dealer prices that ever existed in this market.

[23] In the sense of general reductions in major-company prices in the direction of meeting those of independent companies.

[24] This refers to the increasing elasticity of demand for the product of the individual firm (see chap. iii, p. 23). That is, price cutting by one firm will bring a greater response

which can be expected as an economy proceeds from the war and postwar free-spending stage into the more rational consumer behavior of recessed business conditions.[25]

As mentioned earlier, a serious break occurred in retail gasoline prices in the Los Angeles market in late January, 1950, when Standard Stations, Inc. finally succumbed to market pressure and reduced its retail quotations in "critical areas." This reduction was followed by Standard's Chevron outlets and by dealers of General Petroleum (in their Mobilgas outlets), Union Oil Company, and Richfield. Prices were also reduced by dealers of Shell, Associated, and Texas Company, many of whom had started to cut earlier. The ownership and operation of a considerable number of service stations by Standard Oil Company (Standard Stations, Inc.) provides the company with a certain degree of control over retail prices, although this control is likely to be more effective in decreasing prices than in raising them. The reduction in retail prices in early 1950 amounted to about 2 cents on regular-grade and 2½ cents on premium-grade gasoline.

By mid-1950 the prevailing price for gasoline in major-company stations in the Los Angeles market had stabilized[26] at about 22 cents for regular grade and about 24 cents for premium grade. Variations

---

in terms of amount taken when business conditions are relatively inactive than when they are active, hence, vendors will make increasing use of price cutting.

[25] Two factors, however, which operated in the direction of offsetting this tendency toward open price war should be mentioned at this point:

1. There has been, and continues to be, a substantial expansion of the Los Angeles market, which has the tendency of reducing the need for retaliatory action on the part of major companies despite inroads by independent distributors.

2. A large part of the gasoline sold in this market is supplied by major companies; to the extent that this is true, the volume of sales by major companies—unitwise, at least—would not be affected by the successful competitive efforts of independent companies; hence there would be less incentive to retaliate.

In the opinion of the authors, however, open warfare could not be avoided. For one thing, not all major companies are likely to be sharing equally in the increasing business of the independent companies as suppliers. A company which does not have any subsidiary outlet, or means of selling the product under a second label, or which does not sell for rebrand purposes, is hit harder by the loss of business to the aggressive price competitor than one which possesses such facilities or makes such arrangements. For another, major-company *dealers* derive no advantage at all from the gains made by the independent companies. Indeed, to the extent that independent companies gain volume at the expense of major-company dealers, the latter lose that much business, although, of course, the impact *may* differ greatly among major-company dealers.

[26] Reductions at first varied to some extent among companies and dealers; moreover, the discounts of dealers who had cut previously varied among themselves and were often not in line with the more recent cuts.

from these prices were for the most part fractional; some major-company dealers priced the two grades at 22.1 and 24.1 cents, and others posted prices of 21.9 and 23.9 cents.[27] One exception to this prevailing price of approximately 22–24 cents was found in Union stations where premium-quality (7600) sold for 1 cent higher than market;[28] thus the usual price of gasoline in Union outlets was 22.1 and 25.1 cents for regular-grade and premium-grade gasoline.[29]

In addition to the Union stations a few Shell, Associated, and Texas Company stations were varying from the norm; there was little evidence of such variations on the part of stations selling General Petroleum, Richfield, Standard Oil, and Union Oil products. Unlike the deviation of Union stations, most of these variations constitute reductions below the prevailing price. They typically amounted to 1 cent,[30] although occasionally to 2 cents. These larger cuts are

[27] According to the local reporter for the *National Petroleum News* (June 21, 1950, p. 13): "Many stations have stabilized their prices at 21.9¢ per gallon for regular and 23.9¢ for premium instead of the 22.1 and 24.1¢ which predominated for a long time. That variation was prompted by an obvious psychological motive. A drop of 0.2¢ per gal. made the gasoline look a penny a gallon cheaper."

[28] According to an official of the company, this policy has been quite successful. In fact, our informant stated that the company's sales of premium-grade gasoline have increased relatively more than the total sales of this grade of gasoline on the Pacific Coast. It is his opinion that this policy is consistent with the company's established policy of promoting the quality aspects of its service and product by means of appeals to the higher income market; in other words, the company is endeavoring to attract the type of consumer who does not mind paying an extra cent for a "quality" product. According to one informant, an additional factor making for the company's success in promoting its premium-grade gasoline is the fact that a larger-than-average proportion of Union customers drive cars requiring higher-octane gasoline, namely, Oldsmobiles and Cadillacs.

In a conversation with one of the authors a Cadillac owner stated: "I have to chase around looking for a Union Oil Company station in order to get 7600 every time I want to buy gasoline." The point here is, of course, that this consumer thinks he has to purchase Union 7600 because he believes it is the highest octane gasoline in the market and the only one that will satisfy the requirements of his Cadillac.

[29] One Union Oil Company dealer on Sunset Boulevard in Hollywood, was selling regular-grade gasoline at 23.6 cents and premium-grade at 26.6 cents in July, 1950. He stated that although his competitors were selling gasoline at prices nearer to 22 and 24 cents for corresponding grades, he had noticed little change in the amount of business done by his station. He attributed his ability to maintain volume in spite of charging higher-than-prevailing prices to Union's policy of catering to the higher income groups. In fact this dealer said that over half of his customers were owners of the more expensive automobiles, such as Buicks and Cadillacs, and that these people were not particularly price conscious; he admitted, however, that occasionally one of his patrons complained about his prices.

[30] An Associated station on San Vicente Boulevard was offering gasoline at 1 cent below the prices charged by other major-company dealers in the neighborhood. The owner of this station also owned a Shell Oil Company outlet one block away. He oper-

most likely to appear in highly competitive sections of the market.[31] Thus, there was in mid-1950 evidence of further softening of the market, with a slowly increasing number of reductions from the recently established retail price level (22 and 24 cents). Most stations in the area, including most major-company dealers, were displaying price signs in July, 1950.[32]

Dealers retailing products of subsidiary companies—Rio Grande, Seaside, and Signal—as usual, offered gasoline at essentially the same prices as those at which major-company products were sold.[33]

---

ated the Associated station with just one attendant, and thus was limited in the amount of service he was able to give. When he took over the Associated station (formerly a Signal Oil Company outlet), it had been closed for two months and was in a run-down condition. He said that the 1 cent cut in price was in part a compensation for the limited service given at the station and in part a device for building business. He felt that if he could succeed in pumping sufficient gasoline to pay expenses, other income from the station would provide the profit. He reported that he broke even the month previous to the interview (June, 1950).

[31] According to the local reporter for the *National Petroleum News* (June 21, 1950, p. 13), the competition became so intense in one section of the Los Angeles market area (Victory Boulevard) that a Shell Oil Company conventional-type outlet, located in the midst of a cluster of self-serve stations, reduced its price for regular-grade gasoline to 19.9 cents—2 cents under prevailing prices. Reportedly, this was the lowest quotation on a major-company brand found to be advertised in this area at the time. Latterly, this low price spread to other sections of the market.

[32] An executive of one of the major oil concerns operating in this area stated that one definite evidence of a price war is the posting of promotional price signs on station premises. According to him, price signs are tangible evidence of intensive price competition; indeed, where there are no price signs there is no price war.

Union Oil Company stations, both company-owned and dealer-owned, do not display price signs as a general rule. One of the company officials explained that in the beginning of the present price war, when other major-company stations began to cut prices and put up price signs, Union stations were hurt by a loss of business. He said the company then advised station operators to display signs so that the public would be informed that Union was selling on a competitive basis with other major companies. (Incidentally, most of Union Oil Company's signs advertised the regular-grade gasoline only; Union's premium-grade product was a cent higher than the market price.) Very shortly thereafter, according to this official, the company suggested that the signs be removed. The reason was that Union was not going to try to compete on a level with the price cutters, and that by continuing to display price signs the public would feel that the company was selling on a price basis but could not sell as low as its competitors. Most of the stations representing Union Oil Company did not display signs at the time of writing (July, 1950), and the company was continuing to place emphasis on the quality of product and service.

[33] The authors came across a Rio Grande station, near Santa Monica, which had continued to sell this relatively little-known brand of gasoline at prices that prevailed among major-company stations before January, 1950, when the major-company price structure collapsed. The owner of the station holds the master lease on the station property and has been in the same location for almost twenty years. He has made it a practice to open the station early in the morning and has, over the years, built up a clientele which knows that it can depend on this early morning service. This operator

That is, typically, subsidiary-company dealers in the market as of July, 1950, offered regular-grade gasoline at about 22 cents and premium-grade at about 24 cents. While fractional variations from these figures prevailed, very few substantial differences obtained in this market. Thus, the somewhat questionable policy of subsidiary companies following the lead of major companies in pricing their products seems to be fairly well established in the area under consideration.[34]

The majority of conventional independent stations were selling gasoline in the mid-1950 market at around 20 cents for regular grade and 22 cents for premium grade. Actual quotations varied fractionally, as in the major-company stations, at one-tenth above or below these figures, i.e., 19.9 or 20.1 cents for regular grade and 21.9 or 22.1 cents for premium grade. However, prices of the independent companies varied much more than those of the major companies. A considerable number of independent firms (e.g., Golden Eagle dealers) were selling regular-grade gasoline for 20.9 or 21.9 cents, and an even larger number raised the price of premium grade to 22 or 23 cents, while some were even selling both grades at the same price[35] as major companies.[36] However, some dealers seem to have reversed this trend recently. While the differential between major- and independent-company dealers on regular-grade was fairly well

---

stated that his gallonage ran from 12,000 to 14,000 a month, and that while his business did slightly fall off early in 1950, when the major-company price structure gave way, by July he was doing as well as in the corresponding months of past years.

[34] The policy is questionable on two grounds: (1) subsidiary-company brands are much less well-known than major-company brands, hence cannot command a comparable price from a substantial segment of the market, and (2) the possibilities of using subsidiary-company brands to acquire custom from the price-conscious segment of the market seem to be too good an opportunity to miss.

[35] The president of the Eagle Oil & Refining Company pleaded with his dealers, through paid advertisements in trade papers, to cease price-cutting and concentrate on "merchandising." (*Automotive Dealer News*, March 20, 1950, p. 3.)

[36] One Wilshire Oil Company station, located in West Los Angeles, in June, 1950, was offering gasoline at prices which prevailed before the price war. The operator of the station admitted that his volume of business had fallen off but stated that his supplier company would not allow him to cut price on its principal brand. He added, if he decided to sell one of the company's "secondary" brands at cut prices, he would have to stand the full amount of the loss in margin, since the tankwagon prices for both the principal and secondary brands were the same. One wonders whether his statement concerning absence of subsidization by Wilshire was correct and whether he may not have been rationalizing his position. In any case, he reported that even though he was losing volume on sales of gasoline, his repair business was enabling him to keep the station open.

established at 2 cents, the differential on the premium-grade was not nearly as well defined—amounting probably nearer to 1½ cents on the average.

It is interesting to note that the independent-company dealers were using promotional price signs more freely on regular grade at a low price, and were maintaining a higher price, compared to the major-company stations, on premium quality. This was a reversal in tactics in the use of price signs from the promotional plan of some months before. At that time, the usual sign read "Save 5 cents"; the reference was almost invariably to the saving, or the purported saving, on premium grade which was almost always larger than on regular grade.[37]

Table 20 shows differences, if any, in the retail prices of the representative aggressive price competitors between October, 1949, and June, 1950. Generally speaking, the aggressive price competitors reduced prices only slightly following the reduction in the major-company retailer price level in January, 1950. With the exception of Muller Bros. (whose reduction may have been a reflection of the major-company reduction)[38] and Victory Petroleum Company (whose reduction was more difficult to explain),[39] few of the cuts amounted to more than 1 cent; some of the reductions were much less and some prices even increased.

Major-company dealers cut 2 to 2½ cents from the prices prevailing before January, 1950, but the aggressive price competitors generally reduced their prices only one cent or less; consequently the differential between the prices of major-company dealers and mass distributors was reduced from about 4 cents to nearer 2–2½ cents, with possibly a little greater differential for some of the self-serve stations.[40] This differential is very close to what is considered

[37] As a result of the activity of governmental authorities against misleading price signs (see chap. ix, p. 126, n. 16), retail vendors tended to switch to the posting of actual prices rather than purported savings. It follows then that they would want to publicize their lowest quotation—the price of the regular-grade rather than the premium-grade product.

[38] Muller Bros. distribute Tide Water Associated products.

[39] The cost of regular grade, which was offered at 16.9 cents by Victory stations, was an estimated 16 cents in truck-and-trailer lots "at the rack," and more if purchased in smaller quantities, delivered.

[40] The usual price in self-serve stations was 18.9 cents on regular-grade and close to 20.9 cents on premium-grade gasoline, although here again there was a tendency, as in the independent companies, to keep the premium-grade price relatively higher.

normal between major-company and independent-company gasoline.[41] The narrowing of the differential lends support to the statements of major-company executives that they have been able to recover the gallonage that was lost to other types of competitors.

TABLE 20

GASOLINE PRICES OF REPRESENTATIVE AGGRESSIVE PRICE COMPETITORS IN THE
LOS ANGELES RETAIL GASOLINE MARKET, OCTOBER, 1949 AND JUNE, 1950

	Premium grade		Regular grade		Form of discount	
Aggressive Competitors	Oct., 1949	June, 1950	Oct., 1949	June, 1950	Cash	Other
Consumer's Coöperative...	21.9	(ᵃ)	19.9	(ᵃ)	X	
Craig Oil Company.......	22.9	22.1	21.4	20.1		Coupon
Foster Oil Company......	21.9	23.9	20.9	21.9	X	
Gilmore Self-Serve........	21.6	20.6	19.9	18.9	X	
Hane Bros..............	21.6	20.9	19.9	18.9	X	
Hutton's Shell Service....	23.9	23.9	21.6	21.6	X	
Mark Bloome...........	22.9	21.9	19.9	18.9	X	
Muller Bros.............	25.6	22.0	23.1	20.0		Coupon
Parks Service Stations....	24.9	23.9	23.9	22.9		Coupon
Rothschild Service Stations	21.6	22.0	20.6	21.6	X	
Sears, Roebuck & Company	23.6	22.1	21.6	20.1	X	
Tide Oil Company........	20.9	19.9	18.9	18.5	X	
Urich's Self-Serve........	22.0	20.9	19.9	18.9	X	
Victory Petroleum Company............	20.9	20.9	19.9	16.9	X	

ᵃ No longer in business.
Source: Field survey by the authors.

An existing differential between major-company dealers and aggressive price competitors is no indication of the importance of this latter type as a competitive factor in this market. Actually, the much wider differential that existed earlier (as a result of the deepcutting tactics of the aggressive price competitors) forced major-company dealers to cut prices, and thus reduced the differential.

As mentioned earlier, no prediction can be made at this time with respect to further cuts by various types of competitors. The further

It was not unusual to see 18.9 cents for regular grade and 21.9 cents for premium grade; however, most self-serve outlets were selling premium grade for 20.9 cents.

The local reporter for the *National Petroleum News* (July 5, 1950, p. 15) said: "Often the self-serves barely shade the posted price of conventionals. There is one anomaly of a self-serve proprietor holding to his established price of 19.9 cents while two neighboring conventionals advertise their gasoline at 18.9 cents. Motorists in that area pay a premium of a penny a gallon for the privilege of serving themselves."

[41] The differential which does not make for a serious drawing off of volume one way or the other, usually about 2 cents.

cutting below the mid-1950 structure by a few sellers will tend to make for general cuts over a period of time, if such activities persist. What developments might take place to offset such an eventuality one cannot say. Whatever else might be said, state unfair-practice[42] and locality-discrimination[43] measures will probably be of little avail in controlling price cutting in this market.

Retail Prices of Gasoline at Different Quality Levels

For some years gasoline was offered in the Los Angeles area at three different quality levels—premium grade, regular grade, and third grade.[44] The third-grade product is no longer offered,[45] so

[42] The California Unfair Practices Act (*Bus. and Prof. Code of Calif.*, Secs. 17000 to 17101), which applies to all retail concerns and includes service station operations, proscribes selling at less than cost with the intent of injuring competitors. Cost within the meaning of the act includes invoice cost plus distribution expense; the latter may be determined by a cost survey in the absence of evidence of the particular vendor's expenses. Incidentally, the state of Michigan has a law similar to that of California except that it applies only to sales of bakery and petroleum products (covering both locality discrimination and less-than-cost selling).

One main difficulty here lies in the enforcement of such legislation. Strictly speaking, cost floor legislation is not likely to be violated in the selling of gasoline anyway, because even though a deep-price cutter is cutting his per-unit margin, by this very fact he may be greatly expanding sales, with the result that per-unit costs decline also. Moreover, gasoline is not likely to be used as a loss-leader for the selling of other items—lubricating services, wash jobs, and the like; the reverse is more probable—the offering of services at less-than-cost prices to induce gasoline patronage. Even here, however, few if any actual cases have occurred because the law applies to the sales of goods, and not services.

[43] As mentioned, the California locality-discrimination measure proscribes selling at lower prices in one section of a community or city or any portion thereof, or in one location therein, with the intent of destroying or preventing competition of any regularly established dealer of any article in general use or consumption (including gasoline). (*Bus. and Prof. Code of Calif.*, Secs. 17000 to 17101.) In most instances, however, gasoline is sold at a cut price not by a company-operated station, but by a dealer operating his own station; thus no discrimination is involved. Even where discrimination *is* involved, it is justified by "a meeting in good faith of the prices of competitors."

[44] As was noted (chap. v, p. 58, n. 9), third-grade gasoline was considerably lower in quality than regular-grade, at least on a basis of the antiknock rating. Thus, in November, 1934, third grade averaged 63.9 octane, with a range from 63 to 65, while regular grade averaged 70.75 octane, with a range of 69 to 71. (California Testing Laboratories, Inc., *Gasoline in Southern California 1934–1944* [Los Angeles], 1944.)

[45] As mentioned, third-quality gasoline was introduced by the major companies as a device for capturing a part of the business going to price-cutting independents and as a reflection on the quality of the independent product. The data in table 21 below indicate the differential between regular-grade and third-grade gasoline ranged from 4.6 cents for a brief period in 1933 to as little as 1 cent in 1935. The last of these quotations (just before the war in mid-1941) show a differential of 2 cents, which was the same as that between regular-grade and premium-grade gasoline at that time.

that gasoline is at present found in this market in only two qualities (although some vendors offer what they claim to be a super-quality product in addition to the premium grade).[46]

Generally speaking, regular-grade gasoline fulfills the requirements of most motor cars satisfactorily. The premium-grade product, commonly called *Ethyl*, is offered by a station (a) to supply the demands of those who are not satisfied with anything but the "best," and (b) to take care of the needs of those who must have high-test gasoline for the smooth operation of their high-compression motors. Sales of premium-grade gasoline are an estimated 60 per cent[47] of the total sales of gasoline made through service stations in this market.

Problem of Pricing Different Quality Offerings. The problem of pricing different quality products in a line by one seller—as in the sales of premium-grade and regular-grade gasoline—is exceedingly complex[48] because it involves cross elasticity among the products making up one's own offerings as well as possible shifts in consumer response to the offerings of various sellers. This problem is faced by meat vendors (pricing the various kinds and cuts in order to (1) derive enough revenue to cover all costs and (2) avoid surpluses in some and deficits in others). Somewhat the same problem is faced by impresarios in "scaling" a theater. The problem is complicated for some mass merchandisers, such as Sears, Roebuck, when one model of a line (e.g., of stoves or refrigerators) is used as a "leader" with dependence placed upon personal salesmanship to influence selection in favor of a higher-priced model instead of the one that was featured.

Injudicious price-setting of gasoline at different quality levels may result in (1) a larger sale of premium grade than regular grade or (2) a larger sale of regular grade than premium grade and (3) a net reduction in the amount taken of the product of the particular seller because the type of customer preferring the grade with the unfavorable price will tend to take his custom elsewhere. (This

---

[46] In one instance the "super" premium product contains an upper-cylinder lubricant called "thermo lube." Except for this, there is no detectable difference between this and other premium-grade products offered at retail at 1 cent less per gallon.

[47] See above, chap. v, p. 59.

[48] For an interesting discussion of the problem see Joel Dean's article "Problems of Product-Line Pricing" in the *Journal of Marketing*, January, 1950, pp. 518–528.

assumes that one of the offerings is competitive with those of rival firms, which may not even be true.)[49]

Offhand, one might think that sales of the high-octane motor fuel, instead of the regular-grade product, would be advantageous to the service station operator, because it produces more gross revenue, which aids in the absorption of expenses. This point of view would seem to be vitiated, however, if the increased revenue has to be turned over to the supplier company in payment for this higher-priced product. And, if more than the amount of the retail differential reverts to the supplier, it would seem that the seller would sustain a relative loss. But the concentration on sales of premium-grade gasoline (even at a price netting a per-unit reduction in revenue to the retailer) may yield enhanced volume, and hence gross margin, particularly for a price cutter, because of a possibly greater confidence of consumers in the quality of the product offered by the vendor. That is, the *Ethyl* designation may serve as a standard of quality for price cutters, hence enhance total sales of such outlets and, conceivably, increase net revenue. Of course if the higher-priced product yields a larger per-unit margin, increased sales may result in an even larger profit.

Regular-Grade and Premium-Grade Price Differentials. Because of the willingness of the motorist to pay more for high-octane motor fuel,[50] differential pricing on the basis of quality (which *may* be a form of price discrimination) provides opportunities for differential

---

[49] That is, the premium-grade (for example) may be much the better buy in one station due to the fact that the price of regular-grade gasoline is higher than the price of competitors. This, of course, tends toward a loss of customers of regular-grade gasoline.

[50] One official of a major petroleum firm in this area feels that there is a great deal of "elasticity" between the premium-grade and regular-grade product. Before World War II, when consumers were quite price conscious, statistics indicated that approximately 80 per cent of the gasoline sold by this particular company was regular grade and about 10 per cent premium grade; the remaining 10 per cent was third-grade. However, the situation was altered as the consumer found himself in the midst of more prosperous times, and the proportion shifted to 55 per cent premium grade and 45 per cent regular grade (the third-grade gasoline no longer being sold). This official also mentioned that the preference of consumers for this, in most cases, unnecessary luxury was an example of the lack of complete information on the part of the purchaser. He referred to his firm's then current advertising campaign which was directed at informing the consumer that the premium-grade product is not necessary to the successful performance of his automobile unless he owns one of the few models that require the higher octane rating (such as Cadillac, Oldsmobile "Rocket," Buick "Roadmaster").

gains at both the retail and refinery levels. The actual realization of differential gains depends upon judgments by vendors as to the value of the product to consumer-buyers, the offerings of competitors, and the reactions of consumers to the offerings of rivals.

The figures in table 21 show that the differential between the regular grade ("house brand" so called) and the premium grade has differed considerably over a period of time.[51] The differential in stations selling major-company products and not cutting price was typically 2½ cents just before the outbreak of the price war in Los Angeles. According to our sample of prices in major-company outlets, given above, this 2½-cents differential prevailed only in Standard Oil, General Petroleum, Texas Company, and Tide Water Associated outlets. The Union differential appears to have been somewhat wider than 2½ cents, while the differential in the outlets of other major companies was somewhat narrower. The differential between premium-grade and regular-grade gasoline in Los Angeles at major-company dealer outlets in July, 1950, was typically 2 cents; in Union Oil stations the differential was 3 cents.

The 2- to 2½-cents differential by no means prevailed in all service stations in the Los Angeles area. For one thing, price-cutting major-company dealers sometimes passed the slightly wider per-unit margin earned by the sale of premium-grade gasoline (½ cent) on to consumers, at least in part. For another, independent-supplier price differentials between regular-grade and premium-grade gasoline were often much less than those found in the major-company

---

[51] Before 1940 the price of Ethyl was influenced, if not actually maintained, by the Ethyl Corporation. That is, until about ten years ago sales of ethyl fluid were restricted by the sole producer at the time, Ethyl Corporation, through a system of licensing agreements with gasoline manufacturers and jobbers. By the terms of these agreements, territories were allotted and refiners were permitted to sell treated gasoline only to such jobbers who were licensed by the Ethyl Corporation. Moreover, such jobbers had to maintain the proper price differential in order to be considered as "ethical" and thus to procure supplies of gasoline from the refiner. The court decided in *Ethyl Corporation, et al.* v. *United States*, 309 U. S. 436 (1940), that while the company holding the patent may refuse to sell to dealers who do not maintain prices, it may not by means of agreements with gasoline refiners control the price of the product in the traffic beyond the buyer. Purchasers of ethyl fluid, therefore, were freed from restriction in the pricing of the premium-grade product. Interestingly enough, Ethyl Corporation would not have been able to avail itself of fair trade contracts either, because fair trade laws require that the product so controlled be in "free and open competition,"—but Ethyl Corporation was the only seller of the antiknock compound at that time.

TABLE 21

PRICE DIFFERENTIALS BETWEEN PREMIUM- AND REGULAR-GRADE, AND REGULAR-
AND THIRD-GRADE, GASOLINE ON A BASIS OF POSTED PRICES IN
LOS ANGELES, 1932–1949
(On certain dates for which data are available)

Date	Premium-regular grade	Regular-third grade	Date	Premium-regular grade	Regular-third grade
Apr. 9, 1932	3.0	3.0	Mar. 6, 1934	2.0	2.5
June 27, 1932	3.0	4.0	May 23, 1934	2.0	2.5
Jan. 16, 1933	3.0	(a)	June 26, 1934	2.0	2.0
Feb. 10, 1933	3.0	4.6	Aug. 31, 1934	2.0	2.0
May 9, 1933	2.0	3.6	Apr. 3, 1935	2.0	2.0
June 20, 1933	3.0	3.6	Apr. 13, 1935	2.0	2.0
June 26, 1933	3.0	3.6	June 5, 1935	2.0	2.0
Sept. 6, 1933	2.0	3.5	June 8, 1935	2.0	1.0
Oct. 14, 1933	2.5	2.0	July 1, 1935	2.0	1.0
Oct. 19, 1933	2.0	2.5	Sept. 25, 1935	2.0	1.0
Nov. 3, 1933	2.0	1.6	Oct. 19, 1935	2.0	1.0
Nov. 9, 1933	2.0	2.0	Nov. 27, 1935	2.0	2.0
Nov. 15, 1933	2.0	2.5	Apr. 2, 1936	2.0	1.5
Nov. 27, 1933	2.0	2.5	Mar. 23, 1937	2.0	2.5
Dec. 27, 1933	2.0	2.5	May 28, 1940	2.0	2.0
Feb. 21, 1934	2.0	2.5	May 24, 1941	2.0	2.0
Feb. 28, 1934	2.0	2.5	Nov. 18, 1948	2.0	(b)
Mar. 1, 1934	2.0	1.5	Nov. 22, 1949	2.5c	

a Price for third-grade gasoline not given.
b Third-grade product no longer sold in this market.
c From prices observed by the authors.
Source: Announcements of price changes published in the newspapers—*The Los Angeles Times* and the *Los Angeles Evening Herald & Express*—on or about the dates on which changes were indicated in the price data (for regular grade only) in the *Petroleum World Annual Review* 1949.

set-up, and this same differential often carried over into the retail price structure. The following table indicates the differentials between premium-grade and regular-grade gasoline which prevailed in 14 representative aggressive cut-rate stations in late 1949.

Station	Differential	Station	Differential
	(in cents)		(in cents)
Muller Bros.	2.5	Gilmore Self-serve	1.7
Hutton's Shell Service	2.3	Hane Bros.	1.7
Consumers' Coöperative	2.0	Craig Oil Company	1.5
Urich's Serve Yourself	2.0	Foster Oil Company	1.0
Sears, Roebuck & Company	2.0	Parks' Service Station	1.0
Tide Oil Company	2.0	Victory Petroleum Company	1.0
Mark Bloome	2.0	Rothschild Self-serve	1.0

This survey shows regular-grade–premium-grade price differentials ranging from a high of 2½ cents to a low of 1 cent. Thus, the price structure of major-company dealers as applied to regular-grade–premium-grade differentials is not typical of all pricing situations in this market. Large aggressive outlets offered high-octane gasoline at a premium of as little as 1 cent, with an average of perhaps 1½ cents.

As mentioned earlier, there may be opportunities for greater profits in the sale of premium-grade gasoline because of a wider margin available to those vending it. Such a gain might be earned at the retail level, at the supplier level, or at both levels, depending on the existence of a price-cost differential and where it is found.

Generally speaking, major-company dealers in the Los Angeles market enjoyed a ½ cent per-gallon advantage in the sale of premium-grade over regular-grade gasoline before the price break in 1950; that is, the retail price was 2½ cents higher than the regular-grade price while the tank-wagon price was only 2 cents higher. The situation of the large-scale independent operator was somewhat different. The premium-grade product was available in large lots from independent suppliers in this market at 1 cent[52] above the regular-grade price. Thus, some large-scale retail distributors—those selling premium-grade at more than an additional 1 cent—were deriving a per-gallon gain in the sale of premium-grade gasoline; some, however, were not attempting to exact any differential gain from the sale of premium-grade gasoline—those selling high-octane gasoline at a premium of only 1 cent.

It would appear that the gains made in the sale of premium-grade gasoline by supplier companies are often substantial, particularly in the case of major concerns. The major supplier receives 2 cents more for premium-grade than for regular-grade gasoline sold under

---

[52] The following were prices (including tax) supplied by one of the refining companies for gasoline sold in large lots to the mass distributors.

| | December, 1949 | | July, 1950 | |
	Premium grade	Regular grade	Premium grade	Regular grade
	(in cents)	(in cents)	(in cents)	(in cents)
At rack				
Major-refinery product............	18.00	17.00	17.00	16.00
Independent-refinery product.......	17.30	16.30	16.75	15.75
Delivered				
Major-refinery product............	18.25	17.25	17.25	16.25
Independent-refinery product.......	17.55	16.55	17.00	16.00

his own brand, and the premium grade contains on the average
0.77 cc. more of T.E.L. fluid than the regular grade, valued at 0.159
cents. It would seem from this that the bulk of the 2-cent refinery
differential (2.00 — 0.159 = 1.841 cents) could be retained as profit,
assuming, of course, that there is no additional cost in producing
the stock used for making higher-octane gasoline. Thus, the opportunities for gain in the major-company segment of the market seem
to be largely at the refinery level.[53] However, the price differential
between premium and regular grade charged by the independent
suppliers to those buying in large lots is typically only 1 cent a
gallon. Therefore, the price structure of the independent suppliers
(as applied to large-volume buyers at least) reveals a much smaller
opportunity for a differential gain in the sale of premium-grade
over regular-grade gasoline, although even here some opportunity
to obtain a per-unit advantage seems to exist.

   Where narrower price differentials prevail between regular-quality
and premium-quality gasoline, the consumer-buyer of premium grade

---

[53] The following table is a detailed presentation of the charges for tetraethyl lead
made by the Ethyl Corporation over a period of time.

Dates in force	Royalty charges[a]/ gallon and price of lead/cc.	Dates in force	Royalty charges/ gallon and price of lead/cc.
	(in cents)		(in cents)
1923–10/1/28...............	1.0 (lead)	7/1/33–1/1/34..............	0.24 (royalty)
10/1/28–8/15/29............	0.7 (royalty)		0.35 (lead)
	0.5 (lead)	1/1/34–12/1/34[b]..........	0.33 (lead)
8/15/29–1/1/30.............	0.6 (royalty)	12/1/34–11/1/35............	0.30 (lead)
	0.4 (lead)	11/1/35–7/1/36.............	0.28 (lead)
1/1/30–7/1/30..............	0.6 (royalty)	7/1/36–7/1/39.............	0.26 (lead)
	0.35 (lead)	7/1/39–5/15/40.............	0.25 (lead)
7/1/30–3/1/32..............	0.5 (royalty)	5/15/40–4/1/41.............	0.23 (lead)
	0.35 (lead)	4/1/41–4/1/42.............	0.20 (lead)
3/1/32–7/1/33..............	0.425 (royalty)	4/1/42–7/1/48.............	0.18 (lead)
	0.35 (lead)	7/1/48–10/16/48............	0.20 (lead)

   [a] There were no royalty charges before October 1, 1928, or after December 31, 1933.
   [b] During this period refiners started to put tetraethyl lead into regular-grade gasoline also.

   The cost of the ethyl fluid in October, 1949, was 0.2063 cents per cc. of T.E.L.
On the West Coast, a recent average of T.E.L. content per gallon of premium-grade
gasoline was 2.22 cc. (The maximum amount that may be used is 3 cc.) It is not
correct to use this figure in determining the differential cost of T.E.L. as between
regular-grade and premium-grade gasoline because T.E.L. is also used in regular-grade
gasoline. The average content of T.E.L. in regular-grade motor fuel is approximately
1.45 cc. Therefore, the differential cost, on the average, for premium-grade gasoline
on a basis of lead content only, assuming no difference in refining costs, is about
0.159 cents (2.22 — 1.45 × 0.2063 = 0.159).

enjoys an advantage, assuming, of course, that the price of the premium-grade product was reduced rather than the price of the regular-grade increased. It should be noted, however, that the consumer not requiring the higher-octane product but buying it because it is a bargain, pays more for his gasoline than he needs to. But it is admitted that he may derive more satisfaction from his purchase than he would if he bought the regular-grade product. Consumer education along these lines might result in maximum satisfaction at lowest cost.

XIV

SUMMARY AND CONCLUSIONS

This study has been an attempt to analyze the nature of rivalry in retail gasoline distribution in a relatively narrow market at close quarters. Two types of conclusions may be drawn: (1) Those which result from the findings themselves and (2) those which result from the method used in conducting the research.

A. It is felt by the authors that considerable light may have been thrown by this study on rivalry at the retail level—the importance of demand elasticity on gasoline vendors' policies; the differing behavior of vendors in varying market positions; the influence of suppliers' policies on the competitive activities of retail vendors; the variety of competitive tools available to gasoline vendors, including the use of new distributive techniques; the behavior of prices at different quality levels among geographical areas, over a period of time—to recall only a few highlights of the study.

The Department of Justice[1] to the contrary, there is little evidence of anything but vigorous competition in this market (with the possible exception of conservation activities in connection with crude supply and associational activities of retailers). There is no question about the existence of intense rivalry in the Los Angeles

---

[1] *Complaint, United States* v. *Standard Oil Co. of California, et al.,* Civil No. 11584-C, S.D. Cal., May 12, 1950, pp. 12–15.

gasoline market at the retail level, at least during the period under study. Sharp rivalry exists (1) between independent and major companies as groups, as well as (2) among individual dealers within each of the two groups.

The intensity of competition in the Los Angeles retail gasoline market has increased greatly over the two-and-one-half-year period of our study. This has resulted from a combination of factors which may be set forth as follows:

Demand for Gasoline:

1. Increasing responsiveness to the offerings of price cutters, because of a better market knowledge by the consumer and, with time passing, an opportunity to adjust his buying habits.

2. Increasing responsiveness as a result of growing consumer price consciousness, accompanying a change from favorable to less favorable business conditions.

Supply of Gasoline:

1. Increasing surplus of gasoline stocks which, while having little direct effect on major-company dealer prices, has an indirect effect through lowering prices of supplies sold through independent channels.

2. Increasing number of outlets of the aggressive price-competitor type striving for a share of the total gasoline volume in this market area.

A reversal of this trend toward increasing intensity of competition at the retail level could easily take place if the present (July, 1950) international conditions were to become more acute. In that event the listed tendencies would be vitiated and the "soft" market conditions would disappear.

Independent sellers of the mass-merchandising variety without question furnish the sharpest type of competition in the Los Angeles market; this is in contrast to the grocery field, where mass-merchandising chain concerns provide this aggressive type of rivalry. The deep-price cuts of the aggressive price competitors have been so successful in attracting patronage in the post war period that the normally conservative competitors have been forced to shift emphasis from other than price-competitive devices to the use of price as a major device for wooing custom. This fact, combined with an overbuilding of mass-distribution units (largely self-serve stations),[2] has intensified competition even further, until by July, 1950, all types of sellers were using every competitive device imaginable, including tying offers of every description,[3] two-for-one sales, premiums and cash prizes, product warranties, etc., to attract service station patronage. It is interesting that some of the aggressive vendors have countered the price cuts of major-company dealers with shifts in competitive emphasis from direct-price to the normally less sharp non-price and semi-price schemes.

While the importance of large-scale aggressive price competitors in this market should not be underestimated, it should not be overrated either. It is true that the new large-scale retail units offer perhaps the most vigorous type of competition, but any price-cutting independent provides an aggressive type of rivalry, which is bound to have a depressing effect on the retail price. Thus, even before the advent of the mass-selling outlet, price competition was vigorous in this area. This is evidenced by the existence of price wars in the 1920's and 1930's when mass-selling units did not exist.

In view of the inelastic nature of the demand for gasoline (the generic product), it would appear in theory to be advantageous for major-company vendors to operate under a high-price policy. This, of course, is difficult, if not impossible, to do with impunity while aggressive price competitors exist. It is interesting that a large part of the gasoline sold by aggressive price competitors orginates from major-company suppliers. This provides strong evidence of the existence of active competition among major companies; no one supplier can effectively shut off supplies from the aggressive sellers, since some of his competitors will sell them if he does not. Actually, one firm may have quite a different policy than another in this regard; moreover, one firm might have a much greater need for business than another at a particular time. This may result in competition by major suppliers for the business of the aggressive vendors. There are such cases in this market; for example, Eagle Oil &

---

[2] Keeping in mind that the market for privately branded self-serve products is limited to a relatively small segment of the total market.

[3] Such offers included low-price (and even free) washing, brake adjustment, and cigarettes at 15 cents a package with the purchase of gasoline. Indeed, one aggressive vendor in this market offered a package of cigarettes for 1 cent with the purchase of six gallons of gasoline.

Refining Company's contract with Standard Oil Company of California was no sooner concluded than other sources of supply were found by Eagle (including other major companies).

The question arises what major companies can do about inroads on their retail business by large-scale independent stations. Two ways seem to be open to the major concerns:

1. *The direct method*—competing with the aggressors in price, or making it possible for their dealers to do so. If aggressive price competitors are making inroads on what they think is their share of the business, we would expect the major companies ultimately to move in the direction of meeting aggressive competitors' prices[4] (as they have done). However, we would not expect major companies to switch completely to mass-merchandising on a price basis since they are better equipped to operate in a less aggressive manner. Such a move would be a violation of the whole philosophy of major companies operating conveniently located stations, and offering top-quality service and products. Moreover, locations at present occupied are utilized partly for advertising purposes, and it would be impracticable to abandon them; to convert them into large-scale outlets might be equally impracticable, partly because of limitations of space. One could expect direct methods to be used then, but these would be confined largely, if not entirely, to adjusting prices from time to time as the occasion demands (as has been done heretofore).

2. *The indirect method*—selling the gasoline to the large-scale distributor (as many have done). Although they may lose business to the large-scale outlets, many if not most of the major companies indirectly provide some of the gasoline sold in such stations so that the loss in business to aggressive price competitors is more apparent than real. It would seem to be to the advantage of a major company to sell to cut-raters, either directly or indirectly, assuming, of course, that the cut-raters would acquire supplies from some source, especially if sales were made on a rebrand basis. Actually, this would be a good example of market segmentation. That is, one sells first all he can at a higher price under his own company brand name, and then accepts whatever the market will bring for the same

---

[4] Not actually *meeting* such prices, which would not be necessary in view of the difference in goodwill of the major- and independent-company brands, but merely reducing the differential.

product sold under the less well-known brand name of some independent company.

One may conclude, tentatively, that the distribution of the products of major-companies through relatively few large-volume outlets is both unnecessary and impracticable; however, if pressure became too great they might try operating a few mass-merchandising units, offering a differentiated product (with or without service) to cater to those who are price conscious, while continuing to distribute the bulk of their product through conveniently located stations offering full service. On the other hand, any serious move to sell gasoline at cut-rate in self-serve stations might be considered unfriendly by other major-company dealers whose margins are relatively narrow and who find it difficult enough under normal conditions to operate their stations successfully.

While major companies would not be expected to change completely their competitive techniques, there is little question about the influence of mass distributors on the location, size, and layout of retail gasoline outlets. It seems to be well established that spaciousness of service stations is attractive to gasoline patrons. It is equally well established that advantages derive from placing pump islands perpendicular (or diagonal) to the boulevard or street, from having large-capacity storage tanks on station premises,[5] and from separating free service facilities from those which yield revenue.[6] New light seems to have been shed, also, on the effective use of non-corner locations by large-scale independent operators. Future station design and construction is bound to be influenced by the experience of mass distributors in these matters. It is an interesting sidelight that inde-

---

[5] According to the official of an independent-supplier company, who has had some experience with self-serves, one of the most important contributions the self-serve stations have made to the industry is direct delivery of truck-and-trailer loads of gasoline to retail outlets. This official feels, moreover, that storage facilities large enough to accept truck-and-trailer lots are going to be a first requisite of a good service station before long—that even though a service station pumps only 25,000 gallons per month, the saving in transportation costs will soon pay for the added cost of the larger facilities.

[6] In fact, it has been suggested by one oil man to eliminate free service and in this way reduce the price of gasoline to the consumer. His plan would be to establish "service centers" away from the driveways, such as at the rear of the lot, where for a small fee the customer could purchase the service desired. He believes that this scheme would not only enable the station to charge lower prices for its product, but would in turn increase the gallonage dispensed by enabling more cars to pass through the driveways. (*National Petroleum News*, October 26, 1949, p. 11.)

pendent vendors should have provided this leadership[7] rather than the major companies.[8] On the other hand, it should be recognized that the independent operators are to a considerable extent parasites since they make little or no contribution to the development of the product.[9]

Just one more point: This study has been concerned with gasoline distribution at the retail level. The classification of competitors and all conclusions (except those especially noted) have been based upon this segment of the industry only. It is quite likely (indeed certain) that some modifications would have to be made in the conclusions if the wholesale phase were to be included. The main difference that would develop if one were to broaden the scope of this study to include preretail levels is that the major companies would emerge as much more aggressive with respect to price. This is evidenced by a study of the industry on a much broader basis that is being conducted at present by one of the authors.

---

[7] As of February, 1950, the authors had discovered only two self-serve stations that sold the *branded* product of a major company—one an Associated station, the other a Shell Oil Company outlet.

1. Associated self-serve in Pasadena: A spacious, 12-pump, complete-service layout with islands perpendicular to the street. The owner stated that all companies except Standard Oil, Union Oil, and possibly Richfield were interested in the arrangement but that Tide Water Associated did not have representation in that immediate area. Richfield hesitated because it felt the self-serve might put its station down the street out of business. The station originally did not display a price sign as the company was opposed to it; it advertised "Self-Serve or We Serve You." At the time the operation was observed its price for premium grade was 23.6 cents (a saving of 3 cents from the Standard Oil Company price in Standard Stations, Inc.) and for regular grade 21.6 cents (a saving of 2.5 cents from the Standard Oil price).

2. Shell self-serve in east Los Angeles: This is a four-island, twelve-pump station, on the southwest corner of Slauson Avenue at Holmes. It is on a rather small lot compared with the usual self-serve area but its layout is typical—the islands perpendicular to the street, a small hut for making change in the middle of the lot, and service facilities and washrack in the rear. A blackboard was posted at the back of the lot with the license numbers of cars that had won prizes, such as television sets and automobile accessories. There were no price signs or any sign indicating that it was a self-serve at the time the station was observed; the only advertising posted was the regular Shell Oil trade-mark sign. Men customers were servicing their own cars. The price for Shell premium grade at that time was 23.9 cents (a saving of 2.7 cents compared with the Standard Oil price); regular grade was 21.6 cents (2.5 cents saving).

[8] But perhaps this simply proves that the conservative competitors are indeed conservative. However, to be absolutely fair, there was a trend toward increased size of stations even before the advent of mass-selling gasoline distributors.

[9] Conversely, the evidence suggests that the major part of the credit for the discovery of America's oil should go to individuals or firms which are independent of major-company connection.

B. Turning now to the method of analysis: Generally speaking, the method we have used in studying competitive behavior has been satisfactory. The combining of economic theory with observed market behavior appears to have great possibilities. The scheme of analyzing prices on a multi-dimensional basis possesses great promise as a revelatory device. The plan of placing a segment of the market under a high-powered microscope is extremely worthwhile, if indeed it is not indispensable as a method of discovering the true nature of competition. Such a scheme not only is an effective device for testing hypotheses, but it provides behavior patterns which are beyond the powers of imagination of even the most fertile-minded theorist.

This study, however, reveals a danger in this latter technique— one may not fully realize at the outset the heavy requirements for competent research assistance, and hence is apt to proceed inadequately resourced in this regard with the result that some aspect of the study is given only superficial attention. One should be prepared to move in closer where such a course is indicated, if an accurate and detailed picture of competitive behavior is to be obtained.

The senior author would like to make it clear that he could not have had more willing or intelligent assistance in the prosecution of this study, but had not enough help available to examine all aspects of the competitive picture in sufficient detail. While the investigators went back time after time to seek explanations of various phenomena and even reasons behind reasons in some phases of the study, it was impossible to obtain anything but a first approximation in other phases. The two most important examples falling into the latter category are:

1. The consumer-behavior analysis, where practically no attempt was made to test consumer-behavior patterns inductively. Consumer response, of course, is extremely important as an aspect of competitive behavior. Ideally, such a study as related to gasoline should have been an integral part of this competitive analysis, if only as an aid to the authors in drawing sharper conclusions concerning the effectiveness of competitive tactics. But the scope of a study of this sort is so great that it could not be undertaken considering everything else that had to be done with the limited resources at our command. Fortunately, a study of consumer preferences for various products— including gasoline—is being conducted at present through detailed

consumer interviews in the Los Angeles market area.[10] This should throw considerable light on consumer-behavior patterns.

2. The competitive behavior of individual station operators, where only a superficial analysis was possible. Thus, we have provided little of a definitive nature on the reactions of rivals to varying competitive activities. In order to obtain a detailed behavior pattern the area under observation would have to be greatly limited. The authors hope that they or someone else may be able one day to select a group of stations in a relatively small subarea within the market area under study, and by prearrangement observe any changes which take place in the competitive struggle (e.g., a price reduction by one vendor or the introduction of a new competitive factor such as a self-serve station), and obtain the psychological reaction of the several sellers to such moves, as well as a detailed picture of any counter moves which are made by rivals. In a small segment such as has been indicated, the timing of the sequence of events could be properly recorded so that one could obtain the immediate results as well as those over a period of time. Such a detailed study of the reactions of competing sellers to various competitive activities by rivals, both direct and indirect, should go far toward replacing hypotheses with facts.[11]

Just one more word on methodology. It should be obvious that the limitations of this study discussed above are not inherent in the microeconomic method of analysis. It may not be nearly so obvious, however, that this scheme of making minute analyses of a submarket segment depends to some extent for its success on a somewhat broader study to provide a framework for the more intensive investigation. Thus, an analysis of rivalry among a group of filling stations would be of little use unless it were conducted in the light of some knowledge of the product available, the nature of the demand for the com-

---

[10] See chap. iii, p. 31, n. 47. A generally similar study is reportedly being contemplated by researchers at the University of Pennsylvania, although we do not know whether the study of gasoline is included in the plan.

[11] We would be interested not only in sales of independent-company stations but sales in relation to various competitive influences. The type of thing one might look for is: Effect on competitors of (1) a new entrant in the immediate area; (2) new competition at a distance, especially if operating under price-cutting policy; (3) introduction of some new service device by one or more of the competitors (such as Union Oil Company's "three-finger" service system), or some ostensibly different product (such as "rust-proof" gasoline); (4) expansion of size or change in layout of a station. The impact of these and other factors might be measured in terms of the immediate results as well as over a period of time.

modity, the form of competitive behavior generally found in the field, and so forth. The narrower type of study, therefore, would not take the place of the broader overview type, but would merely complement it by providing detailed information on competitive behavior.

It is hoped that the study will lead toward further exploration into the nature of competition, so that one day there will be a fact-founded body of theory to replace the present highly conjectural hypothetical explanation of competitive behavior. Despite the interesting, and, the authors hope, useful findings coming out of this analysis of the nature of competition in the Los Angeles retail gasoline market, this study could not be considered as having made a maximum contribution unless it resulted in similar investigations in other areas.

www.ingramcontent.com/pod-product-compliance
Lightning Source LLC
Chambersburg PA
CBHW021701210326
41599CB00013B/1476